Warriors and Scribes

Critical Studies in Latin American and Iberian Cultures

SERIES EDITORS
James Dunkerley
John King

This major series – the first of its kind to appear in English – is designed to map the field of contemporary Latin American and Iberian cultures, which have enjoyed increasing popularity in Britain and the United States in recent years.

The series aims to broaden the scope of criticism of Latin American and Iberian cultures, which tend still to extol the virtues of a few established 'master' works, and to examine cultural production within the context of twentieth-century history. These clear, accessible studies are aimed at those who wish to know more about some of the most important and influential cultural works and movements of our time.

ALREADY PUBLISHED

DRAWING THE LINE: ART AND CULTURAL IDENTITY IN CONTEMPORARY LATIN AMERICA by Oriana Baddeley and Valerie Fraser

PLOTTING WOMEN: GENDER AND REPRESENTATION IN MEXICO by Jean Franco

THE MOTORCYCLE DIARIES: A JOURNEY AROUND SOUTH AMERICA by Ernesto Che Guevara

THE GATHERING OF VOICES: THE TWENTIETH-CENTURY POETRY OF LATIN AMERICA by Mike Gonzalez and David Treece

JOURNEYS THROUGH THE LABYRINTH: LATIN AMERICAN FICTION IN THE TWENTIETH CENTURY by Gerald Martin

PASSION OF THE PEOPLE? FOOTBALL IN SOUTH AMERICA by Tony Mason

IN THE SHADOW OF THE STATE: INTELLECTUALS AND THE QUEST FOR NATIONAL IDENTITY IN TWENTIETH-CENTURY SPANISH AMERICA by Nicola Miller

MEMORY AND MODERNITY: POPULAR CULTURE IN LATIN AMERICA by William Rowe and Vivian Schelling

JORGE LUIS BORGES: A WRITER ON THE EDGE by Beatriz Sarlo

MISPLACED IDEAS: ESSAYS ON BRAZILIAN CULTURE by Roberto Schwarz

DESIRE UNLIMITED: THE CINEMA OF PEDRO ALMODÓVAR, New Edition, by Paul Julian Smith

VISION MACHINES: CINEMA, LITERATURE AND SEXUALITY IN SPAIN AND CUBA, 1983–1993 by Paul Julian Smith

FORTHCOMING

BUILDING THE NEW WORLD: MODERN ARCHITECTURE IN LATIN AMERICA by Valerie Fraser

MAGICAL REELS: A HISTORY OF CINEMA IN LATIN AMERICA, New Edition, by John King

AN ARGENTINE PASSION: MARÍA LUISA BEMBERG AND HER FILMS, edited by John King, Sheila Whitaker and Rosa Bosch

THROUGH THE KALEIDOSCOPE: THE EXPERIENCE OF MODERNITY IN LATIN AMERICA, edited by Vivian Schelling

Warriors and Scribes

Essays on the History and Politics of Latin America

◆

JAMES DUNKERLEY

VERSO

London • New York

First published by Verso 2000
© James Dunkerley 2000
All rights reserved

Verso
UK: 6 Meard Street, London W1V 3HR
US: 180 Varick Street, New York, NY 10014–4606

Verso is the imprint of New Left Books

ISBN 1–85984–754–4
ISBN 1–85984–272–0 (pbk.)

British Library Cataloguing in Publication Data
A catalogue record for this book is available from the British Library

Library of Congress Cataloging-in-Publication Data
Dunkerley, James.
  Warriors and scribes : essays on the history and politics of Latin America / James Dunkerley.
    p. cm.
    ISBN 1–85984–754–4—ISBN 1–85984–272–0 (pbk.)
    1. Latin America—Politics and government. 2. Latin America—Foreign
relations—United States. 3. United States—Foreign relations—Latin America. I. Title.

F1410.D84 2000
320.98′09′04—dc21
                                                                                    00–061439

Typeset in Baskerville by SetSystems Ltd, Saffron Walden, Essex
Printed by Biddles Ltd, Guildford and King's Lynn

To the Effendi

Contents

Acknowledgements

Chapter 1 was first published as Occasional Paper No. 2, Institute of Latin American Studies, University of London 1992. Chapter 2 was first published in *New Left Review* no. 206, July–August 1994. Chapter 3 was originally published as Occasional Paper No. 16, Institute of Latin American Studies, London 1998. Chapter 4 was first published in John King, Ana López and Manuel Alvarado (eds), *Mediating Two Worlds: Cinematic Encounters in the Americas*, British Film Institute, London 1993. Chapter 5 was originally published in V. Bulmer-Thomas (ed.), *Latin American Studies in the United Kingdom, 1965–95*, Institute of Latin American Studies, London 1996. Chapter 6 was first published in V. Bulmer-Thomas and J. Dunkerley (eds), *The United States and Latin America: The New Agenda*, David Rockefeller Center for Latin American Studies, Harvard and Institute of Latin American Studies, London 1999. Chapter 7 was originally published as Occasional Paper No. 20, Institute of Latin American Studies, London 1999. I am extremely grateful to all publishers and editors for permission to reproduce this work.

1

Barrientos and Debray:
All Gone or More to Come?

The prominence and popularity of biography in explaining politics have been surprisingly little affected by the advent of social science. Moreover, we have in recent years seen the re-emergence of a rather distinct genre – that of 'parallel lives' – which was most notably developed by Plutarch in the first century AD, with more than two dozen sketches of Greek and Roman figures.[1] Plutarch's influence has, of course, proved enduring, not only through Shakespeare's use of North's translation but also via Dryden, Racine and Emerson amongst others. It is, then, somewhat surprising to discover no mention of him in three modern studies: J.H. Elliott's *Richelieu and Olivares*, Michael Beschloss's *Kennedy v. Khrushchev*, and *Hitler and Stalin: Parallel Lives* by Alan Bullock.[2]

Perhaps this silence on the part of such eminent scholars, at least one of whom received a 'classical education', simply reflects modern acceptance of an approach that Plutarch himself never fully explained or defended. Yet even if this is the case, it is worth quoting the observation of D. A. Russell:

> . . . either character or circumstance may be the basis of a *sunkrisis* (comparison); similar events affecting dissimilar persons and similar persons reacting to contrasting events alike provide a suitable field for the exercise. It is basically a rhetorical procedure; but it is rescued from purely rhetorical ingenuity by its value as a way of concentrating and directing the moral reflections which are the primary purpose of biography.[3]

Of course, I don't have the time to provide even a proper biographical sketch of René Barrientos and Régis Debray. Furthermore, one doubts the contemporary usefulness of an approach as didactic as that of Plutarch with respect to virtue and vice, even when reflecting on the politics of Latin America through the experiences of a conservative general and a radical intellectual.

Nevertheless, Russell's argument is far from wholly redundant for these two individuals, who in fact never met each other and yet were the principal surviving protagonists on either side of the guerrilla staged by Ernesto Che Guevara in Bolivia in 1967. They may, then, plausibly be taken as representative not only of polarised political traditions and outlooks but also of a binding antagonism. Although these phenomena are by no means ancient, memory is frequently tyrannised by fashion, especially when this operates as mercilessly as it does within academic life. At the same time, for most of us Bolivia is a place as obscure as it appears to be exotic. Let me, therefore, look at each man before reflecting very briefly on the proposition that the qualities with which they are most closely associated now belong to a surpassed age and have been rendered redundant and ridiculous by the consolidation of a liberal democratic culture based upon modern capitalism and the hegemony of consensus.

General Barrientos's reputation has not stood the test of time or resisted the invective and denigration of his many enemies. But in the last decade of his life – including four years as President of Bolivia – he possessed an impressive image at home and abroad as a charismatic military strongman or *caudillo*. In his recent biography of de Gaulle – himself scarcely a besuited wimp – Jean Lacouture says that Barrientos's reputation 'made people tremble'.[4] This is exaggerated but unsurprising since the picture abroad was very much that painted by *The Times* in its obituary of 'a handsome ... Airforce general (who) was the target of many assassination attempts, (a) dark-haired president (who) carried three bullets in his body'.[5] This, too, was not strictly true, but it pales in comparison with some of the home-grown descriptions heaped upon Barrientos when he was at his zenith: Condor of the Andean Skies; Creator of the Second Republic; Paladin of Social Democracy; Restorer of Faith in the National Revolution; and General of the People.[6] This last title is also that of a hagiography written for wages by Fernando Diez de Medina, who includes in his 350 pages the phrase, 'Barrientos was Bolivia, Bolivia was Barrientos'.[7]

Such an assertion strikes one as innocently foolish until we recall the declaration made by Rudolf Hess at a Nazi rally in 1934 that, 'Adolf Hitler is Germany, and Germany is Adolf Hitler'.[8] Even if – as is quite likely – Diez de Medina was simply borrowing from the not inconsiderable corpus of National Socialist literature that had made its way into Bolivia in the 1930s and 1940s, this resonance between euphoric nationalist sentiment and personalist political leadership is not uncommon in modern Latin America.[9] Barrientos, for all his authoritarianism, was no Nazi, and he never succeeded in organising a proper political party to replace the Movimiento Nacionalista Revolucionario (MNR), the movement which had led the revolution of 1952, to which he himself had belonged even before that revolution, and which he overthrew in a coup in November 1964 when he was serving as constitutional Vice-President.

René Barrientos Ortuño was born in 1919 in the small provincial town of Tarata in the department of Cochabamba. Not untypically for this region, he was of mixed Quechua and Spanish blood, and his fluency in the Quechua language was later to play a key part in developing both regionalist backing and something of an indigenous identity in one of the two Latin American countries – the other is Guatemala – which still had a majority Amerindian population.

Barrientos's parents were of humble, rather than poor, background, but he was orphaned young and, losing his brother César in the Chaco War against Paraguay, his upbringing was overseen by sisters Corina and Elena, upon whom he later depended heavily. His passage from local seminary to military college was not unusual for somebody of his background. Nor, in fact, was Barrientos particularly distinctive in his admiration for the radical nationalist officers Germán Busch and Gualberto Villarroel, who from the late 1930s attempted to curb the power of large tin companies and reduce Bolivia's political dependency on Britain and the USA. Too junior to belong to the nationalist military lodges that supported these leaders, Barrientos nonetheless opposed the conservatives who came to power in 1946, and he penned a very short and rather uninspiring pamphlet calling for 'the glorious and valiant army to free itself from vulgar obeisance to the tin companies'.[10] Cashiered, but having already qualified as a pilot, he flew missions for the insurgent MNR in the civil war of 1949, and in April 1952, following the party's eventual capture of power in a three-day insurrection, it was Barrientos who volunteered to bring the MNR leader Víctor Paz Estenssoro back from exile in Buenos Aires.

The MNR nationalised the major tin mines, decreed an extensive agrarian reform, and introduced universal suffrage for the poorest country in mainland America. Under strong pressure from the left-wing miners' union, the party had little choice but to acquiesce in the formation of popular militias, which for a while threatened the very existence of the regular armed forces. Perhaps wisely, Barrientos spent a fair part of the 1950s on postings and courses abroad, including, according to his enemies, a spell in a US psychiatric hospital. In all events, it is only in the early 1960s, following the Cuban Revolution and the accelerating division and right-wing drift of the MNR that he came firmly into the public eye. As the party's authority decomposed and its rule became more violent, Barrientos exploited his dual role as commander of the airforce and leader of the MNR's military lodge to promote the restoration of the armed forces, staging a thinly disguised bonapartist campaign that attracted increasing support from Washington and the very private companies against which he had railed in the 1940s. Indeed, once he came to office, the general reversed a great many of the political positions that he had championed a decade earlier.

If Barrientos was widely denounced as an opportunist and traitor, at least he staked out his ground emphatically, using language that manifested little or no modulation:

> The Fatherland is in danger. A vast Communist conspiracy, planned and funded by international extremism has exploited the good faith of some sectors of labour in trying to pit the people against the armed forces . . . It doesn't matter that the snipers, the masters of blackmail, demagogy and lies heap up mountains of calumny against the armed forces. They are frustrated; their epilepsy and maladies do not impress our glorious institution, effectively at the service of the people and against the traffickers who suck on the credulity and good will of the workers.[11]

The same man who expressed these sentiments ensured that he was made a freemason days before coming to office, and having done so promptly appointed eight close relatives to ministries, ambassadorships or directorships of state corporations.[12] He was, perhaps, not overly prejudiced in such a macho culture by the fact that, rather like John Kennedy, he had a high sex drive over which he exercised poor control, although to describe him as Priapic is probably to give his activities an undeserved classical gloss.[13] Only recognising eight children as his own but promising to adopt more than 50, Barrientos was thrice married, once bigamously, to his 'first lady' Rosemarie Galindo – a union that he failed to regularise, he said, 'because of pressure of work', instead contracting nuptials with Cati Rivas a month before he died.[14]

Such antics greatly exasperated the prelates, but the populace as a whole seemed more perplexed by Barrientos's efforts to justify the outlawing of trade unions, manipulations of the Constitution, erratic suppression of opposition parties, and attacks on the student movement:

> 'I am', said the President, 'a man of the Christian left – nationalist in economics, democratic in doctrine. But this democracy is just, active, belligerent, dynamic and profoundly revolutionary because I am seeking only social justice and the happiness of the peasant, worker and middle class majority; in sum, the happiness of the people.'[15]

Of course, one should never underestimate the power of even the most incomprehensible and leaden rhetoric when it is delivered with energy and conviction. And it is to this, I feel, that Barrientos owed his significant popularity. He was, above all else, a man of action for whom heroic feats were essential and sheer movement an adequate substitute for rationality.

Barrientos was by far the most peripatetic of Bolivia's presidents. Often he would conduct essential business in La Paz early into the morning so that he could spend the daylight hours moving around the republic, dropping into the smallest and most isolated communities to shake hands, share a drink or meal, distribute footballs and bicycles, speechify and, above all, ratify the existence of the president. Such paternalism was, of course, an integral feature of traditional patterns of authority, the exchange of hospitality and fealty for gifts and recognition reaffirming identities in a manner that is only partially understood in terms of patron and client. It was all made possible in an exceptionally mountainous country courtesy of the helicopter, first used over the Bolivian *altiplano* in mid-1962 and rapidly adopted by Barrientos, who enjoyed the permanent loan of a Bell craft from Gulf Oil, one of the companies favoured by his 'open-door' economic policies.

One civic-minded citizen concerned at the expense of such activity wrote to the press to observe that in two years these trips must have cost at least $700,000, the president having travelled the equivalent of two-thirds of the distance between the earth and the moon.[16] This comparison is telling because, of course, Barrientos ruled Bolivia, and ruled it from the air, at a time when space travel had captured the global imagination. Sometimes this occurred rather too vividly, as when a puma was reported to have landed from outer space near the town of Ayo Ayo, just a fortnight before Telstar was launched and while John Glenn's capsule was on display in Mexico City.[17] In such a context, though, even an aviator of most illiberal outlook and attachment to 'order' might appear not only glamorous but also dazzlingly modern.

It seems unlikely that René Barrientos would have comprehended Aristotle's bracketing of the virtue of courage with the vice of audacity as well as cowardice.[18] Yet if he vacillated over major political decisions in a manner that belied his impulsive personal style, he could never be accused of bodily cowardice.[19] Indeed, it might even be said that his career hinged on three instances of physical fortitude or suffering.

Barrientos first won widespread popular acclaim in October 1961 when some 20,000 people gathered at the El Alto aerodrome above La Paz to watch a demonstration of parachuting, which had been attempted only twice before in the country – in 1939 and 1947. This event – central to a much-publicised aeronautical week organised by the general – went horribly wrong when the 'chutes of three of the 15 soldiers who made the drop failed to open and they fell to their deaths in front of the crowd. Faced with accusations of allowing his men to use inferior equipment, Barrientos simply invited the press back to El Alto, put on one of the dead men's parachutes and executed a faultless jump himself.[20]

In February 1964 the general staged an energetic but futile effort at the MNR's Ninth National Convention to have himself nominated as vice-presidential candidate for the general elections to be held in August of that year. Upon hearing of his defeat, he got heartily drunk and indulged in a number of emotional outbursts that did not augur well for President Víctor Paz and the apparatchiks who had manipulated the convention. A month later at two in the morning, Barrientos was shot as he left the home of his sister Corina following a meeting with supporters. The attack, which was very probably staged by the MNR's political police, the *Control Político*, seemed finally to have removed a threatening loser as Barrientos, hit in the chest, collapsed to the ground. However, the bullet had struck the metal United States Airforce insignia habitually worn by the general, shattering on impact with the result that no organs were damaged and he suffered only slight flesh wounds, caused by splinters.

Perhaps the most sober lesson which can be drawn from this incident is that the important thing about uniforms is that they are different. But Barrientos and his US friends were taking no chances. At 8.45 am, following a brief operation, he was taken to El Alto, and by 6.15 pm he was in the Panama Canal Zone, recovering in a US military hospital. Víctor Paz, fully able to read the writing on the wall, moved quickly to have the elected vice-presidential candidate resign and, after an enterprising reinterpretation of party statutes, he was able to send a cable to Panama offering Barrientos the position as his running-mate.[21] This was readily accepted, the office being exploited within six months to depose Paz and end a dozen years of MNR rule.

A year later, having taken dictatorial power, the general was again shot, but because he was driving a jeep and wearing protective clothing, of the three bullets that struck him only one caused a major wound – in the buttocks. This shooting took place on the road between Tarata and Cochabamba, and Barrientos was immediately ferried to the house of his sister Elena, where he remained for several days in what appears to have been a deliberately contrived atmosphere of crisis – almost melodrama – as delegations of officers visited him to express their backing and urge a return to the capital. The tenuous gravity of the moment was not assisted by the fact that the detectives sent to investigate the crime had to exclude the general's underpants as evidence because they had, quite fittingly, already been laundered in 'Ace' washing powder by Leonor Lezama, Elena's maid.[22] The tension cultivated during this incident was again exploited by Barrientos, who, having tested his support within the high command, and probably his own self-confidence as well, called a precipitate halt to the truce with his opponents and launched a major offensive against the left.

It is tempting – especially within the academy – to ignore all but the folkloric qualities of such matters. This, though, would be a mistake – one, I sense, made by Che Guevara and Régis Debray in 1967. It is certainly true that René Barrientos had by then become a figure loathed by many in the working class for his violent record of repression, and he was despised by much of a middle class youth negotiating the rapids between the elitism of adolescent Christian Democracy and that of a socially deracinated Leninism. It is also the case that Barrientos himself played a minimal role in the military operations against Guevara. Moreover, his propaganda war against the guerrilla was seen abroad as complete buffoonery. And yet one has to ask oneself why his regime was so little threatened by this insurgency when, despite a multitude of errors made by the radical left, so many of its charges were entirely accurate and widely accepted. Undoubtedly, the calculating young rationalists were spectacularly wrong-footed by an expressive, instinctive politician whose populist edge lay precisely in his unpredictability, and whose vulnerability was masked – not revealed – by his capacity for mouthing gibberish.

Barrientos survived Che Guevara by some 18 months. He died – as might have been expected – in a helicopter crash on one of his dashes around the country. For a while foul play was a suspected – not least on the part of Cati Rivas's ex-husband, the ebullient Captain Faustino Rico Toro – but the laborious autopsies practised on the defunct president could not shake the most sober explanation. Unable to accept this, some, including police Colonel Oscar Vargas Valenzuela, resorted to the astral plane of investigation and consulted the general's spirit – an inadvisable course of action since the Bolivian Church lacks a qualified exorcist, and there stands in the city of Oruro a house, once occupied by German dabblers in the occult, that remains empty and haunted even after the ministrations of officials sent from Rome. As it happens, Colonel Vargas was informed by the general's shade that his death was 'due to a simple accident'.[23]

When he was in the realm of the quick Barrientos had declared, 'to die is part of life. Those who fear death cannot command.'[24] This is one of the few sentiments that he assuredly shared with Guevara. It is also, perhaps, not surprising, in view of his experience in Bolivia 25 years ago, to find in Debray's *Critique of Political Reason* the declaration that, 'Death is the lyrical core of the individual, the site where he discovers that he is irreplaceable.'[25]

In turning to Régis Debray one might legitimately expect some relief from the kinds of excitements that have just been described. This, however, can only be partial for although Debray may properly be described as an intellectual, he was very young when he resolved to harness his analytical skills directly to the struggle for revolutionary socialism. To the best of my knowledge, the only time that he has been fully employed in an academic post was in 1966, in Cuba. It is, then, not entirely surprising that when, on 20 April 1967, Debray was detained by elements of the Bolivian army's Fourth Division near the village of

Muyupampa in the middle of the guerrilla zone of operations his pro-
testations that he was only covering the campaign as a journalist were not
readily accepted. Several days later a rather elated General Barrientos told
the international press that Debray was a guerrilla and agent of Fidel
Castro whose adventures would end in Bolivia.[26] In fact, neither claim was
proved to be true, but the first was more than plausible and, for a while,
the second seemed highly likely.

Jules Régis Debray was born in Paris in September 1940, the son of
relatively affluent lawyers who were soon to become members of the
Resistance. When he was arrested in Bolivia his mother, Janine, active in
conservative politics, was Vice-President of the municipal council of Paris,
on which she had served for 20 years; his father, Georges, a distinguished
attorney, was a member of the Council of Lawyers and a Chevalier of the
Legion of Honour. Such a respectable bourgeois background later proved
vital in promoting a high-profile campaign in Debray's defence, but it did
not apparently provoke an exceptionally talented youth to acts of social
rebellion or idle iconoclasm. Indeed, Régis appears to have fulfilled the
exacting expectations of his parents, receiving the 1957 national philosophy prize for secondary students from his mother's hands and graduat-
ing first from the Lycée Louis-le-Grand in 1959. That year his parents
rewarded him with a holiday in the USA, but when in Miami he diverted
to Havana for several weeks in order to witness the recently triumphant
Cuban Revolution. On his return Debray entered the Ecole Normale
Supérieure to study for a master's in philosophy with Louis Althusser. In
1961 he visited South America for several months; and he returned there
in 1963 for a stay of 18 months, visiting every country except Paraguay.
Subsequently he began to study for a doctorate in social anthropology
under the supervision of Maurice Godelier.

Debray was, therefore, scarcely wet behind the ears when he was
arrested in Bolivia. However, local opinion seems to have been that the
combination of his intelligence and self-esteem – even some sympathetic
commentators talked of arrogance – had transformed the Frenchman into
what is known in that part of the world as a *S'unchu Luminaria* – the sense
of which might be translated as 'somebody whose fine words mesmerise
only momentarily'. Another reaction was that Debray was a *Q'incha Qhara*,
which literally means 'unlucky European' but which can also signify
'European who brings bad luck'. Certainly, as he awaited a court martial
on the eve of his 27th birthday, charged with murder, robbery, grievous
bodily harm and rebellion, Régis Debray appeared to be paying a very
high price for a *folie de grandeur* that compounded the assurance of a
comfortable metropolitan upbringing, the pretensions of Althusser's
Marxist theoreticism, and the presumptions of Cuban revolutionary internationalism. It is a heady mix and – combined with his significant literary

talent – it should remind us that Debray, like Barrientos, can only be taken as 'representative' by virtue of his being outstanding.

A week after he had been arrested, beaten into a coma and threatened with death, Debray, understandably pessimistic about his prospects, started to write down some reflections on his short life. Initial declarations, such as 'Memories don't interest me', reverberate with the petulance with which he responded to his interrogators. But this brief memoir settles down as soon as its author casts his mind back to the regime at the rue d'Ulm and the outlook of the young philosophers at the Ecole Normale Supérieure:

> . . . we thought [he tells us] we could analyse our world and our hearts at arm's length . . . a fine philosopher who was guiding our steps as students, and had introduced us to Karl Marx, gave us the entrée to the kingdom that he was himself exploring, that of theoretical rigour and dialectical materialism, as a theory of general praxis . . . All very fine: theory draws its effectiveness from its rigorousness, and its rigorousness is effective because it separates 'development in reality' from 'development in thought', the 'operation of society' from the 'operation of knowledge'. In other words, all we had to do to become good theoreticians was to be lazy bastards.[27]

Under the circumstances this is a pardonable exaggeration, but it is also a quite justified response to Althusser's progressive elimination of the core philosophical problem of the guarantees of knowledge and truth as well as his relentless invective against the ideological illusions of immediate experience.

This passage is from Althusser's book *Reading Capital*, published in 1965, when Debray was back in Paris:

> We must take seriously the fact that the theory of history, in the strong sense, does not exist, or hardly exists as far as historians are concerned; that the concepts of existing history are therefore nearly always 'empirical' concepts . . . that is, cross-bred with a powerful strain of ideology concealed behind its 'obviousness'.[28]

As Perry Anderson has observed, such a position is an almost exact replica of Spinoza's logical progression from the monist dictum that 'Truth is the criterion both of itself and of falsehood' to the assertion that the primary delusion of humanity is the conviction that individuals are free in their volition, or, as Spinoza puts it, 'Their idea of freedom is simply their ignorance of any cause of their actions.'[29]

It is not too difficult to see how such an approach complicates the issue of political commitment and daily practice for the radical philosopher. Certainly, it places a large question mark over Che Guevara's slogan that it is 'the duty of the revolutionary to make the revolution' – a call to which Debray was exposed even before he was to grapple with Althusser's rejection of 'the empiricist model of a chance "hypothesis" whose verification must be provided by the political practice of history *before* we can affirm its "truth" '.[30]

Combine these two positions and you can readily attempt to make the revolution free of any prior 'historical' verification of your ideas, or, alternatively, you might stoically restrict yourself to contemplation and criticism. Althusser tended to the latter option, albeit at some cost to his real-world relations with the leadership of the French Communist Party. It is, perhaps, telling that on 1 March 1967, just as Debray was making his way from La Paz to the guerrilla zone, Althusser wrote his student a letter, commenting on Debray's recently published book *Revolution in the Revolution?*. Althusser says:

> The struggle poses urgent demands. But it is sometimes *politically urgent* to withdraw for a while, and to take stock; everything depends on the theoretical work done at that time ... Time thus taken away from the struggle may ultimately be a saving of time ... I see this as being the duty of all working class and revolutionary intellectuals. They are entrusted by the people in arms with the guardianship and extension of scientific knowledge.[31]

It was, of course, too late. Debray, like many students, had drawn rather different conclusions from those of his professor. 'The intellectual', he wrote in *Revolution in the Revolution?*,

> will try to grasp the present through preconceived ideological constructs and live it through books. He will be less able than others to invent, improvise, make do with available resources, decide instantly on bold moves when he is in a tight spot. Thinking that he already knows, he will learn more slowly, display less flexibility.[32]

Some might think this observation good for most occasions, but Debray was applying it to guerrilla warfare, with which strategy for the Latin American revolution he had already become closely identified through the publication in 1965 of an extended essay, 'Castroism: the Long March in Latin America'.[33] Perhaps, despite the pious disclaimers just mentioned, he saw in guerrilla warfare more than just a repudiation of the mores and experience of the Ecole Normale Supérieure. Maybe he discerned in the conjunction of intellect and force that praxis about which Althusser had lectured and around which no small part of classical literature revolves?

Whatever the case, Debray's writing on this subject is not essentially original. Despite a distinctive polemical flair and analytical insight, its central thrust is clearly derived from the interpretation of the Cuban Revolution made by Che Guevara, who within months of the overthrow of Batista's dictatorship produced an admirably cogent defence of what became known as *foquismo*. Guevara tells us,

We consider that the Cuban Revolution contributed three fundamental lessons to the conduct of revolutionary movements in America. They are:
1. Popular forces can win a war against the army.
2. It is not necessary to wait until all conditions for making revolution exist; the insurrection can create them.
3. In underdeveloped America the countryside is the basic area for armed conflict.
Of these three propositions, the first two contradict the defeatist attitude of revolutionaries or pseudo-revolutionaries who remain inactive and take refuge on the pretext that against a professional army nothing can be done, who sit down to wait until in some mechanical way all necessary objective and subjective conditions are given without working to accelerate them.[34]

Of course, the disastrous defeat of Guevara's own guerrilla was but the most poignant example of the insufficiencies of this compelling voluntarism, against which the political objections and historical evidence mounted up with tragic velocity. For our purposes there is no need to detail this process, which is the subject of a rich literature.[35] However, it is certainly worth noting that the appeal of a political philosophy rooted so positively in *making* a revolution and overcoming objective constraints through *action* is not limited to periods of radical optimism and advance; it may also – if not equally – acquire a constituency in times – such as our own – of embattlement and despair.

Debray's practical experience of conducting this struggle was short and sobering. Arriving at Che's camp in the first week of March 1967 together with two other foreign visitors, he was initially anxious to become a combatant although he had entered Bolivia officially and as a journalist for a Mexican magazine. Guevara, however, immediately asked him to organise a solidarity campaign in France, and noted pithily in his diary that the suggestion that Debray return to Europe via Cuba was 'an idea which coincides with his desires to marry and have a child with his woman'. A week later Guevara, who gave Debray three interviews, noted that, 'the Frenchman stated too vehemently how useful he could be on the outside' – an account that Debray, to his considerable credit, himself volunteered before Che's diary was published.[36] Indeed, at his trial the Frenchman – whom the guerrillas nicknamed 'Danton' – made an eloquent defence speech around his declaration, 'I regret that I am innocent.'[37] In this he stresses that Guevara even gave his increasingly burdensome visitors a choice of how and when to leave the force – an offer which, given the progressively vulnerable position of the guerrilla, clearly indicated that they were not subject to military discipline.[38]

The fact that Debray was able to make an unashamedly heroic defence speech owes not a little to his lawyer, Raúl Novillo Villarroel, whose enterprising but careful demolition of the loose case made against his

client revealed the determination of the three military judges to pass a
verdict of guilty and impose the maximum sentence of 30 years. This
should not surprise us – a score of young conscripts had been killed
during the seven weeks of Debray's presence with the rebels, and yet now
not only de Gaulle and Sartre but also Malraux, Robert Kennedy and
Bertrand Russell were requesting a pardon and scrutinising the legal
procedures and moral rectitude of their country. Moreover, the guerrilla
had clearly been set up and led by Cubans, and here was this Frenchman
who supported the whole enterprise and yet expected with Olympian
condescension to get off because he had not himself squeezed a trigger.
Recognising the odds – but not, I think, quite why they were so poor –
Debray cast aside caution. In a closed session, following an officially
contrived outburst by spectators, he informed the colonels,

> Each one has to decide which side he is on – on the side of military violence or
> guerrilla violence, on the side of violence that represses or violence that
> liberates. Crimes in the face of crimes . . . You choose certain ones, I choose
> others, that's all.[39]

But it is not quite all, for while a colonel might indeed *commit* a crime,
an intellectual would only *be on its side*. Debray, then, standing on firm
legal ground, makes a moral virtue out of a necessity. 'Guilty of what?' he
asks his judges. 'And on what grounds? Political? Granted. Criminal?
Inadmissable.'

> . . . tell me: 'We are condemning you because you are a Marxist-Leninist,
> because you wrote *Revolution in the Revolution?*, a book that was read by some
> guerrillas in your absence. We are condemning you because you are a confessed
> admirer of Fidel Castro and came here to speak with Che without first
> requesting permission from the authorities . . .' That's fine. I have nothing to
> say.[40]

Debray's wish was not granted. Apart from anything else, the international furore caused by his trial had persuaded Barrientos to execute
Guevara summarily in order to avoid an even worse outcry. Now that
this had been done and still held the world's attention a month
later, there was nothing whatsoever to be gained from indulging the
Frenchman.[41]

Debray spent over three years in prison before being released by a
military president. In February 1968 he was allowed to marry his sweet-
heart, Elizabeth Burgos, who was given visiting rights for 10 days every
three months. He had, of course, nothing to do with the events in Paris
of that year – a fact that might explain his subsequent interpretation that
their 'real meaning' was the establishment of a new bourgeois republic
on a 'modern or American individualist agenda'.[42] Upon his release he

interviewed the Chilean president Salvador Allende, the leading regional exponent of 'the peaceful road to socialism', but whilst there are clear signs of Debray being chastened, he showed no major shift in his line. Indeed, after Allende's death in 1973, the Frenchman wrote in his account of Guevara's last campaign that 'it is right to fight'.[43]

The shift, I think, comes after Debray has settled his analytical accounts with the guerrilla experience in the two-volume work *La Critique des Armes*, the publication of which in 1974 coincided with the onset of dictatorial regimes in South America. Aside from several novels, apparently written for personal catharsis and not without some quite nasty things to say about readily identifiable individuals, Debray leaves Latin America and concentrates upon France itself.[44] It is unremarkable, even from what little has already been described, that he should write a study of modern intellectuals – a survey that was predictably controversial and unusually 'empirical' in its approach.[45] Indeed, it is refreshing to find – even if only in a footnote in the *Critique of Political Reason* – this author declaring, 'no concrete analysis of a given historical period can proceed by deduction (the use of categories). At most it can infer certain localised results and contrast them with a global conception of social history.'[46]

At times the sheer eclecticism and lack of focus of this work put one in mind of Ortega y Gasset's comment of Stendhal – that he 'possessed a head full of theories; but . . . lacked the gifts of a theoretician'.[47] This may sound harsh, but to a non-theorist it looks like pretty good company to be keeping, and the view, I think, is justified by Debray's reluctance to develop theories beyond his immediate polemical needs. This is the case in his latest work, *Que Vive la République*, a quite emotional text that places its author in the tradition of Michelet and Durkheim as he revindicates the state and the collective – even when known or felt through myth – against the particularities of civil society. One does not baulk when Debray effectively fingers post-modernism as landscaped ethnomethodology, but when he protests that the media today pay inordinate attention to the death of a celebrity from AIDS, wondering why it cannot take corresponding interest in the grandeur of a speech by Saint-Just, one feels that this – rather than 'Danton' – would have been a more fitting *nom de guerre* for his earlier incarnation.[48]

Debray, of course, was a servant of the French state for over a decade, first advising President Mitterrand on third world affairs and subsequently joining the Conseil d'Etat as well as serving as secretary of the South Pacific Council. It is, perhaps, a fitting irony that in this latter capacity he not only promoted a new regional university to 'combat Anglo-Presbyterian morality' but also defended the testing of nuclear devices on the Mururoa atoll by approving the detention of protesting squatters, including one Mr Charlie Chang and 17 members of his Taata Tahiti Tiana party who were found guilty under a 1935 statute relating to economic crimes. One does not, of course, imagine that Mr Chang and his followers played any part in Mitterrand's call for other states to follow his 'unilateral' halting of nuclear tests, but one is grateful that the choice of violence on offer was so clear-cut.

Since we have moved on rather precipitately over 25 years from 1967 let me turn briefly to the question raised in the title – 'all gone or more to come?' – which, apart from a not entirely misplaced evocation of infantile loss and deferred gratification, signals the lurking presence of some very grand theory in the shape of Francis Fukuyama's *The End of History and the Last Man*. This text, published in 1992, declares quite unambiguously that the ideal-types represented for us by Barrientos and Debray have no significant role to play in future world events although they may possibly linger on the margins of the stage until market economics and liberal democracy have finally seeped into every last cranny.

This is assuredly not the place to get to grips with Dr Fukuyama's expansive thesis, but we should at least take note of the extraordinary confidence with which it is propounded.

> Technology [Fukuyama informs us] makes possible the limitless accumulation of wealth, and thus the satisfaction of an ever-expanding set of human desires. This process guarantees an increasing homogenization of all human societies, regardless of their historical origins or cultural inheritances. All countries undergoing economic modernization must increasingly resemble one another; they must unify nationally on the basis of a centralized state, urbanize, replace traditional forms of social organization like tribe, sect, and family with economically rational ones based on function and efficiency.[49]

For Fukuyama this is clear because we have already crossed the threshold of 'the end of history'. He is in no doubt that there will be, as he puts it, 'no further progress in the development of underlying principles and institutions because all of the really big questions (have) been settled'.[50] Moreover, he gives Latin America a quite significant role in a transition that nobody could sensibly deny has started to take place but that few would deign to insist – even with such a glorious mélange of borrowed philosophy, poor history and wholesale wishful thinking – is going to end where he says it will, still less that it is the last transition of all. Nonetheless, one has to accept that this is a theory that – rather like post-modernism – has proved quite resistant to the collapse of many of its particular features, reflecting more than a purely philosophical mood. Indeed, it might even bear out some of Debray's laconic ruminations on 'developments in thought' and 'developments in reality'.

There is no need to embark upon a detailed survey to comprehend why the present conjuncture in Latin America might contribute to the conviction that 'liberal democracy remains the only coherent political aspiration' and free markets, or liberal economics, an inevitable destiny.[51] As Victor Bulmer-Thomas showed us so clearly, the last five years in particular have seen an emphatic shift in regional economic policy away from corporatist capitalism towards free market principles, producing in several countries a notable reduction in inflation as well as state intervention; overall economic performance has registered a significant improvement.[52] Moreover, the imposition of invariably harsh and initially inequitable and unpopular deflationary policies has almost everywhere been undertaken by elected civilian administrations – the result of an impressive if still unfinished transfer from dictatorship to constitutional rule over the last decade. Since 1988 every country has held an election, and some – including Bolivia – have been governed by three or four successive civilian administrations resulting from the popular vote. Even in those cases, such as El Salvador and Guatemala, where the electoral process began very much as a US imposition and unashamedly excluded the left, there has been some – occasionally much – progress towards a negotiated truce.

It is surely telling that the region's one Communist state – Cuba – has not made this transition, but it is also a widely held view that spiteful US policy has played a major role in fortifying the nationalist resolve of the leadership in Havana. It may even be that poor Cuba is having to represent her sister republics in defying the arrogant gringo with a kind of dusk chorus of denunciation. If Fidel Castro retains a remarkable popularity throughout the region, this now rests heavily on nostalgia, and in many ways he would serve as quite a passable amalgam of Barrientos and Debray.

Today the internationalist is not a European left-wing philosopher but a conservative North American economist – Professor Jeffrey Sachs of Harvard, who, having presided over the Bolivian stabilisation plan of 1985 proceeded to Warsaw and Moscow, and, although he may perforce have had to dally there awhile, one could readily imagine him pushing on to Beijing via Hanoi.

In the political realm the fact that the Latin American dictatorships were generally able to determine the nature of their departure sets them apart from the experience of the east in 1989 and the west in 1945. It has also left a distinctly disturbing set of dilemmas between revenge and reconciliation that are largely being handled at an official level by a retreat from prosecution to amnesty to outright 'forgetfulness', as well as through a clear shift from the naming of those alleged to have committed crimes to that of those known to have been their victims. This may be successful in terms of statecraft, but it is much less so at the level of civil society, especially for the direct victims of repression and their families. Anybody who knows Ariel Dorfman's play *Death and the Maiden* cannot fail to appreciate this.[53]

The question of human rights has not, in fact, provoked open conflict to the same degree as have economic policy and corruption. Moreover, if a refusal to forget or forgive remains at the core of both survival and deterrence, it is worth noting José Woldenberg's observation that as the victims and their repressors die the objective effects of this sentiment necessarily decline. In the case of Latin America, where the savagery of dictatorship has occurred very recently, the more likely scenario for *de facto* acquiescence is the coming maturity of a generation too young to have remembered – half the present population of Chile, for example, was born after Pinochet's coup in 1973.[54]

This picture may not fully accord with Fukuyama's bouncy predictions, but it would appear to herald the disappearance of the likes of Barrientos and Debray. On the one hand, the warrior who grasps office with scant regard for policy and holds it by a combination of dashing deeds, demonisation and unabashed political dependency. And on the other, the radical thinker for whom foreignness and the terrible risks of failure on the insurrectionary road to civilisation are strictly secondary considerations in a decisive culture of commitment. Whether or not we deem these attributes even partly worthy, they are widely seen to be anachronisms. One is reminded of that passage in Gabriel García Márquez's *The General in his Labyrinth* where Bolívar admonishes a Frenchman: '. . . stop doing us the favour of telling us what we should do . . . Damn it, please let us have our Middle Ages in peace!'[55] Except, of course, that after 160 years the Middle Ages are over, and, Fukuyama assures us, there is now on earth no apparent problem that is not soluble on the basis of liberal principles.[56]

Some caution is evidently called for. In the first place, not even Fukuyama's sources concur on whether the linear ascent of human history to this felicitous apogee will greatly reduce the incidence of warfare. As a result, we might expect the ancient disparities between the warrior and the scribe to continue for a while yet.

Secondly, it is typical of intellectuals to assign transcendent importance to underlying principles when ordinary folk are far more concerned with the tactile reality pressing in on them every day. One should not, then, underestimate the indisputably harsh price being paid by Latin America's poor for economic stabilisation or the cholera that is presently afflicting them or the sense of injustice over past violations of human rights and present corruption. It would be even more unwise to assume that these are consciously traded for acquiescence in liberalism on the belief that this is the true 'development in reality'. Unlike in eastern

Europe, a great deal of what is currently occurring has been seen before and illusions are more modest in a region that has been far more and much longer market-oriented than some theorists – right- and left-wing alike – recognise.

Against the impressive quietude of Argentina and Chile in the early 1990s one must pitch the eruption of popular fury in Venezuela and the suspension of constitutional guarantees and government in Peru. Furthermore, one might note that in this latter country a particularly violent and remarkably resourceful insurrectionary movement – Sendero Luminoso – is headed by a man – Abimäel Guzmán – who has not been seen in public for over 10 years, suffers acutely from diabetes, and is the author of a thesis on Kant's theory of space. These are not obvious components of a charismatic leader although among several Bolivian figures who exercise an influence well beyond the customary parameters of public respect I would single out Eduardo Nava Morales, for many years Dean of Economics at San Andrés University in La Paz, a man whose work on Keynes in the early 1950s had an influence on the MNR, and who now, with the loss of his middle ear aggravating a famously bad temper, poor eyesight and a tendency to obesity, may be seen each day being assisted down the street to his classes by students whom he will shortly berate.

It is, though, much more often a combination of healthy physique and oratorial energy that one associates with charismatic authority, as illustrated by the description given in the Mexican daily *La Jornada* of Comandante Hugo Chávez, the officer who led a violent coup attempt in Venezuela in February 1992 against the deeply disliked regime of Carlos Andrés Pérez. Given Chávez's subsequent popularity, it would seem clear that many people shared *La Jornada's* view of him as

> young and slim. His trim and clean *mestizo* features highlighted a smooth sensuality. The contrast with the pallid and flaccid masks of the parliamentary bureaucracy was striking ... the sense of self-control and military discipline, honour and serene conviction in the face of uncertain destiny distinguished the soldier as a classic hero ... his words invoked with tenderness the name in which independence is rooted: Bolívar ... the soldier accepted full and absolute responsibility for the events of the night – something which surprised public opinion, tired of a political system that, in the name of anonymity, permits social crimes to be committed with impunity.[57]

This contrast, which is not too exaggerated, evokes that between Barrientos and the MNR. More importantly, however, the inclusion of Bolívar's name in the title of the rebel movement underlines the dangers of adopting Fukuyama's unproblematic division between ancient and modern, or the post-historical. For the fact is that in Latin America the two are not separate – not even parallel – but passionately entwined. It is not, then, simply a question of arguing that Latin American 'modernity' began in 1922 with the publication of César Vallejo's poem 'Trilce', or in 1946 with the opening of the Volta Redonda steelworks, or in 1973 with the coup in Chile. Rather, it is a matter of unburdening ourselves of the unilinear perspective that confuses the 'development' of political economy with the 'nature' of a society in its entirety.

Last month I attended a clandestine meeting in an industrial suburb of Mexico City where a man known as El Hermanito and reckoned to be inhabited by the spirit of the great lord Cuauhtémoc conducted major surgical operations with a regular household knife and without anaesthetic on patients who included qualified doctors and computer programmers as well as peasants and street-sellers. As a result, I am probably too impressed by and indulgent of the regional propensity for metaphysics in general and rebirth in particular, but one ignores such phenomena at the cost of gravely misunderstanding the people for whom they possess great meaning. There is undoubtedly a quality of innocence about the persons and activities of Barrientos and Debray; they belong to a bygone age. Yet innocence is defiantly relative.

I want to finish by upholding the claims of 'the third man'. By this I mean a representative of those who died in defeat, as opposed to Barrientos, a victor felled in his prime, or Debray, one of the vanquished who was spared to ruminate. 'All gone' means 'disappeared', which in Latin America is immediately understood to signify physically executed with the body destroyed or hidden. As a result, there are very many names that one could pin on this third figure, but today I choose Jorge Ríos Dalenz – a man whom I never met and who does not appear in the report of the Rettig Commission set up by the new Chilean government. This is because investigation of those killed under Pinochet depended upon a submission by family or close friends, and Ríos was a Bolivian without relatives in Chile.

Chichi Ríos Dalenz, a member of the Movement of the Revolutionary Left exiled from Bolivia two years earlier, was executed at the same time as the singer Víctor Jara – on 15 or 16 September 1973 – in the Estadio Chile, where they had been held for three days.[58] Once described as 'the flower of the Bolivian left' for his restless creativity and organisational energy, he is now little more than a sentimental footnote in the past of Jaime Paz Zamora, who was his friend, admirer and party comrade, and who today subscribes to many of the views held by Fukuyama and is President of the Republic of Bolivia.

It is testimony to the generosity of the people of Chile that last year Jorge Ríos and the other foreigners who died in the Estadio Chile were each remembered in song alongside their compatriots as that place was subjected to a secular and remarkably optimistic 'purification', or exorcism. Perhaps a response more fitting to the present occasion would be to reserve a quota of doubt with respect to both the inevitability of history and the full identity of its authors.

1992

Beyond Utopia:
The State of the Left in Latin America

Alice got up to leave. We are still here . . . and we sing . . . still.[1]

One bleak Saturday, a year or so after Pinochet had handed office back
to the civilians, I found myself sheltering from a storm in Valparaiso's
Plaza Victoria. The square was deserted except for the sentries outside the
imposing HQ of the Chilean navy and a solitary, well-groomed figure in a
typical businessman's grey suit, clutching a briefcase and struggling
against the driving rain. 'That,' I proclaimed to my companion, 'is why
Chilean capitalism is so strong: these entrepreneurs go to work in the rain
at weekends.' Two days later we attended a meeting in Santiago at which
some independently-minded Communist Party militants who had just
freed themselves from the formidable dominion of Corvalán and Teitel-
boim were trying to resolve their precarious organisational status and
political direction. Simultaneously renouncing and perfecting the discourse of orthodoxy, these comrades, who hail from one of the most
loquacious of radical currents, entered into a prolonged tussle over
whether they should retain their independence or enter the rightward-
moving Socialist Party, now a junior party in the government, and become
tribunes for genuine radicalism in a still significant forum. Wearying of
the predictable points of order, we made to leave, only to be accosted at
the door by the quartermaster of one of the factions, anxious that he was
about to lose two vital votes. It was the man in the grey suit. The figure
that I had so confidently identified as representing capitalist prowess was,
in fact, one of its dwindling band of opponents, his urgent weekend
labours significant in an entirely different sense.

Jorge Castañeda has peppered his marvellous, sprawling book with pen-
portraits and vignettes that are a good deal livelier than this, but all share
a profoundly elegaic air.[2] None of the figures to whom we are introduced

retains both their early radical convictions and their optimism; more than a few are burnt-out guerrilla fighters. Perhaps this choice is unsurprising from an author who insists upon the continued relevance and importance of the left but who is also prepared to declare openly what many believe yet will not state: 'The only thing left to fight for is a future that is simply the present, plus more of the same . . .' (p. 234). In fact, Castañeda's book is brimming with ideas, concrete proposals and creative insights, but he is clearly at pains to depict the scale of the defeat of the left – both in Latin America and abroad – as starkly as possible so as to dispel any illusion as to the corresponding scope of the challenge that still confronts it. It is both a weakness and a strength of the book that its author endeavours to fight on all fronts, providing us over nearly five hundred pages with a synoptic history of the region's left between 1959 and 1993; an assessment of the balance of forces following the end of the Cold War; a primer on the political economy of development; a treatise on democracy; and a portfolio of precise policy proposals. The extent of the text's ambition certainly renders it prey to criticism on a variety of technical and stylistic grounds, but an altogether more prominent feature resides in its gener-osity – Castañeda is not in the game of composing sophisticated jeremiads; if he identifies a problem he also suggests a solution, however humdrum or unpalatable that might be.

A Mexican academic who was educated in France, has worked in the US and writes a regular column for *Newsweek*, Castañeda has assembled a book that is neither strictly scholarly (although there is an exceptional range of written and oral sources) nor populist, but rather, written in a mid-range, plain-speaking tone that assumes little of the reader (certainly not that they know the patois of leftism), imparts calm confidence, and progresses with an almost disturbing fluidity. This makes for maximum accessibility and registers the quite distinct politico-intellectual sensibilities of Europe, North and Latin America, but it does not always permit a proper focus. The same voice used to condense the ideas of Gramsci and Foucault is employed to describe guerrilla feuding in El Salvador, outline the problems of import-substituting industrialisation, and assess the char-acter of Fidel Castro. Not everything emerges unscathed, the politics doing better than the ideas, the micro faring less well than the macro, and the contemporary winning out over the past. Yet despite the book's generalist expression, its organisation suggests a target audience that is either Latin American or already quite knowledgeable. There is no summary presentation of the region's political history; it is some two hundred and fifty pages before we are given proper statistics for modern economic performance, and four hundred before the social structure is fully illustrated. This arrangement has led some critics to combine the (plausible but misleading) description of Castañeda's work as 'social

democratic' with the unfounded charge that he undervalues the power
and destructiveness of neo-liberal capitalism.

The book is organised in three broad sections. The first surveys the
record of the left – understood in a very general, relational sense – since
the Cuban Revolution. The second discusses Latin America's distinctive
intellectual tradition and its modern social movements in rather broader
terms, and then assesses the political balance of forces in the conjuncture
opened by the collapse of Communism in 1989. The final part of the text
draws on – and occasionally recapitulates – these to address the three
issues that Castañeda identifies as crucial to the radical cause – nationalism, democracy and the formulation of a new economic model – each of
which is treated in first a diagnostic and then a prescriptive chapter. In
my view this final section, which comprises some two hundred pages,
could stand alone as a coherent and compelling text, and as such it would
assuredly serve a more directly *political* purpose, at least within Latin
America. Yet the book deserves to be taken in its rich, controversial
entirety with the aim of reviving a debate presently in some danger of
being made moribund by the mutually reinforcing strains of twisting neo-
scholasticism and bone-headed recitation of doctrine, both of which
prosper on distress and neither of which offers tangible reward.

Insurrection and autocracy

For Castañeda the basic record of the Latin American left in the modern
period is that it won two revolutions (Cuba and Nicaragua) and lost one
(Nicaragua); that Cuba's endurance is sustained at a quite unacceptable
price both in terms of the plight of its people and with respect to the
wider claims of socialism; and that the Chilean tragedy – about which he
is not quite so forthright – was in more than small measure the result of
an extremist sabotage characterised less by calculating malevolence than
by foolish pursuit of unwarranted maximalism. This is a familiar perspective, and it still allows for recognition of the exceptional human cost
involved as well as the critical fact that the overall impact of the left's
endeavour has been greatly to improve the human condition of the
Americas. On both scores Castañeda is generous, although it is his
tendency to declare the left's strengths in general and to itemise its
weaknesses in detail. At the same time, he is not alone in identifying the
specifically Communist heritage as 'congenitally alien [to] Latin America'
(p. 25) and the Communist parties as much less influential than Marxist
ideas in general.[3] On the other hand, his assessment of the left's capacity
to engage with the electoral phase of politics from the early 1980s as
having important origins in the Communist parties' pursuit of legal

strategies in the post-war era is both fair and useful. In essence, though, Castañeda sees Latin American Communism as too weak to constrain the insurrectionists who came to dominate the radical tradition after Cuba and too publicly bonded to the USSR to be able to dwell for long in legal politics and engage effectively with reformism before Washington and local reactionaries chopped it down.

Partly as a consequence of this, Latin America's experience of reformism has largely been at the hands of the nationalist-populist 'left', which sometimes embraced Communist allies but more often shied away, as with Peronism, Getúlio Vargas in Brazil, Peruvian Aprismo, the Bolivian MNR and the Mexican PRI (understandably not on Castañeda's list but surely worthy of mention in this connection). Castañeda does not go far down the treacherous path of defining populism, but he captures both its essence and the core features of the environment in which it flourished by describing it as 'a compromise between limited political will to impose reform from above, and limited capacity to fight for reform from below' (p. 46). He also draws from Alain Touraine a critical insight with respect to this current: 'the direct appeal to the people eliminates forms of political representation common to the West.'[4]

What, at root, this means is that the same economic policies associated in Europe with social democracy were pursued in Latin America by authoritarian and corporatist movements that often involved mass participation but very weak attachment to democratic procedures. Yet by the 1990s many such currents were proving perfectly capable of escaping both their origins and institutionalised accountability, reviving a spurious 'anti-politics' through demagogy and preaching deliverance through sacrifice to win – fairly or otherwise – the elections that now had to be held. This occurred with the MNR in 1985, when it introduced the subcontinent's 'exemplary' neo-liberal shock adjustment; with Menem's mutant version of Peronism from 1989; with the PRI under Salinas after 1988; and with Acción Democrática under Carlos Andrés Pérez's second term from 1989. Should Fernando Henrique Cardoso win the elections of October 1994 it is likely to occur in Brazil, and one may discern important elements of the populist tradition's 'convocatory' appear in the reactionary authoritarianism practised by Alberto Fujimori in Peru (successfully) and Jorge Serrano in Guatemala (unsuccessfully). It is undoubtedly the case that the travails of the last decade have thrown up two potent radical challenges in the Mexican PRD and the Brazilian PT, both of which Castañeda assesses at some length, but the protean nature of populism, and its general passage from the left to the right in the post-war period, deserve greater attention.

In moving to the unambiguously left-wing experience of Cuba and Nicaragua, Castañeda treats a much clearer object of study and criticism.

In comparison to the Soviet model he sees Cuba as 'freer, more democratic, disorderly, tropical and spontaneous as well as being intellectually
more diverse and politically more liberal' (p. 74). However, he is really
more concerned with the Cuban model of the 1960s and 1970s for the
revolution in the rest of Latin America that was characterised by its
hemispheric ambition; socialist nature, emphasis on armed struggle,
attention to the role and requirements of leadership, insistence on the
foco theory of guerrilla warfare, and repudiation of Communist Party
claims to vanguard status. At the same time, Castañeda reminds us, the
Cubans wanted to keep one-party rule, full expropriation of the means of
production, and the objective of social homogeneity. He does not make
an issue of Havana's moral crusades and keeps the focus on the militarist
elitism associated with 'Castroism'.

This ground has been well trodden, not least in this *Review*; we need
no renewed rehearsal. Nevertheless, at some thirty years' distance from
the apogee of 'guerrilla-ism', one might perhaps cast a more cautious eye
at the now received belief that such matters are the exclusive property of
a bygone age, the grotesquely contrived 'universalisation' of a piece of
sheer luck in Cuba, and an almost adolescent compulsion to militarise
politics. Contemporary views on the left about electoral politics possess all
the assurance of those that previously elevated armed struggle. But who
on the left could raise serious objections to the campaign waged in
Chiapas by the Zapatistas in terms of either the need to take up arms or
the manner in which this was done or, indeed, its impact upon the entire
edifice of political control in Mexico? Perhaps even more compelling –
what are the objections to insurrectionary activity in Haiti against the
murderous regime of Cédras and François? Has not the level of terror,
and exhaustion of alternatives, rendered armed struggle an option to be
considered seriously, if not a necessary undertaking? If the claims for
guerrilla-ism were generally inflated and misguided, they were not always
so and even now retain some sad validity.

Castañeda is right to set his face against the conceits of clandestinity,
which he illustrates vividly, but this has much deeper roots than post-war
radicalism. Almost all oppositional politics in the subcontinent were
perforce secret even into the republican era as a result of the autocratic
and patrimonial substrate laid by Catholic absolutism. The customs and
practices of lodges and brotherhoods correspond not only to oligarchic
proclivities but also to the needs of unseating tyrants and the preservation
of embattled popular cultures. More recently, the terrorist capacity of
even regimes as corrupt and narrowly personalist as those of Somoza,
Trujillo, Batista and Duvalier compelled any meaningful opposition to go
underground or resign itself to sacrifice. And if there were miserably few
exceptions to this Caribbean tradition, the sheer frenzy of the South

American coups of the 1970s brutally extinguished sophisticated theories about low-cost political change in the region's most advanced societies. One does not wish to reintroduce a specious rationale for the nobility of guerrilla-ism by the back door, but Castañeda passes over its extenuation in the Southern Cone rather too rapidly, and if the achievements there were limited almost exclusively to symbolising a spirit of resistance, armed struggle in Central America proved both necessary and very far from fruitless.

In fact, the book's treatment of the Nicaraguan Revolution and the guerrillas in El Salvador and Guatemala is discernably kinder than that of Cuba, even though Castañeda sees the FSLN as winning power very much as a result of exceptional circumstances, which allowed them 'to pass . . . off tactics as strategy' (p. 111). In the same vein, he later views the Sandinistas as taking an 'instrumentalist' approach to liberal democracy, and relying excessively on police powers in the knowledge that they could justify this to supporters at home and abroad in terms of the US embargo and sponsorship of the Contra counter-revolution. In 1990, 'when they found themselves rejected by the voters, their true colours – undemocratic, not congenitally or intrinsically corrupt – peered through the olive drab uniform' (p. 347). This decidedly harsh appraisal will still infuriate many and is not sufficiently supported with hard evidence to convince the agnostic. Castañeda, who underwent the exasperating experience of being an adviser to the FSLN when their *braggadocio* was at its zenith, may be thought – to use his own phrase – to be having his *enchilada* and eating it when he reflects that the Sandinistas 'behaved much better than most ousted Latin American rulers, but much worse than they should have' (p. 351). Yet the extensive expropriation and distribution of property by the party after it had lost at the polls and before it left office – the '*piñata*' – was never defended persuasively enough by the leadership to counteract the loss of *mística* this caused amongst the rank and file.

However, Castañeda's charges against Sandinismo are much less about corruption than about autocracy, and he makes telling points over the critical role played by both the FSLN and the Cubans in the fatal feuding that beset the Salvadorean FMLN in the early 1980s. For some the issue was restricted to the need to maintain discipline at a time of civil war, but here it is strongly argued (albeit largely from anonymous sources) that the killing of FMLN leader Marcial in 1983 (by his own hand or otherwise) owed less to the requirements of upholding democratic centralism than to those of Havana's and Managua's foreign policies (p. 352ff). The charge, effectively, is one of brutal opportunism, and it fits depressingly well with Castro's prolonged preferment of Joaquin Villalobos, the most aggressively pragmatic of the FMLN's commanders, and a man who many believe murdered his comrade the poet Roque Dalton in 1975. This is dirty linen that we were once told we couldn't wash whilst the fighting continued – ten years ago a book of my own was rejected by a Mexican publisher simply because it addressed this issue – and now the inference is that these were 'historical errors' that may be absolved. Castañeda does not labour the point, but he does not let us forget.

It is, then, no little irony that one of the central problems facing the two contemporary movements which Castañeda palpably admires – the Mexican PRD and the PT in Brazil – is that their leadership is in each case gravely complicated by formation from disparate groups, lack of programmatic precision, and the necessary promotion of internal democracy to support demands for its proper practice in national politics. The PT will almost certainly have to modulate its stance in order to win the 1994 poll, but the tumultuous events in Mexico have shown Castañeda to have been too pessimistic about change there, even if some on the left still underestimate the value placed by many Mexicans on the order and continuity represented by the PRI. The analogies with the Soviet Union are inexact but more telling than some will allow. Castañeda is worried that the radical cause in both Brazil and Mexico will be prejudiced by 'the dynamic of confrontation' whereby electoral logic and right-wing provocation condemn it to ever more shrill expressions of a familiar denunciatory discourse. Indeed, this concern pervades the book as a whole although it does not extend to support for the kind of accommodation practised by the Chilean Socialist Party, which Castañeda seems disinclined to consider as left-wing at all any more (p. 169). Here it is not clear if he sees the Chilean experience as being an exaggerated version of the regional pattern because of the tangible insufficiencies of Unidad Popular and the exceptional combination of prolonged terror and economic growth registered under Pinochet, or whether it is simply because the Chilean Socialists have tried to emulate European social democracy – an option that Castañeda believes futile now that Communism has collapsed (p. 172).

Intellectuals and movements

Some non-Latin Americans might think the allocation of a 30-page chapter to intellectuals – as distinct from their ideas as such – rather strange, even self-serving. But Castañeda is justified in this and quotes Carlos Fuentes to good effect:

> In a continent like Latin America, with countries characterized by weak civil society, the intellectual finds exaggerated responsibilities foisted upon him . . . a member of parliament, a labour leader, journalist, a redeemer of his society

in the absence of functions that civil society should fulfil . . . Latin America has
been . . . governed by elites, by a power elite and a critical elite, with a sort of
dialogue between the two. (p. 180)

This, of course, is a notoriously two-way street. One thinks of erstwhile
radicals: Mario Vargas Llosa, who tried to become president of Peru on a
fiercely right-wing platform in 1990, and Octavio Paz, who excoriated the
Zapatistas as no more than unwashed psychopaths. Both men have been
attacked by Manuel Vázquez Montalbán for propagating a 'theology of
neo-liberalism' through their heavily syndicated newspaper columns.[5] Yet
ranged against them are the likes of Fuentes himself, the more retiring
García Márquez, Eduardo Galeano, Carlos Monsiváis, Elena Poniatowska,
Osvaldo Guayasamín, Adolfo Gilly, Chico Buarque, Jorge Amado and
Arnaldo Orfila, who as founder of the (still flourishing) Siglo XXI
publishing house in Mexico, probably did more to advance the course of
radicalism in the subcontinent than did the Trotskyist workers at the (now
closed) Siglo XX tin mine in Bolivia.

Intellectual history is a peculiarly exigent undertaking at the best of
times, and Castañeda asks rather too much of his limpid textbook prose
to engage convincingly with the state/civil society relation that his concerns and Fuentes's reflection place at the centre of the scene. However,
even a curtailed discussion yields reward, and one would like to see more
made of the near-coincidence of the 'French School' (Foucault, Lacan *et
al.*) rejection of the autonomy of civil society and the onset of the
dictatorships in South America which made the 'invention' of this sphere
a vital political and psychological resource. Such an apparent disjunction
between theory and practice is not peculiar to the region, and although it
took on a particularly consequential form, there still remains the thorny
question of limits, or as Castañeda puts it, 'terminological haziness'
(p. 198). Of course, even if Foucault's monism is set aside, neither Hegel
nor Gramsci will provide us with clear and fixed limits, the parameters
being highly mobile, even mercurial.

In April 1952 the miners of Siglo XX, having backed a three-day armed
uprising in which the Bolivian army was defeated and the oligarchic state
overthrown, insisted that whilst the local garrison was taken over and its
arms distributed to the populace, some of the soldiers were not to be
demobilised. These were the bandsmen, who had been contracted to play
at local *fiestas* through the important winter cycle of saints' days. Their brass
instruments were valued above autochthonous pipes, and their uniforms
lent 'occasion' to the revelries. In time, of course, a regular army would be
reconstructed around these remnants, and it would eventually overthrow
the revolution. Equally, a populist tradition remains rooted in the Bolivian
military (just as the *quena* pipe is today prized above the bugle).[6] Nor is it

always a matter of capillary action between collectivities, ideas and institutions. The rapid elevation of the Guatemalan human rights ombudsman
Ramiro de León Carpio to the presidency of the republic in June 1993 as
the result of a thwarted coup attempt is the most stark of recent instances
of individuals representing 'civil society' acquiring, by virtue of that func-
tion, state office. As in this case, it is often an emblematic transfer in which
conduct is sacrificed to image, but this does not exhaust all its significance.
At the same time, it is not entirely inconsequential that some politicians –
including de León for a few weeks – become known by their first name.
This is almost typical of Brazil (Getúlio, Tancredo, Lula, etc.), which is
supposed to have a weak state and a strong civil society, but elsewhere it
can also signal a more than notional diminution of the space between
public and private domains. Quite how far this line of inquiry is taken
depends on the weight one wishes to give 'psychopolitical' considerations.
(I imagine that many British revolutionaries could reflect with some profit
on why they chanted against 'Maggie' Thatcher.) Although he touches on
such matters, they are not a major concern for Castañeda in a way that they
might be for refugees and relatives of the disappeared in the Southern
Cone or Central America, where the scale of violence and exile and
displacement was so great.[7]

The 'grassroots explosion' from the 1970s of social movements, or what
Castañeda rather tentatively calls the 'social left', is treated favourably but
quite formally. It is perhaps indicative that the pen-portraits that preface
most of the book's chapters include only one representative of the social
left, and Castañeda's final platform pays no sustained attention to the
kinds of issues that concern the rank and file and for which no elite
ingenuity can substitute mass experience in the formulation and implementation of policy. There is frequent mention of women's organisations,
health, education, housing, human rights, and so on, but scant consideration of the often highly innovative, cooperative and egalitarian experiments that the region has thrown up in these areas over the last two
decades. Naturally, the last thing one would want is a shopping-list – and
it is not as if we lack popular testimony, which has become a vibrant genre
even in translation – but instances of resource at this level both inspire by
example and help creatively to subvert the tenacious assumption that
when formulae fail they simply need reordering. There is also some
danger in resisting critical examination of the social left just because it
does spring from popular experience. Here, for instance, Castañeda
simply welcomes the holding of the congress of continental indigenous
and popular organisations at Quezaltenango (Guatemala) in October
1991, when that meeting was, in fact, the occasion of fierce – sometimes
bitterly destructive – debate over how to respond to the five hundredth
anniversary of the Spanish conquest – a debate that deserves consideration

every bit as much as do the finer points of electoral reform and industrial strategy discussed here over tens of pages.[8] Equally, he is surely correct to identify the non-governmental organisations (NGOs) as 'now a reality, and an integral, important part of the regional Left' (p. 234). Yet one of the key consequences of the economic recession and neo-liberal offensive has been the elevation of the NGOs not only into parastatal bodies in many poor areas but also into conduits for political favours and clientelist control. This is not just true of the plethora of religiously-funded bodies, and many of the secular currents of the political left have taken refuge in the NGOs from both dictatorial oppression and repudiation by rank-and-file movements that fear 'ideological colonisation'.

Towards a new platform

Castañeda approaches the challenge of constructing a new radical platform for Latin America very much within an international framework, and most specifically in the light of the collapse of Communism, which he sees as providing almost as many opportunities as problems. The last third of the text also shifts into a more polemical gear: 'People do not die, go to prison, resist torture, or devote years of their lives to fighting for something that cannot be visualized or thought of in concrete terms, something that is not definite' (p. 242). I'm not at all sure about this form of words, which courts some risk of obscuring – if not denying – the emancipatory needs of and for political imagination. It is, though, precisely the utopian or fantastic qualities of Latin American radicalism that Castañeda feels have burgeoned to excess in the past and must be tamed. He is right to identify the potent regional Catholic tradition as a critical – maybe even determinant – complement to the teleological strain in Marxism, with the result that it was a good portion of society, not just some wild-eyed members of the elect, who subscribed to a future which 'included redemption, revenge, and final reckoning where good would triumph over evil, the poor over the rich, the autochthonous over the alien' (p. 242).

Latin American radicals were able to cleave with marked resilience to Bolshevik symbolism because their own history of insurgency against state-based autocracy allowed a kind of parallax. Even after the Cuban Revolution, which in practice and then in rapidly and energetically propagated theory contradicted a great part of the Marxist-Leninist prospectus, it proved relatively easy for embattled leftists to 'read' their past, present and future positions through the prism of Russia/USSR and to a lesser – but still critical – extent, China.

Castañeda may be going too far in trying to disturb this tendency when he declares:

> The most powerful argument in the hands of the Left in Latin America – or
> anywhere else – has never been, and in all likelihood will never be, exclusively
> the intrinsic merit or viability of the alternative it proposes. Its strong suit is the
> morally unacceptable character of life as the overwhelming majority of the
> region's inhabitants live it. (pp. 254–5)

Although the fluent *Newsweek* prose dampens the effect, this passage
suggests a kind of Bernsteinian presumption and abdication that Castañeda plainly rejects in its most irresponsible guise, but about which he is,
apparently, rather unsure, as becomes clearer nearly two hundred pages
later:

> The fact that the Right and the Centre, which have been governing most of
> Latin America for the last half century, have not proved up to the task, does
> not mean that the Left has the benefit of its adversaries' failure or that the task
> is unfulfillable. (p. 426)

This general problem has acquired particular importance in Latin America precisely because the neo-liberal right had established a powerful
record in the region under *both* dictatorial and constitutional regimes well
before the collapse of Communism. There are, then, two rather distinct, if
still complementary, phases to the right-wing challenge: the first that,
from at least the debt crisis of 1982, laid siege to the longstanding statism
of the region's corporate capitalism which the left had broadly viewed as
a basis for reform; and the second, after 1989, when the whole ideological
edifice of what Castañeda consistently calls 'socialism' came down. The
local neo-liberal campaign was assisted by the defeat of the Sandinistas in
1990 and what many reckoned to be the protracted death-throes of Cuban
Communism, but the real strength of the right lay in its claims precisely
not to have awaited the implosion of collectivism and statism but, rather,
actively to have demonstrated a superior model of production and distribution, *thereby* contributing to the erosion of socialism.

How does Castañeda propose that the left counter such claims? He
sees three broad areas where the rectification of past errors, the opportunities offered by the global balance of forces in the mid-1990s, and the
searing human cost of a decade and more of rampant neo-liberalism
could, in harness, provide the basis for a left-wing renaissance based
primarily upon material issues and driven by a constructive – rather than
denunciatory – energy. These are: a reformulated nationalism; an
expanded and deepened democratic vocation; and a blueprint for economic growth and equity combining different existing models of capitalist
development.

Although the last of these propositions would seem to be by far the
most controversial for those on the left, the first is scarcely less contentious
in that it runs against deep-seated social custom whereas, in practice, the

region is already tightly enmeshed in one model of capitalist development and, as Castañeda puts it, the left 'can reasonably hope to persuade millions of Latin Americans that another type of market economy . . . is preferable to the status quo' (p. 431). In sum, changing the economic prospectus in this manner may not be so radical, but it might well secure popular support and could even be seen as viable. Whether nationalist identity could be adjusted quite so readily is a moot point. Here Castañeda concedes – on one of too few occasions – that Latin America is in many respects as diverse as it is united, but he proceeds from the general understanding that:

> For many, if not all, of the developing countries, time has run out to construct nations like others: with their own national language, administration, market and currency and with a truly autochthonous ruling elite. (p. 287)

This is, for Castañeda, as true of Latin America as of the rest of the 'third world', although it is clear that the strong local tradition of anti-imperialism, the enduring culture – if not the precise tenets – of dependency theory, and the fact that these were primarily directed against the US, all make for powerful obstacles to any revisionist campaign in this sector. It is true that, even before the Cuban Revolution, the left stoked up nationalist rhetoric well beyond its capacity to control the consequences, but is it the case that it was only, as Castañeda puts it, 'because of its rivalry with the Soviet Union [that] the United States had no choice but to be hostile to anti-US nationalism in Latin America' (p. 295)? Might there not have been other, more residual factors? I also feel that Castañeda may again have been too affected by his Mexican nationality in reading the real strength of nationalist identity, since in few other countries has this been so exhaustively manipulated by the state (although in the Mexican case Washington's provocations certainly justified a good part of this, as Castañeda demonstrates with a rare display of unalloyed anger).[9] It is arguably not just the left but a significant sector of Latin American society as a whole that has deepened its nationalist self-image and vocation since 1945, very often in terms of 'community' rather than in more strictly economic fashion but most frequently through the matrix of a readily sanctioned anti-Americanism. Thus, whilst Castañeda makes a good case for a 'less attitudinal' and 'more policy-oriented' approach to nationalism – an approach he calls 'longitudinal' because it is primarily related to the US – he accepts that this can only be partial: 'because nation-building in Latin America is incomplete . . . the Left . . . has no choice but to remain nationalistic' (p. 298).

Sovereignty, integration, democracy

Two main proposals are derived from this conclusion. The first requires
a resilient assertion of sovereignty on issues 'involving domestic non-
economic affairs, such as drug enforcement, immigration control and
extraterritorial law enforcement of any type' (p. 304). Although it is
precisely in these areas that Washington has been expanding its ambitions
since 1989 – including the invasion of Panama at the end of that year –
Castañeda sees a more equitable future as the US is foisted with the
consequences (and fear of much greater costs) of what he calls 'intermestic' issues – accelerated immigration, environmental degradation, drugs
trafficking and debt boomerangs – which result from the recession and
are no longer conducive to treatment in simple internal/external (and so
bilateral) terms. On such matters it is necessary for the left to learn how
to 'work Washington', seeking out sympathetic constituencies and the best
portfolio of policies for mutual interest on specific issues, rather than
adopting a general defensive stance derived from (undeniably) inequitable relations, particularly in economics. It may well be that Castañeda
has overestimated the potential of 'global civil society' associated, for
example, with the Rio conference of 1992 on the environment, and he is
under no illusions as to the arrogance that pervades the US political elite,
regardless of the occupant of the White House. But his pragmatic solution
clearly amounts to more than extracting a tentative virtue from an
overbearing necessity.

The second proposition in this regard – regional integration – is
already in sight, albeit in a form (NAFTA; Mercosur) that Castañeda does
not endorse. The left should take up the banner of regional economic
integration because this 'represents an intermediate solution between a
largely unsustainable status quo and a highly harmful progression towards
the dissolution of sovereignties and social options for the developing
nations ... conserving the nation-state as the prime area of economic
activity appears impossible' (p. 313). The European left, in particular, is
also familiar with the real world challenge of the transition between
nationalism and internationalism on a non-socialist basis. And it is clear
that Castañeda, who greatly admires much of the existing model for
European integration, has drawn quite heavily on it to propose for a
much poorer (and more emphatically imbalanced) region a strategy that
includes:

> compensatory financing funded by windfall profit taxes and duties, labour
> mobility, a common external tariff to protect sectors of industry and agriculture
> that are jointly considered strategic and worthy of support, subsidies and credit

facilities in order to make them competitive in a business–government alliance and industrial policy along East Asian lines, a social charter or its equivalent and an environmental charter that harmonizes up, not down, and includes financing provision for the adoption of superior norms. (p. 317)

Here we are introduced to elements of the text's economic programme, but from a purely political viewpoint it is worth noting that Latin America possesses some keen advantages, not just in terms of language and culture but also with respect to a historical trajectory in which independence was secured under a federalist-regionalist impulse. This was too weak to resist the subsequent creation of nation-states for primarily parochial reasons, but it was still sufficiently robust never to be left wholly absent from that process of nation-building which Castañeda sees as unfinished. Under the Panamerican Union, the Rio Treaty of 1947, the Organization of American States and sundry subordinate entities, US hegemony was so prominent that it is more appropriate to talk of overt control. The final ratification of NAFTA confirms the persistence of this domination, but it now obtains in conditions of some insecurity, probable 'over-reach', and with a number of countervailing examples locked into the record and present mindset. The first tentative expression of these – all of which post-date the Cuban Revolution – was the Andean Pact; later instances included the refusal of the OAS to countenance a US-led peacekeeping force in Nicaragua to stop the FSLN coming to power, inconclusive summits over debt renegotiation, and more successful efforts at hectoring Washington into reconsideration of its supply-side interdiction-led approach to narcotics control. Whilst Castañeda rightly warns that any regionalist association must involve surrender of some sovereign rights (p. 321), it is not taxing to imagine most Latin American electorates endorsing the equivalent of the Maastricht Treaty, provided that this does not include the US, to which real (if not formal) rights have already been surrendered in such profusion as to endow a modern Bolivarian project with a strong popular mandate.

As might be inferred from his attitude to revolutionary Cuba and Nicaragua, Castañeda is convinced that the Latin American left possessed a fundamentally 'instrumentalist' attitude to liberal/'formal' democratic systems, even after the onset of the dictatorships of the 1970s.[10] As a result, he not only insists on the issue of internal democracy (taking many sobering pages to illustrate the nature and cost of its absence) but also launches a direct attack on Cuauhtémoc Cárdenas, Lula and Villalobos for refusing to engage in unqualified criticism of the Cuban regime. This makes for clean, logical lines, but it is disingenuous and a cheap point. The question of Cuba is no simple, cathartic 'duck-test' but a profoundly taxing challenge in which the legacy not just of the Latin American left but also that of the Soviet bloc and a far more vital North American imperialist vocation – Washington 'liberated' Cuba 19 years before the Bolshevik revolution – are combined in a manner that places a real premium upon diplomatic and logistical skills if change is to be secured without a horrible massacre, let alone with a modicum of equity. One does not have to subscribe to either notions of 'popular democracy' or Havana's estimate of the threats it faces to recognise that a Cuban transition to competitive politics will combine very few of the advantages and almost all of the setbacks experienced in eastern Europe and elsewhere in Latin America. On these grounds alone there is little reason to be sanguine, but it should also be possible to express a concern that the Cuban people do not pay other people's bills as well as that run up by their own CP without being deemed a party to despotism.

Such reservations about Castañeda's position would seem to be fortified by his citation of the Peruvian sociologist Julio Cotler to suggest that representative democracy 'means the open expression of the formerly disenfranchised mass's economic and social demands' (p. 334) – a proposition of breath-taking assurance even when measured against the more flighty of de Tocqueville's passages, not to mention the reality currently confronting today's supposedly enfranchised poor – some 270 million people according to the World Bank. Nonetheless, despite this marked over-reaction, Castañeda has not made common cause with that growing band of academic 'transitionalists' whose enthusiasm for the procedures of liberal democracy blots all else from the landscape, and he makes an unusually sharp critique of the closed, quasi-oligarchic and ultimately corrupt nature of the 'pacted transition' in Venezuela that was held up as a model for the subcontinent for the better portion of three decades.

As demonstrated by the election results of 1992 and 1993, the Venezuelan left has built an impressive base of popular support and – in the shape of Causa R – should make a strong challenge for presidential power in 1998. This is because over the last few years Venezuelan radicals have prosecuted campaigns against both corruption and neo-liberal policies as well as for honest and socially responsive local administration. Very similar reasons lie behind the quite unexpected success of the left-dominated Frente Grande in the April 1994 poll in Buenos Aires, the victory of the Frente Amplio in the Uruguayan capital Montevideo two years earlier, and those in a number of important Brazilian municipal polls by the PT at the start of the decade. It is true that the Salvadorean FMLN did poorly at local level in the March 1994 poll, but this may be explained at least in part by a far greater 'fear factor' than exists elsewhere (with the eternal exception of Guatemala). Such a pattern of retrieval – uneven but perceptible and likely to be greatly strengthened should the left be allowed to win as well as contest (even local) elections in Mexico – cannot be explained solely by Washington's acceptance of political competition, the collapse of Communism or a serious engagement on the part of the left with the problems and possibilities of electoralism. Radical advances in this sphere also reflect deep popular dislike – occasionally uncontainable hatred – of the revival of practices common to an oligarchic system of 'facade democracy' that has deeper roots than in eastern Europe and itself explains the left's previously carefree attitude towards formal liberties. Here again the radical record would be both better understood, and more fairly appraised, if it were placed in historical perspective as well as judged by its reaction and subjective rationalisation.

Castañeda's programme for the left in this sphere is unremarkable in its stress on electoral propriety, state accountability and encouragement of the expression of civil society. He lays emphasis on the need to expand democratic culture beyond the customary parameters of liberal institutions into the media, labour movement and civil service, where either private enterprise or the enormously powerful regional tradition of patrimonialism (public posts as property to be distributed/inherited on partisan criteria) have continued to prevail well beyond the ending of autocratic government. The case of Mexico illustrates the persistent danger of electoral fraud, but even where this has been greatly diminished there have been only slight advances in guaranteeing a non-partisan civil service, for which there exists a huge reservoir of popular support in a culture that habitually bureaucratises public activity. Without such a separation of state and government, which many on the left thought mere window-dressing for bourgeois hegemony, one cannot envisage a meaningful division of powers and the sweeping judicial reform required to permit the oversight and observance of human rights, proper administration of justice, and institutional bulwarks against impunity. The idea that anti-dictatorial struggle ended with the fall or replacement of the autocratic regimes is absurd – it now centres on the administration of justice as law.[11] Castañeda appears to have underestimated the degree to which this issue remains pending throughout the region, and in general he has little to say on the military question, which should be approached with a radical programme for the removal of its legal privileges (*fueros*) and its role in civil administration, and a large reduction in its budget in addition to the civilian trial of those charged with war crimes and violations of human rights.

Matters relating to the legislature and judiciary used to be thought either part of a 'minimum programme' (and so not worthy of profound consideration; the natural province of reformist fellow-travellers) or – more consequentially – the thin end of the wedge of 'parliamentary cretinism' (and so to be denounced, and exploited solely for that purpose). Castañeda's detailed proposals are open to debate – he advocates

proportional representation and an independent central bank without
much supportive argumentation – but they usefully synthesise the best of
current thinking and experience on the ground as well as reflecting the
direction being taken by a movement deeply scarred by arbitrary behaviour of a most murderous type.

Economic reform and welfare

Castañeda prefaces his blueprint for economic policy with an eclectic but
richly illustrated appraisal of the region's experience of neo-liberalism.
His obvious starting-point is recognition that 'no nation in Latin America
has been able to attain both growth and equity in recent history, if ever'
(p. 392). The failure of the populist regimes of both the post-war years
and the recent period to sustain either side of the growth/equity equation
is presented as no less self-inflicted, being the result of deliberate sabotage
by big business. However, Castañeda does identify a critical characteristic
of the Latin America bourgeoisie in that 'the internationalization of
politics and capital flows have given Latin American elites options their
predecessors [in other countries] did not possess: ask for help or leave'
(p. 404). The fact that recourse was made to both options frequently and
often with success reflects not just on US influence but also on the
peculiarities of entrepreneurial culture in the subcontinent and on some
of the difficulties associated with the idea of a 'national bourgeoisie' that
has underpinned a raft of radical analysis and policy over the last fifty
years.

Although Castañeda is sharply critical of traditional corporatist over-
taxation and staffing of the public sector, he makes a properly fierce and
detailed case for fiscal reform and identifies the state as playing a crucial
role in economic management and development. He captures the current
craze for privatisation in two telling sentences:

> What everyone was doing [was] selling assets to pay debt, with the hope that
> when the sales came to an end, as they inevitably would, someone else would
> take up the slack . . . The almost unavoidable result of dozens of governments'
> virtual bankruptcy was presented as a deliberate, freely adopted policy choice,
> applauded by ideologues in Washington and local beneficiaries. (pp. 418–19)

This auction follows on from more than a decade of 'structural adjustment
programmes' in which virtually all the adjustment came on the spending
side with infamously catastrophic consequences for the majority of Latin
Americans. Although many have secured survival through emigration,
involvement in the drug trade or contraband, petty commodity production and informal trading, these are precisely the 'intermestic' issues

which Castañeda reckons the US will be obliged to recognise as a strategic danger, and they can in no sense be depicted as a radical solution to the neo-liberal destruction of the corporate economy, still less as a model for the future.

Castañeda's alternative departs from three clear but exceptionally demanding tasks: the need to maximise the differences between existing models for market economics; the need to exploit the leverage given by globalisation (particularly of third world poverty); and the need to promote recognition within the US and the capitalist class that conservative economics in Latin America after the debt crisis has deepened the gap between rich and poor to such an extent that this now threatens a social explosion (p. 428). He then proposes an inter-market type of transition, whereby 'the Left can blend . . . the social corrections imposed upon the market by West European capitalism with the business–government complement to the market developed by Japanese capitalism' (p. 434). 'Export industries would be forced to compete abroad but would be protected at home as long as they made significant gains in competitiveness' (p. 464).

Drawing on Alain Lipietz's defence of worker 'implication' in the production process to address the issue of industrial relations under capitalism, Castañeda proposes a growth strategy of export-led industrialis-ation of the domestic market governed by a state sector defined by 'protection without full-scale protectionism, regulation without stifling the market, state ownership without a command economy, competition without savage capitalism' (p. 441). This, it should be recalled, is envisaged within the context of regional integration, and one cannot imagine Paraguay, for instance, pursuing the same path as Brazil, although Casta-ñeda does appear so strongly wedded to industrialisation that he is in some danger of missing the potential for both growth and equity in agriculture in (reformed) domestic as well as export markets. Neverthe-less, the rebuttal of autarky and the revindication of industrialisation clearly challenge sterile orthodoxies on both the left and the right. Such a prospectus is sure to draw the perennial response that it constitutes nothing more than a prettified social democracy. However, in addition to requiring that export-led industrialisation be environmentally sustainable as well as the engine of regional growth, Castañeda's core platform includes the establishment of an authentic welfare state to be funded by a thorough-going fiscal reform, effective international forgiveness of the debt – now probably in the order of $500 billion – and the slashing of military expenditures. If such policies are 'social-democratic' they are also exceptionally radical (and not only by virtue of their simultaneous common sense and repudiation by all governments of the region bar Cuba). Indeed, after some four hundred pages dedicated largely to a critique of utopianism, it is somewhat gratifying to reach such a bold conclusion.

Castañeda understandably devotes much space to the corresponding objection that his model is itself utopian since Washington could not tolerate it even if sections of local capital might. He is, after all, requiring that 'the US be neutral in its support for one economic and social programme or another – far-reaching debt relief (virtual condonement, in fact), international cooperation on tax reform, access to markets without draconian reciprocity and significant transfers for sustainable development' (p. 446). In return, 'the grand bargain of the millennium' offers the North, and the US in particular, 'the implementing of environmental and social policies in the Third World that deter jobs from fleeing en masse from the high-wage countries to the low-wage ones while at the same time ensuring more job creation and investment in the Third World' (p. 466).

Many might think that such a 'bargain' will never be recognised as such by the North before it is too late, not least because Castañeda's 'intermestic' issues can be faced down with short-term aggression and manipulated into a fin-de-siècle 'great fear' of a barbarian global underclass. The purely economic and managerial objections are, of course, legion, but Castañeda's sheer nerve and eschewal of cynicism are highly invigorating and deserve to be debated as widely as possible.

The fact that the left can now command at least a quarter of the popular vote in Latin America's two largest states – Brazil and Mexico – and has established an important presence through the ballot box in Venezuela, Argentina, Uruguay, Nicaragua and El Salvador suggests that such a debate would be advanced and far from abstract. The region is, indeed, highly diverse, and in some countries the combination of neoliberalism and populism has dwarfed the radical option; Chile remains cowed by its history, and in Peru Sendero Luminoso have made a savage case for historical exceptionalism, but the prospects in mid-1994 might be thought surprisingly bright in view of the state of play four years earlier.

July–August 1994

The 1997 Bolivian Election
in Historical Perspective

The poll of 1 June 1997 in Bolivia might, perhaps, be thought outstanding only for its result – the constitutional election to the presidency of a man, General Hugo Banzer Suárez, who had taken that office by bloody coup 26 years earlier and held it for seven years as a dictator. Yet Banzer's election and the strong position of his party, Acción Democrática Nacionalista (ADN), in the congressional poll and its subsequent formation of a '*megacoalición*' (ADN/CONDEPA/MIR/UCS) may be seen as expressions of a wider 'consolidation' of the institutions of liberal democracy in Bolivia, marking an important shift away from the post-war pattern of corporatist politics 'by ultimatum'.[1] That pattern had reached its peak in 1980–85 with, first, the anarchic and drug-related dictatorship of General Luis García Mesa (1980–81) and, then, the weak constitutional administration of the Unión Democrática y Popular (UDP, 1982–85), which fell prey to syndicalist and radical demands which it could neither meet nor suppress. The poll in 1997 was the fourth national election to be held according to constitutional order since 1985, when the UDP had been obliged to leave office a year early. As a result, the election could be said to confirm a new pattern of political behaviour whereby conservative and populist forces negotiate electoral and administrative pacts and coalitions without facing stringent constraints from other domestic political forces. Yet neither Banzer nor his several allies in the '*megacoalición*' which took office in August 1997 were extravagant in their celebration or claims of achievement – a sobriety echoed by most commentators, if not the university Trotskyists who cosily issued a call for armed insurrection to oust 'the fascists' from power.

That call to arms jarred particularly in the context of the exhumation of the remains of Ernesto Che Guevara and six of his guerrilla comrades to be returned to Cuba on 12 July 1997, just a few weeks short of the thirtieth anniversary of their execution. The youth of the contemporary

radical left seemed blind to the popular rejection of the politics of
violence, despite a dozen years of strict neo-liberal policies, fiscal parsi-
mony, and only modest success in reforming a centralised and patrimonialist state, in which corruption was widespread, if not endemic. Indeed,
the smooth operation of the election and the lack of conflict attending
both its result and Banzer's inauguration is all the more remarkable given
the instability and violence that had prevailed for several years previously
in neighbouring Peru and the fact that Bolivia's own indigenous communities have never been properly included within the culture or institutions of a liberal state which still exhibits a marked racism. Although no
administration since 1985 has been able to avoid suspending the constitution under states of siege, in order to restrict popular protests at the
high social cost of deflation, those mobilisations have not endured or
grown. No serious guerrilla force has taken root since the days of Guevara,
the once powerful trade union confederation (Central Obrera Boliviana,
COB) is divided and disoriented, and the legal left is but a shadow of its
former self. Taken together with Banzer's past and the high profile of
entrepreneurs in his government, this scenario would seem to suggest an
uncomplicated victory of the right, but that victory is certainly complicated, in terms of ideology as well as institutions.

The electoral system

Elections have been held intermittently in Bolivia since the 1840s, but
they did not become meaningful in terms of the competitive allocation of
office until the 1880s, and the urban masses only became actively engaged
in the holding of polls from the 1920s. During the 1930s and 1940s
military governments subordinated – but did not entirely eliminate –
electoral contests, which could still affect local structures of power and
influence in the towns and mines.[2] However, the restriction of the vote to
those who could read and write effectively disenfranchised the rural
population, which accounted for the great majority of the inhabitants of
the Republic. As can be seen from Table 3.1, the election of May 1951 –
the last before the revolution of April 1952 – excited the active participation of less than 130,000 people: a 38 per cent abstention rate by
registered voters when these constituted a tiny segment of the total
population.

This level of participation was in keeping with a social system in which
urban trams hauled platforms behind them on which to carry those
wearing indigenous dress, and in which free personal service of a servile
nature was still common on the manorial estates of the Andean *altiplano*
and valleys. The extent to which the 1952 revolution altered the 'formal

Table 3.1 **Electoral participation, 1951–89**

	Pop.	Potential voters	Reg.'d	Votes cast	Abs. (%)
1951	3,019,031		204,649	126,123	38.4
1956	3,250,000		1,119,047	955,349	14.6
1966	3,748,000		1,270,611	1,099,994	13.4
1978	4,850,000		1,922,556	1,971,968	+2.6
1979	5,253,623		1,876,920	1,693,233	9.8
1980	5,570,109	2,525,000	2,004,284	1,489,484	25.9
1985	6,429,226	2,931,123	2,108,457	1,728,365	18.0
1989	7,125,000	3,191,000	2,136,560	1,573,790	26.3

Source: J. Lazarte, *Revista de Estudios Políticos*, no. 74, Oct.–Dec. 1991. Annex. 3.

political nation' can also be seen from Table 3.2, which shows the geographical distribution of the electorate following the introduction of universal suffrage by the Movimiento Nacionalista Revolucionario (MNR) when it took power through the revolution. (Table 3.2 also shows the decline by the 1990s of the old mining and agricultural centres in the southern Andean region of the country and the contemporary concentration of social power in the triangle of La Paz–Cochabamba–Santa Cruz.)

Although the first poll under universal suffrage – that of 1956 – may be used as a point of comparison for voter eligibility and participation, it scarcely offers us a useful, or even valid, reference point in comparing precise results or party performance. The same may be said of the elections of 1960 and 1964, which were similarly held under the revolutionary hegemony of the MNR, when competition was far from free and fair. This was particularly true in 1964, with the party splitting internally

Table 3.2 **Eligible voters by department, 1951–97**

Department	1951	1956	1966	1997
La Paz	72,512	260,443	436,049	1,068,900
Cochabamba	36,834	203,407	270,622	527,100
Santa Cruz	25,981	94,940	138,236	733,600
Chuquisaca	15,233	57,002	97,434	196,700
Oruro	26,116	62,485	79,057	172,200
Potosí	41,161	125,059	151,074	251,800
Tarija	16,281	29,563	44,406	157,400
Beni	10,093	15,385	40,474	132,800
Pando	2,009	3,046	8,408	19,200
Total	246,220	829,556	1,265,754	3,260,100

Source: C. Mesa, *Entre Urnas y Fusiles*; Corte Nacional Electoral.

Table 3.3 **'Pre-transition' election results** (% vote; major parties only)

	1951	1956	1960	1964	1966	1978	1979	1980
MNR	42.9	82.3	74.5	85.9		10.8	31.1	20.2
ASD	32.1							
FSB	10.5	13.7	8.0	—	12.5			
PL	5.2							
PIR	5.3							
MNRA			14.1		8.6			
FRB					61.6			
PDC						8.5		
UDP						24.6	31.2	38.7
ADN							12.9	16.8
PS-1							4.2	8.7
Blank		1.5	1.2	5.7	5.8	1.8	3.2	11.2
Null		1.1	1.2	6.5	2.4	0.9	10.0	6.3

Sources: Mesa; Corte Nacional Electoral.

at the same time as it won a proportion of the vote almost on a Soviet scale (see Table 3.3).

Yet, just as the victory of the British Labour Party in May 1997 cannot usefully be compared with any poll prior to that of 1929 if *both* participation *and* results are taken as variables, so in Bolivia not a single poll before 1979 – 15 years after the collapse of the MNR's 'National Revolution' – properly stands the test of comparison. This is because the succession of military regimes that followed the MNR (see Table 3.4) either excluded the opposition and sharply restricted election campaigns (as in 1966) or simply fixed the results (as in 1978, a fact clearly shown by the 'excess voters' identified in Table 3.1). Nonetheless, in both 1979 and 1980 the MNR still retained the support of a considerable sector of the population, albeit at a level well short of a majority or one allowing the formation of a single-party administration (Table 3.3). Moreover, given that at the time of the polls of 1979 and 1980 the UDP was still strongly identified with the left-wing of the MNR, one could argue that the revolutionary party of the 1950s continued to enjoy an 'historical primacy' but was no longer able to translate this into coherent ideological advantage or electoral victory. This, however, is something of a theoretical observation since the coups staged in 1979 and 1980 overthrew the election results of those years.

As a consequence of those interventions and the dictatorships they set up we cannot talk of any election before 1985 being 'fully democratic' in the combined terms of participation, free competition, fair result and full social acceptance of that result. For this reason I have identified all earlier

Table 3.4 **Bolivian governments, 1951–85**

1951	M. Urriolagoitia (PURS)
1951–52	H. Ballivián (military)
1952–56	V. Paz Estenssoro (MNR)
1956–60	H. Siles Zuazo (MNR)
1960–64	V. Paz Estenssoro (MNR)
1964	V. Paz Estenssoro (MNR)
1964–69	R. Barrientos (military)
1969	L. Siles Salinas (PDC)
1969–70	A. Ovando (military)
1970–71	J.J. Torres (military)
1971–78	H. Banzer (military)
1978	J. Pereda (military)
1978–79	D. Padilla (military)
1979	W. Guevara (PRA/MNR)
1979	A. Natusch Busch (military)
1979–80	L. Gueiler (PRIN/MNR)
1980–81	L. García Mesa (military)
1981	Military Junta
1981	C. Torrelio (military)
1982	G. Vildoso (military)
1982–85	H. Siles Zuazo (UDP/MNRI)

elections as 'pre-transition'. The watershed is certainly partial in terms of popular participation and party competition, but it is important when these are taken within the context of institutional continuity. One could certainly argue that the transition begins before 1985 – for instance, with Banzer's overthrow in 1978 – but it is only at that point that the transition became a profound process. Equally, one may wish to describe the position prevailing in 1997 less as 'democratic' than as 'polyarchic' on the grounds that there has not yet been a transformation from institutional continuity to a culture and popular expectation of pluralist behaviour within civil and political society.[3]

Within this evolution the poll of 1997 incorporated the result of disparate efforts to settle on electoral arrangements which would prove socially fair as well as institutionally efficient. To some degree, as in 1986 and 1991, changes in electoral law were the outcome of pragmatic – even opportunist – political trade-offs; these should not be treated as emanating from disinterested 'statecraft'. On the other hand, the electoral system put in place over the three years before the 1997 poll was generally the consequence of informed debate over constitutional reform and the relative merits of 'presidentialist' and 'parliamentary' political systems in the post-authoritarian era. Although the MNR had firm control over the

Table 3.5 **National elections, 1985–97: vote**

Party/Front	1985	1989	1993	1997
MNR	456,704 (26.4%)	363,113 (23.1%)	585,837 (36%)	396,235 (18.2%)
AP			346,865 (21%)	
ADN	493,735 (28.6%)	357,298 (22.7%)		485,705 (22.3%)
MIR	153,143 (8.9%)	309,033 (19.6%)		365,005 (16.8%)
CONDEPA		173,459 (11.2%)	235.427 (14%)	373,528 (17.2%)
UCS			226,826 (14%)	350,730 (16.1%)
MBL			88,260 (5%)	67,244 (3.1%)
IU	10,072 (0.7%)	113,509 (7.2%)	16,137 (0.9%)	80,806 (3.7%)
PS-1	38,786 (2.2%)	39,763 (2.8%)		
Total	1,728,363	1,573,790	1,731,309	2,177,171
Sitting:	Siles (UDP)	V.Paz (MNR)	J.Paz (AP/MIR)	Sánchez (MNR)
Elected:	V.Paz (94)	J.Paz (97)	Sánchez (97)	Banzer
Loser:	Banzer (51)	Sánchez (50)	Palenque (16)	(unopposed)
Pact/Coal.:	MNR/AND	MIR/AND	MNR/MBL/UCS	'*Megacoalición*'

Note: Figures in brackets after names of elected and losing candidates refer to the number of votes cast in Congress for each candidate in the vote for the presidency.

executive and legislature, there was broad agreement that the electoral changes it introduced would address the difficulties of the proportional representation systems previously used: up until 1986, the D'Hondt formula, which could reward a party that won less than 1.5 per cent of the vote with up to three seats in the 130-strong lower house; thereafter, the St Laigue system, more favourable to larger political formations. The new system is very similar to that currently used in Germany and known in Europe as the 'additional member' mechanism, whereby half the deputies are elected from a party list ('plurinominal') and half as individual candidates for constituencies ('uninominal'). Under the law of 2 August 1996, article 60 of the constitution was amended to divide Bolivia's 424,000 square kilometres – slightly less than the size of France, Germany and Great Britain combined – into 68 constituencies in an effort to match rising localist sentiment, to curb some of the patronage power of the central party apparatchiks, and to enhance constituency affiliation and responsiveness as a factor in parliamentary behaviour.

As can be seen from Tables 3.5 and 3.6, this new system did not greatly alter the result of the poll in terms of the pattern of the vote from 1985 onwards (the 1997 results given in Table 3.5 are those for the *plurinominal* vote, which enables comparison with earlier polls). However, as an individual variable for the allocation of seats it was of some consequence (Table 3.7) since it enabled *uninominal* candidates of more regionally focused parties, such as CONDEPA in La Paz, to benefit from the strength of their

Table 3.6 **Elections, 1985–97: seats** (130 deputies; 27 senators)

Party/Front	1985	1989	1993	1997
MNR	59	49	69	30
ADN	51	46		43
AP (MIR/ADN)			43	
MIR	16	41		30
UCS			21	23
CONDEPA		10	14	22
MBL			7	5
PS-1	5			
IU		11		4
Eje			1	
Arbol			1	
Others	26		1	

Source: Corte Nacional Electoral.

slate as well as permitting celebrated individuals to buck the weakness of any party slate with which they were attached (Juan del Granado, the prosecutor of General García Mesa in La Paz for the MBL, Evo Morales, the leader of the coca growers' movement for IU in Cochabamba). Table

Table 3.7 **CONDEPA/MBL/IU: slate and constituency votes**

		CONDEPA	MBL	IU
La Paz	pl.	289,175	13,146	9,113
	uni.	228,086	38,969	11,430
Santa Cruz	pl.	11,233	12,170	2,521
	uni.	9,915	24,328	873
Chuquisaca	pl.	12,249	16,378	2,257
	uni.	6,870	23,759	5,869
Cochabamba	pl.	13,115	8,155	59,036
	uni.	9,164	12,087	54,416
Oruro	pl.	24,596	1,987	960
	uni.	18,257	5,277	3,214
Potosí	pl.	17,706	8,258	3,864
	uni.	12,489	11,427	3,733
Tarija	pl.	3,774	4,503	655
	uni.	2,933	11,185	585
Beni	pl.	1,321	2,196	134
	uni.	1,167	2,572	879
Pando	pl.	359	451	55
	uni.	957	491	2

Source: Corte Nacional Electoral.

Table 3.8 **Presidential election 1997 (% slate vote by department)** (not rounded)

	ADN	MNR	MIR	UCS	CON.	MBL	IU	VS	Eje	PDB
La Paz	20.3	12.9	11.1	9.7	37.5	1.9	1.3	1.8	0.6	0.4
Santa Cruz	24.9	24.2	16.0	25.9	2.2	1.9	0.4	1.5	0.4	0.6
Beni	32.7	32.5	8.6	18.5	1.4	2.3	1.0	0.2	0.1	0.1
Pando	38.3	26.9	15.9	9.9	3.2	2.8	0.4	0.2	0.3	0.1
Oruro	21.9	15.6	17.5	15.0	20.5	1.7	1.8	1.8	0.5	0.4
Potosí	19.6	16.7	21.8	14.9	10.9	3.6	2.1	1.0	2.9	0.5
Cochabamba	23.7	11.7	19.9	16.2	4.3	2.2	15.9	1.0	0.4	0.6
Chuquisaca	20.8	18.2	19.7	14.0	9.4	9.5	1.4	1.1	0.8	0.4
Tarija	10.7	26.5	41.9	9.6	3.0	3.7	0.5	0.4	0.5	0.1
National	22.3	18.2	16.8	16.1	17.2	3.1	3.7	1.4	0.8	0.5

ADN – Acción Democrática Nacionalista; CONDEPA – Conciencia de Patria; Eje Pachakuti; IU – Izquierda Unida; MBL – Movimiento Bolivia Libre; MIR – Movimiento de la Izquierda Revolucionaria; MNR – Movimiento Nacionalista Revolucionario; PDB – Partido Democrático Boliviano; UCS – Unión Cívica de Solidaridad; VS – Vanguardia Socialista.

Source: Corte Nacional Electoral.

3.8 shows the geographical distribution of the plurinominal vote for the different parties.

This new, two-tier system operated with remarkable smoothness on polling day, the large majority of the electorate completing both the *plurinominal* upper half of the ballot paper for president, senators and slate based deputies as well as the lower *uninominal* section. The efficient logistical preparation of the poll was notable, including the allocation of a mobile phone to urban electoral stations and extensive distribution of clear preparatory guides to the new system. It is, however, hard to comment with authority on the degree of 'tactical voting' indulged in by the electorate. In part this is because the system was completely untried in 1997, and in part it derives from the fact that the voters were generally aware that since the 1960s no single party had won the 50 per cent of the vote required by the constitution to enable it to take power directly. Consequently, as stipulated by the constitution, the new Congress would elect the president from the front-runners, thereby placing a premium on the pre- and post-election pacts that will be discussed shortly. In 1997 there was a general anti-MNR sentiment amongst the populist and conservative parties as well as on the left, but there was no pre-poll public agreement to form a coalition. As a result, the electorate could reasonably vote against the MNR in the expectation that this would probably change the government but not necessarily to the advantage of their preferred party, even if they voted for slate and constituency based candidates from the same organisation. Equally, it should be noted that the composition of the Senate is calculated by yet another system, by which the winning party takes two of the three seats for each of the country's nine departments and the second-runner receives the remaining one. It defies belief that even the most psephologically sophisticated electorate could have calculated the probabilities of these three routes to the legislature (congressional *plurinominal*, congressional *uninominal*, senatorial) in addition to those of undeclared post-poll pacts whilst retaining the option of delivering a '*voto de castigo*' against the incumbent regime and, perhaps, reserving a separate vote for a favoured individual. In sum, it seems reasonable to suggest that the electorate simply voted according to general experience and proclivity with its calculations being no more detailed than those allowed by a broad estimation of the popularity of the alternatives.

Two other changes in the system deserve mention and may yet acquire more than formal importance. The first is the extension of the presidential term from four to five years. This is in keeping with a general Latin American pattern of extending executive mandates, either in themselves or – most recently and controversially in Peru and Argentina – by enabling the serving of successive terms. In Bolivia the question of re-election is not likely to become such an issue, partly because of the coalition nature of all governments over the last 12 years, but also simply because no government in that period ever succeeded in getting itself re-elected. It is, however, possible that Gonzalo Sánchez de Lozada, who left the presidency in 1997 – having previously lost the polls of 1989 and 1993 – could return as a strong candidate for the MNR in 2002. Since Sánchez de Lozada – popularly known as 'Goni' – was a leading architect of the 1985 economic stabilisation plan which has so strategically underpinned the political transition, his presence has become one of the most notable features of public life. However, it should be stressed that he neither seeks a 'populist' niche of the type created by Fujimori and Menem nor, indeed, does he possess great interest in the type of 'charismatic' politics so often counterpoised to the administration of neo-liberal policies.

Secondly, reforms to the constitution required that at least 30 per cent of all candidates in the 1997 poll be women. This unusual experiment in affirmative action proved relatively uncontroversial, perhaps because it did not result in any significant shift in the gender balance of representatives. Eventually, women accounted for 31 per cent of all candidates, 13 being elected to the 157-strong legislature (10 as *plurinominal* candidates; two as *uninominales*; and one senator). If the stand-bys (*suplentes*) for successful candidates are counted, a total of 34 were elected (all these coming from the party lists but not gaining enough votes to gain a seat under the quota assigned to their party). In 1989, 14 out of 157 legislators (or 7 per cent) were women; in 1993 the number was 12 (with four *suplentes*). At present 135 out of 1,625 municipal councillors are women although in some cities, such as Sucre, women are a clear majority of voters.[4] Local elections were held in 1987 for the first time since 1949 and then at two-yearly intervals, every other contest falling in the year of the national election but being held six months later, as in 1993 and 1997, which will serve as the first real test of the new system of local government discussed below.

Finally, in this regard, it is worth making a brief comparative comment. I have chosen to do this with reference to the systems pertaining to the British Isles, but not simply because both the Irish republic and the UK held general elections within weeks of that in Bolivia. There is a broader sense in which the study of Latin American politics is stymied by comparisons being limited to the region or to those extra-continental states deemed to be undergoing a similar political experience (for example, in terms of transition from authoritarianism, Spain and Portugal in the 1970s and eastern Europe in the 1990s). Yet the debate over the British electoral system has sharpened markedly over the last decade, to the extent that the Scottish Assembly approved by referendum in 1997 will be elected according to the additional member system, combining party lists and Westminster constituency MPs. Furthermore, had the Labour Party not won such a resounding victory on 1 May its leadership might have been obliged to succumb to the significant lobby for the introduction of proportional representation in the UK as a whole.[5] Table 3.9 shows what the effect of the main electoral systems would have been on the composition of the House of Commons.

Equally, whilst the Irish adoption of the single transferable vote (STV) for popular elections to the most powerful chamber of the legislature (the Dail) is far from unique in Europe, it possesses a greater comparability with Bolivia than most. Ireland only experienced her revolution three decades earlier, the absence of subsequent military intervention allowing a prolonged competition between large and generally conservative movements, Fianna Fail and Fine Gael, to which the contemporary leaderships

Table 3.9 **UK General Election of May 1997: actual and simulated results**

Party	1st past post	Alternative	STV	Add. member
Conservative	165	88	189	207
Labour	419	452	346	303
Liberal Democrat	46	90	87	111
Others	29	29	37	38

Alternative: 2nd pref. votes by constituency; STV: single transferable vote in large, multi-member constituencies; Add. member: 50 per cent MPs chosen from party list and 50 per cent from single-member constituencies.

Source: *Economist*, 20 September 1997[6].

Table 3.10 **Eire: General Election results 1951–97 (% first preference votes; Dail)**

	Fianna Fail		Fine Gael		Labour		Sinn Fein		Progressive Democrats	
	%	seats	%	seats	%	seats	%	seats	%	seats
1951	46.3	69	25.8	40	11.4	16				
1954	43.4	65	32.0	50	12.1	19	0.2	2		
1957	48.3	78	26.6	40	9.1	12	5.4	4		
1961	43.8	70	32.0	47	11.7	16	3.0	0		
1965	47.7	72	34.1	47	15.4	22				
1969	44.6	75	33.3	50	16.6	18				
1973	46.2	69	35.1	54	13.7	19				
1977	50.6	84	30.6	43	11.6	17				
1981	45.3	78	36.5	65	9.9	15				
1982 (Feb.)	47.3	81	37.3	63	9.1	15				
1982 (Nov.)	45.2	75	39.2	70	9.4	16				
1987	44.2	81	27.1	51	6.5	12	1.9	0	11.9	14
1989	44.2	77	29.3	55	9.5	15	1.2	0	5.5	6
1992	39.1	68	24.5	45	19.3	33	1.6	0	4.7	10
1997	39.3	77	27.9	54	10.4	17	2.5	1	4.7	4

Others: Greens: 1987 0.4% (0)
                    1989 1.5% (1)
                    1992 1.4% (1)
                    1997 2.8% (2)
Democratic Left 1992 2.8% (6)
                    1997 2.5% (4)

Source: Richard Sinnott, *Irish Voters Decide*, Manchester University Press, 1995.

of the ADN and MNR might aspire. In the same way, both the MIR and the MBL might see in the Irish Labour Party an example of an influential junior coalition role although in 1997 Dick Spring's party was punished for its pragmatic alliance with Fine Gael only slightly less severely than was Antonio Aranibar's MBL for backing the MNR in 1993–97 (Table 3.10). What is clear from the recent Irish experience is that the small parties have failed to make an impact on the position of the traditional movements to the same degree as have the new populist formations in Bolivia. However, this might well not last if the remarkable health of the Irish economy in the 1990s starts to fail – a fact so obvious that it should remind us that electoral systems may indeed matter but, ultimately, they merely translate decisions determined in a world made up of different measurements and estimations.

Parties and blocs, 1985–96

As can be discerned from Tables 3.3 and 3.4, the MNR was the dominant party in the political landscape of 'pre-transition' Bolivia: between 1952 and 1985 only one (very short) civilian government was headed by a president who was not a serving or past member of the party. If, as has sometimes been argued, the Bolivian party system is 'inchoate' this must have more to do with the fragmentation than the institutional longevity of its core political movement.[7]

Nevertheless, the return to prominence of the MNR after 1985 cannot be explained simply by its long-standing bedrock of support so much as by its capacity to exploit this in response to the economic and social crises presided over by the UDP coalition between 1982 and 1985. The key element in this regard was the *movimientista* jilting of expansionist and corporatist policies associated with the 1952 revolution and its imposition of a severe deflationary programme through Decreto Supremo 21060, introduced by President Víctor Paz Estenssoro on 29 August 1985, less than a month after coming to power. That measure succeeded in driving down the hyperinflation that had prevailed under the military dictatorships and the UDP and, despite sporadic popular opposition and mobilisation, the decree continued to operate as a constant in macroeconomic policy under all governments thereafter. This continuity has been partly due to the fact that the programme was initially designed and later implemented by non-members of the MNR, such as Juan Cariaga and Juan Antonio Morales. It also resulted from the decision of the ADN – which had publicly campaigned for this policy in the 1985 elections whereas the MNR had been distinctly pusillanimous about it – to accept with good grace the purloining of its programme as well as to support the Paz administration under a formal agreement known as the 'Pacto por la Democracia'. This might be deemed the single most important instance of elite consensus in the Bolivian transition; it certainly enabled the government to withstand the extended popular reaction against the stabilisation plan and the collapse of the tin price at the end of the year. It is doubtful if the administration could have survived either pressure had the unions grouped in the COB not already over-reached themselves in contest with the UDP, but the experience of conservative collaboration from late 1985 onwards was itself very important.

Under Víctor Paz the MNR effectively reversed the economic policies of 1952–56 with which the president had once been so intimately associated. It is highly unlikely that Hugo Banzer could have achieved this, if Congress had recognised his heading of the 1985 poll and elected him to the presidency on the grounds of his modest yet perceptible victory in the popular vote (Table 3.5). Banzer was not seen as a 'monetarist' in the Pinochet mould, but he was still identified with military rule, and he possessed few links with other parties with which to build an alliance; in August 1985 only the ADN congressmen voted for him (Table 3.6). As an elder statesman and the erstwhile *compañero* of Hernán Siles Zuazo, the outgoing UDP president, Víctor Paz combined association with a radical past, unparalleled experience, and 'imperial' style that enabled him to pick up the votes of the many small parties which won seats in this first truly post-dictatorial poll. Such a 'super-presidentialism' befitted a man in his eighth decade, and it has been depicted as the magisterial manner of closing a career of 50 years. It was, though, more consequential than that. In the first place, Paz was the only figure in the political landscape to whom Banzer could at that moment defer with grace whilst retaining his political capital; Paz's presence allowed Banzer to lose the presidential run-off in style and yet hold the legal right together. Secondly, although the vagaries of the electoral system had given the MNR a lead over the ADN in terms of seats, the *movimientistas* did not seek – and could barely hope – to repeat the run-off vote throughout a four-year term. Instead, they sided with the ADN to form an unassailable majority in Congress over the very parties who had just voted for Paz; this alliance guaranteed the passage of virtually all legislation through Congress (Table 3.6). Thirdly, as a result of these factors, Paz was able to hand day-to-day management of economic policy to his finance minister Gonzalo Sánchez de Lozada, who scarcely needed to worry himself with the problems of parliamentary alliances or sustaining popularity as he piloted through Bolivia's remarkable stabilisation and sought, with much less success, to fire up its desultory growth.

The combination of a strong ideological and parliamentary conservative alliance, the presidency in the hands of a 'father of the nation' figure, and a highly able and confident manager of the economy was certainly felicitous for the implementation of public policy. Indeed, it may have saved Bolivia from becoming authentically 'inchoate' as the majority of its population suffered wretchedly under the impact of deflation, the collapse of the tin industry, the far from perfect rules of competition in *narcotráfico*, and the initially weak poverty alleviation programmes. Yet the strengths of this truly transitional administration spawned a backlash as well as encouraging hubris within the MNR, which predictably put Sánchez de Lozada up as its presidential candidate, and unpredictably broke off the Pacto por la Democracia prior to the poll of 1989. We still lack a detailed and authoritative explanation for this move, but all the indications are that, having benefited so handsomely from coalition politics, the MNR seriously misconstrued the reasons for this, mistakenly assumed that it would be rewarded by the voters for reducing inflation and could therefore jettison the ADN and move behind the electoral pendulum to the centre. Under the circumstances, it is remarkable that the party was not more severely punished at the 1989 poll, and although it lost both the presidency and a congressional majority, it was able to constitute a vocal opposition and retain many appointments in the state sector, particularly the senior ranks of the judiciary.

However, in 1989 the defeat of the MNR was less notable than the manner in which the new administration was formed – an experience which gave rise to the popular story that, on visiting the shrine of the Virgin of Urkupiña, Sánchez de Lozada asked that he might be granted his wish to win the election, Jaime Paz Zamora that he be made president, and General Banzer that he be allowed to run the country, and that all three had their wishes fully realised.[8] As can be seen from Table 3.5, the MNR headed the poll, just ahead of the ADN, with a considerable improvement in the vote of Paz Zamora's Movimiento de la Izquierda Revolucionaria (MIR), a centrist movement which had quit the UDP government as soon as it entered crisis, despite the fact that Paz Zamora was vice-president of the Republic. No longer at the head of the poll, now plainly unable to ally with the MNR, and with the smaller parties located firmly on the left of the spectrum, Banzer played kingmaker by backing Paz Zamora, the third-placed candidate, to be president. Despite the closeness of the MIR's result to those of the front-running parties, this decision aroused acute controversy over the legitimacy of the congressional vote for the presidency, and the constitution was later amended to restrict the run-off to the two candidates leading the popular poll.

Banzer, whilst punishing his erstwhile allies for their fair-weather friendship, refused to enter into another formal agreement. Nonetheless, the loose Acuerdo Patriótico (AP) between the ADN and the MIR lasted up until and through the poll of 1993, and its strong parliamentary majority fortified the image of a benevolent ex-dictator generously backing a party formed 18 years before precisely in order to overthrow his regime. Again, coalition politics had contrived to throw up a strangely complementary pairing – this time in terms of generation and partisan reconciliation. The AP would not seriously tamper with the macroeconomic strategy established in 1985 whilst it strove to project a more balanced approach to stabilisation and a more relaxed, modern and 'inclusive' style of government.

The fact that this failed to consolidate over the following four years owes a good deal to the role of the MIR, which was the junior party of the alliance despite holding the presidency. With its roots in radical Christian Democracy and the insecurely radical urban middle classes of the late 1960s, the MIR had never been tempted for long to dwell within the hard, 'Leninist' left of Bolivia that had such a rigorous programmatic pedigree, proletarian constituency and unsated appetite for sectarianism. Its role as a 'bridge-party' of the centre, able to operate flexibly with the populist derivations of the old MNR and the orthodox left rooted in the unions had made the MIR a vital element in the UDP and, arguably, delivered victory to that coalition in 1980. Now, though, the MIR sought to hold both the centre ground and power by blocking with the right. The tensions caused by this shift had already split the party in 1986 between a pragmatic officialist wing and a 'principled' group under the leadership of Antonio Aranibar that went on to form the Movimiento Bolivia Libre (MBL). Three years later, with its vote doubled and supported by the ADN, the MIR seemed to have extracted maximum advantage from its relocation in the political spectrum. However, it is telling that the MBL (which fought the 1989 poll as part of the left-wing pact Izquierda Unida) began to describe itself as 'trigo limpio' – a phrase which artfully differentiated it from the rising reputation for placemanship and corruption acquired by the Paz Zamora faction, now distributing the offices and favours of the state with an energy exclusive to those who have never previously availed themselves of the rewards of the patrimonialist circuit.

This sense of corrosion in a still incipient, fragile system was hardened by a serious dispute between the legislature (controlled by the AP) and the Supreme Court (dominated by the MNR) that came to involve impeachment of the justices of the court and a dangerous stalemate over interpretation of the constitution, blocking much government business. The fact that the result of the elections and political manoeuvres could so readily destabilise ostensibly non-partisan institutions of the state was both generally disruptive and a specific warning to the MNR that, just as it could not expect to win elections outright or make and break alliances at will, nor could it simply transfer the tasks of opposition to those sections of the state apparatus that it happened to control with an indifferent or neutral effect on the constitutional order as a whole. The eventual solution of this crisis in May 1991 included the exchange of a new electoral law for retention of the justices in their posts. But, as might be expected, this did not presage the comprehensive reform of the judicial system advocated by modernisers from all parties (including the MNR's René Blattmann, who managed to introduce some important changes in custodial policy and sentencing procedure in the 1993–97 government).[9]

Both official placemanship and the crisis over the Supreme Court revealed the extent of drug interests in the political parties and the state, the question of *narcotráfico* returning to the top of both domestic and diplomatic agendas after a relatively low profile in the mid-1980s (despite the fact that receipts from cocaine had readily entered the banking system and palpably palliated the impact of structural adjustment). In this respect it is important to recall that Jaime Paz Zamora and the AP administration took office in August 1989, on the very cusp of the collapse of the Soviet bloc, and that this government would witness the collapse of Communism in the company of the Bush administration in the United States, which sought to implement a comprehensive anti-drug campaign in the western hemisphere. The prior preparedness of the Paz Estenssoro government formally to collaborate with high-profile interdiction operations – such as 'Blast Furnace' in 1986 – that involved deployment of US forces on Bolivian soil had given the MIR what seemed to be a low-cost nationalist platform, from which it continued to proclaim in office that 'coca is not cocaine'. This was a popular enough motif at home, and it played well with those sections of the international community convinced that Washington was seeking to shift to the south the economic, social and political costs of its anti-drug campaign by emphasising the problems of supply over those of demand. However, Paz Zamora misjudged a balance of forces that was, indeed, exceptionally mercurial. In addition to the wider international instability, including the de-escalation of the Central American civil wars that had so preoccupied Washington, his cabinet had to make sense of the unprecedentedly violent intromission of the cartels into Colombian politics; the extensive operations of Sendero Luminoso in neighbouring Peru; and the emergence there of Alberto Fujimori as a regional political figure of maverick qualities but critical importance for La Paz. Even with the invasion of Panama at the end of the year, it is not difficult to imagine how in such a scenario a policy of avowed autonomy towards the USA might commend itself, especially if conducted in harness with collaboration in practice.

Although drug scandals over the last decade have involved members of all the main parties together with the police, armed forces and judiciary, Washington's attention focused on the MIR, particularly once combined pressure from the embassy and press forced Interior Minister Guillermo Capobianco from office in March 1991. After the MIR left government in 1993, the party's number two, Oscar Eid, was jailed for four years for protecting traffickers, and Washington refused to issue visas to either Jaime Paz Zamora himself or to Carlos Saavedra, a senior minister in the outgoing government and effectively Eid's replacement in the party hierarchy.[10] This probably did the MIR little harm in the 1997 poll since it enabled the party to make a positive virtue out of its necessary distance from the USA, but it has further complicated an already critical aspect of public policy for several years. As can be seen from Table 3.11, interdiction operations and reduction of the *cocales* were maintained under the Paz Zamora government with roughly the same results as those registered by its predecessor and successor. These have been distinctly modest in the sense that between 1986 and 1996 the overall area under coca has been reduced little, if at all. But given that Bolivia is, in Washington's estima-

Table 3.11 **Drugs and US aid**

Anti-drug operations, Bolivia 1991–97

Detained/destroyed	1991	1992	1993	1994	1995	1996
Processing plants	1,386	1,052	938	1,613	2,131	1,660
Distillation vats	2,531	1,913	1,727	2,753	3,077	2,819
Persons	1,047	1,226	1,376	2,634	2,494	2,585
Cocaine base (tons)	9.48	10.19	9.51	8.82	9.5	10.0

Source: FELCN.

Coca cultivation and eradication

Year	Cultivated (estimated hectares)	Eradicated (hectares)
1986	25,800	
1987	30,646	
1988	38,400	
1989	41,816	
1990	44,462	
1991	39,086	
1992	36,746	
1993	35,500	2,400
1994	35,000	2,240
1995	30,000	5,492
1996	25,000	7,575

1997/8 target set by USA – 7,000 hectares by May 1998 –
agreed by *cocaleros*, 2 September 1997.

Source: *Presencia*, 20 July 1997.

US aid to Bolivia ($m)

	1993	1994	1995	1996
Economic support	59.5	31.0	16.7	15.0
Development	26.9	19.8	30.0	28.2
Food aid	43.2	36.0	19.9	21.3
Total		129.6	86.8	66.6

Source: USAID.

tion, the world's second largest producer of coca and cocaine – and that cultivation of the former nearly doubled over the period – the expenditure of some $200 million in eradication and interdiction might be said to have yielded some success.

A significant degree of compliance with Washington was always necessary for the simple reason that the USA accounts for over 30 per cent of

Bolivia's foreign trade. However, the prominence under the Clinton administration of the policy of 'decertification', whereby disbursement of US aid is conditional upon local acceptance and realisation of eradication targets, has sharpened the relationship, not least because World Bank loans – and much private investment – would also be put in jeopardy. As Table 3.11 shows, under the Sánchez de Lozada government Bolivia received a diminishing amount of aid from the USA, largely as a result of economic recovery. However, the most vulnerable funds – those for development – have not reduced and could have been frozen or with-drawn had the administration in La Paz not been so warmly disposed towards Washington and generally able to deliver compliance on the part of the most reluctant *cocaleros*, who have replaced the miners as the most vocal and independent sector of the populace. It is telling that, once it had issued a 10-point 'ethical charter', the first public challenge faced by the Banzer government in 1997 was to extract from Evo Morales and the coca-growers of the Chaparé an agreement to meet the US-ordained targets.[11] Indeed, the initial weeks of the Banzer government reflected in raw form the exigencies of fiscal policy imposed by external conditionality – Vice-President Quiroga had almost immediately to attend the Hong Kong conference of the IMF and World Bank. This increasingly familiar 'globalised' scenario, however, included much less violence than in Colombia or even Peru or Mexico. The Bolivian experience of *narcotráfico* has at no stage involved guerrilla groups, and it has rarely thrown up producers or traders whose operations consistently depend upon violent activity. Interdiction on the scale indicated in Table 3.11 has inevitably involved loss of life, and the specialist anti-drug forces have regularly been accused of human rights violations (under the 1993–97 government 22 people died, 105 were wounded and 2,002 were detained in public order operations).[12] Yet, the dichotomy between corruption and violence is as false as it is simplistic, and the ideological and institutional trajectory of national politics from 1985 onwards cannot be seen in isolation from – or as simply parallel to – the character of the local drug economy, especially its connections with the semi-legal cultivation of the coca leaf that directly underpins the subsistence of tens of thousands of poor people. The national election of 1993 reflected this state of affairs in confirming the serious nature of the challenge to the traditional parties from two new movements of strong 'populist' vocation and style: Conciencia de Patria (CONDEPA) led by ex-folk musician and La Paz television proprietor Carlos Palenque, who had polled well in 1989, and the Unión Cívica de Solidaridad (UCS), set up by the Cochabambino beer magnate Max Fernández, who was equally of humble origin. Although CONDEPA began its existence as an urbanised Aymara movement focused on the poorest sectors of El Alto and La Paz, whilst the UCS was less regionally restricted and appeared to gain more success in the provinces, both parties had clearly emerged and developed in response to the deflationary climate and restructuring begun by DS 21060. Headed by charismatic figures, driven by loose rhetoric and sharp expression of complaint, invoking threats to community and cultural values, dependent upon the reputation of being as well as representing 'outsiders', these movements sought national as well as local office but rarely propounded precise policies that might form the basis of a platform for government. Indeed, although much interesting analysis has been devoted to their ambiguous origins, declamatory discourse and contradictory impact on cultural identity, it is possible to view both organisations as vehicles for a machine politics run by a new entrepreneurial sector of *mestizo* background.[13]

In 1993 each of the populist parties won nearly a quarter of a million votes (14 per cent of the turnout), in part at the expense of the AP coalition – which could only muster half of the votes that the ADN and MIR had won by running separately in 1989 (Table 3.5) – but also partly by swallowing up the support of the small, radical, regional and personalist parties. These had secured 26 seats in the 1985 Congress and were now all but eliminated from the scene by a 'catch-all' oppositional offensive which eschewed traditional ideology and yet did not sacrifice rhetorical energy to the pursuit of state position, thereby expanding an already formidable capacity to deliver clientelist favours. The 'professional' politicos had little difficulty in disparaging Palenque's reliance upon the 'culture of complaint' stoked up by his TV programme 'Tribuna Libre del Pueblo', and they could plausibly doubt the solidity of support for Fernández based upon liberal distribution of free beer. Yet the 1993 poll clearly established popular proclivity for these options – whatever the degree of protest this entailed – and that of 1997 would confirm their presence on the scene, notwithstanding the recent death of both leaders and the involvement of both parties in government (CONDEPA in the municipal administration of El Alto and La Paz; UCS in the national coalition led by the MNR).

If the 1993 election result required the conservatives to negotiate with the new populist organisations, it also indicated a recurrent tendency on the part of the electorate to punish the incumbent administration, this time more severely than it had the MNR in 1989 (repeating this result in the local elections of December 1993 – see Table 3.12). On that basis Gonzalo Sánchez de Lozada readily won both the highest popular vote and the congressional run-off, in which Banzer did not even figure. However, the *movimientistas* had learned the lessons of 1989, and they went to some lengths to construct a coalition which would include not only the centre-left MBL (itself engaged in a pragmatic pirouette of a type it once scorned so severely) but also the UCS, which lacked any

track-record or ideological basis for rejecting the lure of office, and, as
vice-president, Víctor Hugo Cárdenas Conde, who headed the Movimiento Revolucionario Tupaj Katari de Liberación (MRTKL). This last
appointment was seemingly a very generous sop to the rather stiff but
talented and honourable Aymara intellectual who held a very modest
constituency in the northern *altiplano*. However, it transpired to be one of
Sánchez de Lozada's more inspired gambles in that Cárdenas, with an
awkward combination of idealism and *realpolitik*, single-mindedly promoted the idea of a multi-ethnic state through the representation of
indigenous identity, this form of 'cultural politics' proving remarkably
popular at home and abroad. The impact on hard policy was slight in the
extreme – as Cárdenas's initial supporters were quick to point out – but
the longer-term influence could be much more consequential, forming a
piece with Bolivia's avoidance of the type of social disintegration and
violence witnessed in Peru.

The Sánchez de Lozada administration

The MNR needed to form a coalition in 1993 in order to control both
houses of Congress. In the event, it assembled an alliance which mustered
97 of the 157 seats at stake – more than the number needed for amending
the constitution, which would be required if Sánchez de Lozada was to
realise his ambitious programme of reforms, the 'Plan de Todos'. This
had initially seemed little more than flamboyant campaign rhetoric, but
'Goni's' reputation as an innovative *técnico* easily outstripped that of
Banzer or Jaime Paz, whose coalition had become mired in 'sleaze' and
inertial tinkering with the earlier MNR programme. Moreover, one should
not underestimate the degree to which the decision by Cárdenas and
Aranibar (separately) to cross the traditional ideological divide both
encouraged a popular view of the new administration as a post-Cold War
government and gave Sánchez de Lozada himself the resolve to pursue
his own programme with non-partisan energy. In the event, neither of
these minor coalition allies salvaged much from the experience of
1993–97 if this is measured narrowly in zero-sum, partisan terms: the
MRTKL was unable even to stand in 1997, and the MBL was severely
chastised by the voters. By contrast, the UCS, which was the least creative
and disciplined member of the government, escaped the backlash entirely,
perhaps because it was so 'semi-detached' that it never became associated
with a programme that went well beyond DS 21060 in dismantling the
institutional and macroeconomic legacy of the 1952 revolution.

The two axes of the 'Plan de Todos' lay in administrative decentralisa-
tion and privatisation, but both were designed with greater attention to

mass 'participation' than most policies of this type, now familiar in the subcontinent because of their popularity with the large multilateral organisations, particularly the World Bank. Although neither policy had been fully implemented by 1997, the electorate had clearly registered their initial impact. In the case of the Ley de Participación Popular of April 1994 there had been a significant distribution of fiscal revenue from the central state to the 311 Organizaciones Territoriales de Base (OTBs) established across the country to administer health, education and other local services. In 1990 Bolivia's total municipal budget had been $22 million; by 1996 it was over $150 million – more than 30 per cent of total public expenditure. Between 1994 and 1995 municipal expenditure per capita rose from $11.2 to $41.1, but it should be noted that a full 46 per cent of the population was concentrated in just seven municipalities.[14] The establishment of comités de vigilancia was supposed to give local support for the statutory restriction of spending on wages to 10 per cent of each OTB's budget as well as to provide more general oversight. To the inevitable incidence of poor organisation in the transfer of services and 'windfall' exploitation of confusion and change by local caudillos and crooks, one should add the no less predictable conflicts over resources both within and between OTBs. It is as yet difficult to gain a firm sense of the impact on local structures and dynamics of power. Government propaganda was often highly exaggerated. Many communities did certainly receive income for the first time, and others now managed enhanced resources, but, by the same token, their new duties implied a far greater expenditure. The electoral out-turn of this root and branch alteration of the country's local government was not sensibly predictable beyond the early success registered by the parties of the governing coalition in the December 1995 local poll as a result of a huge publicity campaign (Table 3.12).

Sánchez de Lozada dubbed his government's privatisation policy one of 'capitalisation' (Law 1544 of March 1994), insisting that the sale of 50 per cent of the stock of public companies, together with transfer of full managerial powers to the private sector, was essential in order to overhaul inefficient entities. This sale was depicted as being a necessary complement to the stabilisation policy of a decade earlier in renovating the legacy of 1952. By the time of the poll nine companies had been sold for a total of $1.7 billion (not all of which was in liquid form). These included the national airline, Lloyd Aereo Boliviano (to the Brazilian VASP); ENTEL, the weak but potentially very profitable telecommunications company (to the Italian STET, which was soon subject to regulatory fines); and two sales that aroused controversy on the grounds of national security – the national railway company to the Chilean Cruz Blanca corporation (which immediately closed down the Sucre–Potosí branch-line) and

Table 3.12 **Municipal elections, 1993 and 1995**

Party	1993		1995	
	%	Concejales	%	Concejales
ADN-PDC	7.8	262	11.4	233
ASD	1.8	10	—	—
CONDEPA	19.6	323	15.5	131
EJE	0.6	15	1.8	25
FRI	2.2	17	3.1	27
FSB	2.1	10	—	—
IU	0.8	8	3.0	58
MBL	11.7	213	13.3	216
MIR	9.4	245	9.3	138
MKN	—	—	0.2	4
MNR	34.9	1,330	21.3	478
MPP	—	—	1.9	8
MRTKL	0.2	2	1.2	33
UCS	8.4	372	17.5	231
VR-9	0.2	3	0.5	2
Total votes	1,119,854		1,716,007	
Null/void	70,042		89,625	
Registered	2,231,945		2,840,492	
Abstentions (%)	47		36	

YPFB's oil and gas distribution branch (at $263 million, worth around 30 per cent of the company's total value) to ENRON-Shell. The prior performance of many of these companies was sufficiently poor to limit popular protest within a society generally sympathetic to the idea of public ownership. Moreover, the rise of new foreign investment from $35 million in 1990 to $520 million in 1996 lessened the impact of charges that Sánchez de Losada, himself a wealthy entrepreneur, was stripping the state of assets on behalf of the business community.[15]

If this policy was both more predictable and controversial than 'popular participation', there can be little doubt about the novelty (and strong electoral potential) of the government's proposals for the use of the receipts of privatisation – distribution to the public in the form of pensions. This required a considerable logistical undertaking since the central Bolivian state had previously run only one very modest pension system – for the veterans of the Chaco War against Paraguay (1932–5), now covering only 8,603 *beneméritos* and 13,571 widows (subject to unusual assessment in case of matrimony on fraudulent grounds by '*cazabeneméritos*').[16] In the event, the reorganisation of pension funds (AFPs) proved to be more restrictive for savers than even the much-vaunted Chilean system since membership of one of the two private systems in La Paz, Santa Cruz and Cochabamba and the one reserved for the rest of the country was obligatorily assigned (although mandatory levels of contribution could be enhanced in all). The closure of some substantial professional schemes was not accompanied with full guarantees for their transferred assets, and it was fiercely resisted by, for instance, the national medical association, which witnessed serious problems in public sector clinical provision as a result of the attendant amalgamation of professionally associated hospitals and clinics. The military, by contrast, quickly accepted the proposals but appear not to have grasped the full consequences of closure and amalgamation – something that may be subject to review in the wake of Banzer's election.

By far the greatest attention was focused on the payment of a pension (Bono de Solidaridad – Bonosol: a sunny enough term to throw a shadow over any affinity with the Mexican public works system set up by Carlos Salinas) to those over 65 years of age. The plan was to pay the equivalent of $248 to some 300,000 pensioners in 1997. This, it should be stressed, represented a considerable sum to many inhabitants of a country with such a low average income (some $800 per head). Indeed, the promise soon flushed out many new 'citizens'; there were 614,000 more registered voters in 1997 than in 1993, including two men of 93 and 107 years in the La Paz town of Ancoraimes who had never previously acquired any documentation from the state.[17] With its capacity for simple registration under pressure – let alone its actuarial skills – the state managed to pay pensions to only 150,000 people by the time of the poll, and substantial doubts remained as to the capacity of the AFPs to meet early expectations despite the fact that they had overnight become some of the most powerful and protected bodies within the national economy.[18] On the other hand, efforts within the MNR to exploit the Bonosol for party ends were largely contained, and Banzer was able to identify himself closely enough with a system the details of which he criticised – for example, by promising to lower the rural retirement age to 55 – so as not to lose electoral advantage.[19]

As with the other main planks of government policy, the brief record of the pension reform was not so poor in either conception or execution to suggest that the administration would be seriously penalised by the voters. There were understandable doubts concerning manipulation of unfamiliar systems and institutions – a response equally elicited by new agrarian reform legislation. In the past, such statutes have proved highly and justifiably controversial, especially in the *altiplano* and valleys, but the new law appeared to be wholly favourable to community and small-owner interests in its abolition of low-level taxation, the guarantees given to collective title, and the privileges advanced to the communities in terms

of allocation of public lands. Nevertheless, the statute was treated in many
sectors as being a contemporary expression of a free-market lineage
stretching back to Bolívar's Trujillo decree, Melgarejo's piratical expropri-
ations of 1866, and the decisive Ley de ex–vinculación of 1884. Certainly,
neither the MNR's authorship nor the support of Víctor Hugo Cárdenas
led to a widespread conviction that the law was a simple development or
improvement on the agrarian reform of August 1953.

Perhaps in all these cases the imbrication of public and private spheres
– the admixture of community and individual interest – was indeed
recognised, being viewed as both potentially efficient and equitable, but it
was not yet trusted to work. It has been observed that Sánchez de Losada
could be seen more as a 'legislator' than a 'governor',[20] but even had he
and his government expended more effort on the tasks of reassurance as
opposed to celebration, it may be doubted whether they would have
greatly soothed a popular disquiet which, as in 1985–89, had less to do
with rational calculation than a more profound insecurity.

Something of the same reaction may be found in the voters' response
to general economic performance, which was formally solid enough to
give grounds for the 'feel-good factor' that has so attracted Anglo-Saxon
psephologists in recent years. As might be expected, given his experience
as finance minister for Víctor Paz Estenssoro, 'Goni' kept inflation under
tight control, obtaining an average of 10 per cent over 1993–96 and a
level of 8 per cent – the lowest in 20 years – over the 12 months prior to
the poll. At 3.9 per cent the rate of economic growth was less impressive,
especially with the population expanding at 2.4 per cent. However, as we
have seen, investment was quite healthy in terms of Bolivia's distinctly
modest record in the past, and recent export performance was relatively
satisfactory – $1.2 billion in 1996 with decreased volume but increased
value in minerals and reduced sales of some non-traditional products
(coffee, vegetable oil, artisanal produce) matched by increases in others
(soya, Brazil nuts, wood). Moreover, confirmation of substantial reserves
of natural gas (up to 9 trillion cubic feet) available from 1999 was capped
by the signing of a 22-year contract to supply Brazil with gas worth up to
$500 million a year through a 3,150 km pipeline under construction
between Rio Grande and Puerto Suárez.[21]

These, of course, were big and generally distant issues, often learned
about from the mass media rather than sensed directly in daily life. On
the street and in popular consciousness the image and experience of
'progress and modernity' was far more ambiguous. This can be seen in
the manifestation of the market-as-modern-retailing, with the establishment in La Paz of a string of new or expanded supermarkets – Ketal;
Hypermaxi; Zatt; Bonanza. By mid-1997 these had captured some 15 per
cent of urban grocery sales but not on the classic grounds of the

economies of scale and loss-leaders, their prices failing to undercut those of the traditional street and covered markets across a range of 32 basic necessities, and being markedly higher on prime cuts of meat. It is unlikely that higher standards of hygiene account for this market share, which probably owes more to the pleasurable sensation of supermarket shopping, even if that currently constitutes an 'event' based on novelty or becomes part of a more differentiated strategy of buying by consumers. There are still millions of dollars tied up in highly profitable 'cholo' wholesale and retail enterprises in the streets and alley-ways in the north of the city and El Alto; Bolivia is very far from adopting 'mall culture' even if its most affluent suburbs may embrace the idea and institute their own mini–versions of it. However, the process is more advanced in Santa Cruz, and McDonald's decision to establish a restaurant in the capital cannot be seen as $2 million lightly expended in a society dedicated at all levels to traditional heavy lunches. In the same vein, the growth of the telecommunications sector by over 11 per cent in the last two years – compared with the general rate of 4 per cent – is, as elsewhere, to a large extent accounted for by cellular phones. Increased use of personal computers amongst the urban middle class, together with rapid rises in the rate of connection to the Internet in both private and public spheres, suggest that this is a strong complementary source of expansion and a possible conduit for the poorest nation in South America to short-cut some of the arduous routes out of 'underdevelopment'.

The need to escape that condition is underlined by its very extremity. In 1996, as we have noted, the average per capita income in Bolivia was $800 per annum; life expectancy stood at 60 years, and the official infant mortality rate at 75 deaths per 1,000 live births. The fact that 38 per cent of children under five are malnourished indicates the principal reason for such an appalling statistic. Basic sanitation, control of diarrhoea, pro-motion of breast feeding, and access to paediatric care are low-cost essentials for child survival – especially in the first 12 months of life – but these remain largely dependent upon foreign aid and NGOs. The public health system is, in fact, more disorganised than it is subverted by malfeasance, but the level of corruption, clientelism and favouritism is seen as high throughout the state as a whole. In 1997 the company Transparency International ranked Bolivia as the 36th worst case of corruption in the world (Nigeria coming last in 54th position). The methodology employed in this exercise was criticised as being clumsy and 'subjective', but the ranking of Chile at half Bolivia's level does not strike one as a travesty, and objections to the league table from La Paz were not unreservedly fortified by the simultaneous announcement by the local police that they had broken a major car-ring operated out of the navy offices by one Captain Clever Alcoba.[22] In fact, even within the legal sphere attention to the division of the spoils remains sharp enough to suggest only a very slight reduction in patrimonialist practices. Following Banzer's victory the press reported that his allocation of the senior offices of state had resulted in the ADN receiving 54.14 per cent of the ministries and CONDEPA 14.28 per cent. At one level this is no more than a contemporary expression of Bourbon punctiliousness, but it does also suggest an instinctive suspension of belief in public service.[23]

One recent instance of the retrograde nature of partial 'modernity' can be seen in the case of five members of the small Uru-murato ethnic group who were arrested in August 1994 for hunting birds protected by law in their traditional grounds of Lake Poopó. Held in jail for a year without trial, they were eventually released on bail, but after three years had received no sentence from Judge Ana Rosa Quiroga; during this period one of those held, a 78-year old man, had died – 'of fright' according to his co-defendants, who were freshly charged with 'ecological crimes' in September 1997.[24] An equal sense of the pertinence of the past could be found in the limited success of the arms amnesty offered to the Laime people of the north of Potosí by the local prefect in the week before the election. Although the authorities celebrated the hand-over of several modern weapons by the community, this was the third such agreement in two years and seemed most unlikely to pacify a region which had experienced violent land disputes throughout the colonial and republican eras. There was certainly nothing in the new agrarian legislation that offered relief on that score.

On the other hand, the continuing cultural and economic power of the Entrada del Gran Poder in La Paz, and the rise to prominence in recent years of the Entrada Universitaria represent confident and energetic expressions of indigenous tradition, no less impressive for the inclusion of Afro-Bolivian rhythms or the participation of young white women pirouetting in baroque *mini-polleras*. The idea of a 'pluri-multi-ethnic state' still languishes in the imagination of intellectuals bailed from detention in a Cold War mind-set, but civil society is increasingly proud of its non-hispanic culture, which is now sufficiently integrated into the mainstream to lose the tag of 'folklore' and foment an appreciable market. Even the notoriously Europhile and circumspect middle class of Santiago de Chile expressed admiration at the passage down their *alameda* of a large contingent of Bolivian dancers in 1995, and in the last few years La Paz tailors have become an essential element in the economy of the Rio carnival. This was the backdrop to CONDEPA's electoral success, as it was to the smooth integration of Víctor Hugo Cárdenas into the MNR government of 1993–97. It is also surely an important contributory factor to the absence of a racially charged violence that could rock the dominant market and state (sometimes described as 'Americanised' because of their integration into the wider US circuit but better understood as being 'European', rather than indigenous, in origin).

The 1997 campaign

The election campaign of 1997 enveloped and expressed these powerfully contradictory features as well as the more explicit display of party and personal conduct. The fact that the UCS leader Max Fernández died in an air crash in 1996 and CONDEPA's Carlos Palenque expired of a heart attack in the midst of the campaign could well account for the high vote of those parties in the June poll, just as it might explain any subsequent decline and extinction. It is unlikely, however, that the general 'style' of these parties will disappear from the national scene, regardless of the success experienced by the Fernández and Palenque children in handling the inherited *vitalicio* leadership of their parents' organisations.

The continued salience of the MIR in electoral calculations was underscored by its ability to bisect the vote of CONDEPA and the UCS. The MIR's 21-point programme opened with an appeal for 'confidence in ourselves', and it ended with the slogan, 'Solutions – Yes; Experiments – No', which is arguably in contradiction with the first point but unarguably rhetoric of the most vapid type. This characteristic feature of the MIR's politics was to some degree offset by thinly veiled nationalist sniping at the USA, and the party did not have to concern itself greatly with radical challenges. The representative of the orthodox left, Juan de la Cruz of Izquierda Unida, campaigned on the grounds that Bolivia is a state without a nation; that it needs to be socialised, and that the only way to rid it of corruption is to throw out the entire current system. His most detailed proposal was that parliamentary business should be conducted in indigenous languages – not itself a very novel idea and equally unappealing when so few parliamentarians were bilingual or even understood Aymara, Quechua or Guaraní. The precise prescriptions of Leninism had been removed from the socialist prospectus, but their rectilinear clumsiness was retained and simply given a graft of autochthonous allusion. The left appeared anachronistic and conservative rather than radical and innovative; its diagnosis of the country's ills was exceptionally broad, and it lacked precise propositions which might give it a more than denunciatory presence. Its only success lay in the election of individuals, such as Evo Morales and Juan del Granado, who had a record of strong personal conduct in opposition.

Nevertheless, it is the case that, between them, the MBL and IU won over a quarter of the vote polled by the MNR, which received slightly more votes in absolute terms than in 1989 but a much reduced proportion

of the total ballot. This was a decisive defeat for the *movimientistas*, whose
following almost fell to that of the second-string parties – CONDEPA, MIR
and UCS. The MNR clearly suffered from the now predictable 'pendulum
effect', whereby the outgoing administration is conclusively repudiated, as
well as from direct distrust of the economic and administrative reforms,
and possibly, through this, some recycled aversion to the social cost of
stabilisation a dozen years earlier. In addition, the party's original presidential candidate, René Blattmann, was precipitately replaced by the more
traditional figure of Juan Carlos Durán, who was a competent minister
and dependable campaigner but always looked as if he was loyally leading
the party into a period of opposition.

The scale of the MNR's defeat in the popular vote was magnified by
the manner in which this was converted into seats; it would seem to have
suffered disproportionately from the introduction of the additional member system. Equally, it is easy to exaggerate the dimensions of the victory
won by Hugo Banzer and the ADN, who were only narrowly ahead in a
system that privileges marginal advantage as much as it compels coalitions.
Furthermore, the ADN is so close to the MNR in ideological terms that it
was possible for the electorate simultaneously to vote against the MNR
and to retain its economic model.[25] Finally, of course, whilst the populist
movements could amass considerable support, theirs remained a largely
expressive politics, lacking both the programmatic coherence and administrative expertise to sustain a serious challenge for government. They still
required the catalyst of an orthodox state manager in order to win
ministries, and, as has been suggested, it is far from clear whether, after
the death of their leaders, they can maintain momentum. Should one of
them fail, it is doubtful that the other would automatically reap the
benefit. The 'populist moment' may not have disappeared, but one potent
electoral manifestation of it could well have passed.

These factors place the ADN's victory in context, but that party itself
depended heavily on the figure of Hugo Banzer Suárez, and he overcame
several important personal obstacles to win the presidency. The first of
these concerned the rise in nationalist sentiment that has for some time
tracked the debate over *narcotráfico*, and which was particularly stoked up
by the regional 'Copa de América' soccer championship held between the
poll and the inauguration (Bolivia eventually being beaten into second
place by Brazil despite great hopes of repeating the famous home victory
by the 1963 national side). As a traditionally pro-USA soldier trained in
Argentina, and as a man who had warmly embraced General Pinochet at
Charaña in 1975 in an abortive effort to open discussion of Bolivia's most
important and contentious boundary dispute, Banzer was vulnerable on
this front. His position was not assisted by the decision of Peru – at fierce

odds over its border with Ecuador – to withdraw completely from all disputation over its southern border resulting from Chile's victory of the War of the Pacific (1879–84). This decision prompted the emergence in Bolivia of the popular saying, 'Never trust Chilean honour, Peruvian fraternity, or Bolivian justice', a sentiment which might not have stuck long in popular consciousness were it not for the high profile of the Chilean companies in the privatisation market.

Reflexive patriotism found fuller expression still as a result of Bill Clinton's decision to lift the 20-year old US ban on advanced weaponry to the Southern Cone countries, which prompted fears of a regional arms race. The threat of renewed tension between Chile and Argentina, together with the revelation that Chile had planted hundreds of thousands of land-mines along its northern borders, must, of course, be seen in a post-Malvinas, as well as a (partially) post-dictatorial and post-Communist scenario. The difference between the Bolivian military budget of $149 million and Chile's of $1,970 million amounts to far more than the cost of a proper navy; even under authoritarian regimes the Bolivian armed forces have never held or seriously aspired to the resources and status of those in Chile. It is widely accepted that access to the sea by retrieval (or exchange) of sovereign territory can only be gained through diplomatic initiative. This very recognition could have pumped up the rhetorical atmosphere from mid-1997, but the *froideur* of pronouncements – civilian and military alike – from Santiago might well have had something to do with Banzer's apparent agreement in 1978 with the Argentine high command to permit offensive operations across Bolivian territory into that of Chile. Whatever the case, and even if the new president's early waspish exchanges with the ex-leftists directing foreign policy in the Frei government stemmed directly from his electoral needs, there is reason to doubt whether the two countries will seriously seek to restore diplomatic relations in the short term.

The more publicised and serious challenge faced by Banzer was that he authorised the killing of scores of people and violated the human rights of thousands under the *de facto* regime of 1971–78 – acts for which he remained unpunished; the strong implication being that he retained a vocation for dictatorship. This latter point was not weakened by the fact that Banzer himself never disputed the general existence of repressive activity and the suppression of civil liberties in the 1970s and had made no expression of atonement or apology for them; he openly argued that they had been justified by the circumstances of the time. However, he was evidently able to persuade nearly half a million voters that they could support him as a leader in a democratic system. Moreover, there are strong reasons for supposing that he was supported by the bulk of this constituency precisely as a democratic leader. That is, in terms rather distinct from those of his own result in 1985 or the support given to Generals Ríos Montt in Guatemala and Pinochet in Chile.

In the first place, the Bolivian political scenario in 1971, when Banzer took power, was undeniably one of social polarisation, political insurgency and the widespread collapse of law and order. His coup was amongst the most violent in national history, but it was not manifestly so because of his personal leadership. The subsequent regime could plausibly be presented as 'of its time', and was – unlike Pinochet's – generally less murderous and restrictive than the coup which opened it. Moreover, Banzer was thrown out of office by his own peers, and was not subsequently seen as representing a consensus of either the officer corps or conservative opinion. However, it is more important that his regime was followed by the anarchic dictatorships of 1980–82, which exhibited a greater proclivity for delinquency than ideology and which went some appreciable way to suppressing the memory of anterior tyranny. Nothing like this, of course, happened in Chile, where Pinochet imposed himself upon the succeeding regime by constitutional fiat, whereas in Guatemala, the regime of Mejía Victores could afford to be milder than that of Ríos Montt and understood the transition to civilian rule as an essential counter-insurgency measure.

Thirdly, Banzer's conduct in the post-dictatorial era was exemplary. In 1982 he had accepted the reintroduction of the 1967 constitution and the restoration of the 1980 election victory of the UDP (which contained ministers from the Communist Party), and, as we have seen, he acquiesced in his 1985 loss of the congressional run-off despite winning the popular poll. In 1989 he fulfilled a minority role in government with sobriety, and even if he seemed to have decided to go into retirement, his conduct in opposition under the MNR administration of 1993–97 gave no cause for concern. These democratic *bona fides* had been won through a combination of high- and low-profile roles, in and out of office, but they had been accumulated very largely through the acceptance of disappointment and defeat.

At the same time, it should be noted that General Banzer had been subjected to an energetic and detailed impeachment by the radical leader of the PS-1 Marcelo Quiroga Santa Cruz, who was assassinated in García Mesa's coup of July 1980. The staging of that indictment, together with the failure of the governments of 1978–80 to proceed against the ex-president in the courts, seems to have bled off a portion of the earlier popular demand for a settlement of accounts and punishment. It stands in marked contrast to the treatment of García Mesa, who was jailed for 30 years for political crimes committed before, during and after the 1980 coup. The fact that, shortly after coming to office, President Banzer authorised an official investigation into the killing of Marcelo Quiroga

Santa Cruz and the whereabouts of his remains could be seen as a theatrical flourish and a further low-cost display of the general's lack of animus. Nevertheless, it is worth noting that at the time the sentiment was circulating quite widely that Banzer, having lost both his sons in accidents, had now paid a personal price for his own actions, whatever he said about the past and however genuine his avowed dedication to the rule of law.

In short, Banzer may not have been liked or even respected, but he was no longer extensively distrusted or hated. It was almost as if, by osmosis, the Bolivian electorate discerned that to be a democrat it was not necessary to share ideas or values, or even to have a pleasant past; the sole requisite is that one accept all the rules of the game. Very often these self-same rules require – formally or practically – a settlement of accounts over past conduct; but in Bolivia they were not applied to Banzer in this manner, and there is little expectation that they will be so. Banzer's election belies the notion that liberal democracy requires a consensual rewriting of history; there are absolutely no guarantees that it will lead to any greater social convergence (or *concertación*). It should, instead, be viewed as the outcome of a series of tough, pragmatic decisions by a political society at least as mature in its calculations as some supposedly more sophisticated electorates.

Che Guevara and the importance of historical memory

During the late 1970s, after the death of General Franco, a poster of Ernesto Che Guevara circulated in Spain on which the 'classic' heroic portrait by Alberto Díaz Korda was accompanied by a slogan: 'I shall return, but not as a poster.' This proclamation carries a strong echo of the last words attributed to Tupaj Amaru, executed by the Spaniards for leading the rebellion of 1781–83: 'I may die, but I shall return as millions.' The idea of a *Pachakuti* – a total cycle, renewal, even millennium – has particular resonance in the southern Andes, where it lies at the centre of a cosmovision and goes well beyond the notion of redemptive reincarnation of fallen heroes. These slogans were posthumously assigned to both men as supposed self-fulfilling prophesies, and if they possess a certain unsettling power in our day of quantifiable certainties, it is because they have not proved to be wholly false. The great insurgent leader from Cuzco had his name appropriated by the Uruguayan guerrillas of the 1960s and those of Peru in the 1980s whilst Che, of course, has never ceased to be present as more than an icon. Moreover, when he did finally return in material form through the uncovering of his skeleton near Vallegrande in July 1997, there was even a certain diminution in the power of that poster image. Discovery, return to Cuba and eventual re-interment in a phar-

aonic mausoleum at Santa Clara – the site of his greatest military victory –
provided the kind of private relief and settlement of accounts so ardently
sought by the relatives of those who have been 'disappeared' in recent
decades in Latin America. Yet it also brought the public Guevara down
from the sphere of myth, where many had been more than happy to keep
him.

The fact that the discovery of Guevara's bones stemmed from the
researches of a biographer rushing to meet a deadline that would enable
publication before the thirtieth anniversary of his execution throws light
on the forensic power of the contemporary chronicle.[26] At the same time,
however, the story of the exhumation occluded reappraisal of the life
itself, the commemoration prompting celebration of a man who was
heroic in the cause of a collectivist anti-heroism. This paradox did not
stand alone; the response to the discovery of Che's remains excited
commentary that was generally disconcerting in that – rather like that
attending the death of Princess Diana two months later – it revolved
around the symbolism of exemplary or sacrificial spirits, wherein rationality stands at less than a premium. Earlier debates over the more prosaic
contradictions of his life – those of an Argentine youth in the post-war
years; of a franciscan lover of the good life; of the 'straight-talker' locked
into a world of conspiracy – were now subsumed into this grander theme.
However, the incongruity of the pulsating commodification of such an
ascetic egalitarian did not seem to be drawing to a close, even in the
desultory effort to create a tourist industry around the makeshift shrine at
La Higuera and the sites of the bloody skirmishes around it.

In the event, most dignitaries of the continental and international left
shunned the activities organised at Vallegrande, preferring to attend the
large concerts and ceremonials organised in Buenos Aires and Santiago
de Chile as well as Havana. It is understandable, in simple logistical terms,
why a man so dedicated to rural guerrilla warfare and who died in the
countryside should be celebrated in large cities; there is no real anomaly
in the 'otherness' of heroism. Equally, one should not be surprised that
amidst all the reflections and analysis there was little consideration of
what Guevara meant for Bolivia itself, now nearly reduced to that spot on
the globe where an internationalist coincidentally happened to meet his
destiny. This is not the place for a full discussion of the character of the
anniversary of Che's death, still less the substance of his life, but a few
brief points can be made from the perspective of Bolivia and the elections
held there a few weeks before his exhumation.

There is now strong evidence to suggest that Guevara had only gone to
Bolivia in late 1966 as a step in a planned combative return to his
Argentine homeland. It is also unlikely that his choice of this neighbour-
ing country as a guerrilla site relied wholly on the advice of Régis Debray,

even if his consultant's *normalien* assurance would have then seemed much less the construction of an *idiot savant* than it does today.[27] Che had already been in Bolivia himself, on tour 13 years earlier as a recently graduated doctor and before he had acquired the radicalism that crystallised the following year in his witnessing the overthrow of the Arbenz regime in Guatemala. There is, however, some hint of his developing attitude in a letter written to his father at the end of July 1953, just before the introduction of the agrarian reform which at the time provided a sharp sense of the weakness of the state but would later prove to be a critical dyke against social radicalism:

> I am a little disillusioned about not being able to stay here because this is a very interesting country and it is living through a particularly effervescent moment. On the 2nd of August the agrarian reform goes through, and fracas and fights are expected throughout the country. We have seen incredible processions of armed people with Mausers and Tommy-guns, which they shoot off for the hell of it. Every day shots can be heard and there are wounded and dead as a result.
>
> The government shows a near-total inability to retain or lead the peasant masses and miners, but these respond to a certain degree, and there is no doubt that in the event of an armed revolt by the Falange ... they will be on the side of the MNR. Human life has little importance here, and it is given and taken without great to-do. All of this makes this a profoundly interesting situation to the neutral observer.[28]

In the light of this, it is tempting to read much into Che's visit, on the day of the agrarian reform, to the Bolsa Negra mine outside La Paz. The miners had, quite naturally, taken the day off work to go to town and participate in the celebrations with *campesino* contingents (the reform was formally signed by Víctor Paz at Ucureña, Cochabamba). Having toured the silent shafts of Bolsa Negra, Che passed the returning miners on his way back to the city, again being impressed by the explosions of dynamite and discharge of guns. It strikes one as particularly odd that during his month in the country the young Argentine should have contrived to miss both the agrarian reform celebrations and the extraordinary experience of Bolivia's proletariat in its Andean engagement. Indeed, this failed *rendez-vous* might be interpreted as reflecting less a proclivity to favour the rural over the urban than a general clumsiness when it came to 'being there'. Certainly, in 1966–67 Guevara categorically misjudged the mood, social resource and political capacity of both rural and industrial working people. In itself this probably did not cost him his life, but the lack of sensitivity and sobriety in assessing local detail always meant that escape was the best outcome awaiting the guerrillas.

By 1997 the social constituency (the 'big motor') that Che's *foco* (the 'little motor') was intended to ignite had been scattered by a comprehensive deindustrialisation and the dismantling of the corporatist institutions of the 1950s. The miners are now numbered in their hundreds, the confused COB is split over the degree of collaboration it should offer the new Banzer government, and Mario Monje, the Communist leader who once disputed Che's appropriation of the radical vanguard in Bolivia, lives out an isolated old age on the outskirts of Moscow. Yet the overall picture is far from clear. Banzer's insistent refusal in public to treat Guevara's endeavour as anything more than a red invasion appeared backward-looking and ungenerous; it was not widely echoed, even in conservative circles. Nor did the government's ostentatious listing of the 54 soldiers and civilians killed by the guerrillas and declared heroes in 1967 strike a chord of anything but sadness. In keeping with the nature of Banzer's own election a few weeks earlier, there was a marked lack of adversarialism in the political atmosphere (in November Fidel Castro did not hesitate to stand next to Banzer for the photo-call at the Seventh Ibero-American summit in Venezuela). A similar mood appears to have prevailed in Buenos Aires and Santiago; an epoch had passed, and if Che was returning, it was not as an exemplar of a precise form of insurgency but as the embodiment of higher values and ideals.

In Vallegrande and the village of La Higuera, where he was shot, Che is evidently more than a celebrity. Elsewhere in the country he might be said no longer to be an 'outsider', a source of embarrassment (or pride) in that he was killed in Bolivia. Perhaps Banzer's observations found scant response because Guevara was now seen less as an internationalist fighting against global reaction in a local setting than as somebody who had misconstrued the nature of nationalism in Bolivia – who had made a specific mistake in interpreting the country. In this he might almost be described as truer to his origins as an Argentine than to his mature convictions as a Communist. Furthermore, one gains the sense from a longer historical perspective that whilst the 1966–67 guerrilla never came to pose a serious threat of ideological conquest, it did raise fears of dismemberment of a type wearily familiar to a populace well schooled about the reduction of their national territory through wars – that of the Pacific (1879–84); in Acre (1899–1901); and in the Chaco (1932–35) – in addition to cut-price sales to Chile and Brazil by the likes of President Melgarejo. These experiences have been the traumatic testing-grounds for any logic that might lie behind the existence of a country deemed by some – not least Chilean generals and US diplomats – to have nurtured too many problems to be worthy of existence. This existence may have been upheld on the simple grounds that no neighbour has historically sought outright conquest and merely opted for maximum annexation of land with lowest social intake, but the state now confronts a new challenge in the integration of regional markets, particularly through Mercosur, of which Bolivia is an associate member.

These circumstances go some way to explaining why so much controversy should be aroused in the weeks around the 1997 election by the publication of a work of amateur history, *La Mesa Coja* by Javier Mendoza.[29] Making extensive use of the notes of his father, the great archivist Gunnar Mendoza, the author proposed that one of the founding documents of the nation – the 1809 proclamation of the Junta Tuitiva in La Paz – was not, in fact, signed or even composed by the members of that body, as had widely been believed for 150 years. Rather, according to Mendoza's methodological mix of strong documentary deduction and psychological induction, that document was a later 'creation'/forgery, and the real original derived from dissident jurists and priests in Chuquisaca (Sucre), who had far greater need and desire to form a state independent of Peru and the Viceroyality of La Plata than did the merchants of La Paz. In effect, Mendoza was revindicating the place of Sucre as the capital of the nation, impugning *paceño* claims to have promoted the birth of the nation, and reviving a debate which was widely thought moribund because it had no contemporary relevance.

The exchanges over this issue combined a ferocious abandonment of common sense by traditionalist politicians with a pained reservation on the part of professional historians, for whom Mendoza's approach was too glib by half. But all participants passed without comment over the critical point that – whoever might have been responsible for the start of the independence struggle – it was completed by a Colombian (Sucre) assisted by two Irishmen (O'Leary and O'Connor), a German (Braun) and an Englishman (Miller) in the execution of a strategic plan drawn up by a Venezuelan (Bolívar). This internationalist presence at the very origin of the state has always been the source of some ambivalence. However, modern nationalists may find some solace in a sentiment expressed by Bolívar to Santander in a letter of October 1825, on his first and only visit to the country just named after him: 'if Brazil invades, I will fight as a Bolivian – a name I had before I was born'.[30]

Simón Bolívar accepted the existence of Bolivia, and probably for better cause than on account of it bearing his name; and he did so despite the fact that its establishment created another obstacle to his federalist design for the subcontinent – an objective and idiom so similar to those of Guevara. Moreover, it could be argued that Bolívar's secular, militarist republicanism savoured very much of that practised by Che 135 years later. Neither man would surely have much difficulty in interpreting the election of 1997 in the terms of their day. For Bolívar, Banzer's election does not quite vindicate his 1826 'Message to the Assembly of Bolivia', but it could be recognised as the intervention of a *caudillo* to sort out the *política criolla* of the lawyers and harness their disputations to the higher needs of the nation. For Che, the campaign would surely have amounted to little more than the squabbles of temporising liberals at the service of US imperialism as they extinguish the depleted legitimacy won in 1952. However, one suspects that neither man would fully grasp how and why many Bolivians could both concur with these assessments and yet still place such a politics above the emphatic pursuit of utopia to which these two historic 'extra-Bolivians' were pledged.

1998

'All That Trouble Down There':
Hollywood and Central America

Hollywood's response to the crisis in Central America following the Nicaraguan Revolution of 1979 had been more muddled and interesting than might have been expected or, indeed, than some of the sharper critics are prepared to allow. It may certainly appear a trifling achievement, but during the 1980s relatively few feature films displayed the unquestioning codes of affinity and antipathy recycled from the first Cold War by a president whose political rhetoric was almost entirely couched in B-movie cadences and who was seemingly as obsessed by Central America as he was by anything else.

Here one should make proper allowance for the fact that the Sandinista overthrow of the Somoza dictatorship and the outbreak of civil war in both El Salvador and Guatemala raised the threat – diligently nurtured by Reagan and Haig during the 1980 US election campaign – of the deployment of US troops just as the first wave of post-Vietnam films, headed by *The Deer Hunter* (1978) and *Apocalypse Now* (1979), had made a major impact. Equally, it is worth noting that the tight 'bipartisan consensus' in Washington over Central American policy until the Iran–Contra scandal (November 1986) was never mirrored in California, where political and economic refugees from Mexico and Central America dominate the burgeoning Hispanic community, giving it a more progressive character than that, for example, in Florida. Given the success of a film such as *Stand and Deliver* (Ramón Menéndez, 1988), one suspects that consideration of their 'local constituency' by the moguls of Burbank may not have been completely tangential. In the event, it is safe to say that regional and conjunctural factors combined with more extensive political and cultural developments since the early 1950s to ensure that the contested and often confused images of Central America that existed within the populace at large were also represented on film.

This does not, of course, mean that either Hollywood or the independents avoided producing a massive amount of rank tat, still less that the terrible conflicts of the isthmus engendered the making of outstanding movies. Indeed, while it is valid to insist on the contrast with the 1950s with regard to formal political culture and base propaganda, in most other respects the record is very depressing. In the first place, although opinion polls throughout the 1980s registered an alarmingly high ignorance about Central America and the Caribbean on the part of the US public, unprecedented coverage in the media heightened simple awareness of its existence as a site of conflict. This, allied with the long-standing manipulation of standard 'banana republic' motifs by Hollywood, made the region a natural successor to South-East Asia as an arena for the post-Rambo generation of killer-heroes.[1]

At one level this deserves little comment, since one set of steaming deciduous foliage is as good as another for the purposes of staging twig-snapping hunts and crashing chases or prompting glistening starlets to lose their shirts. But the replacement of the inscrutable oriental by the carelessly cruel Hispanic as the villain of the piece is not without some consequence. This is perhaps most notable in the predictably increasing attention to the drug trade in such films, which are primarily (often exclusively) aimed at the video market. If this audience is captive, it is still only on remand since the 'action and adventure' sections of the rental stores are as capacious as they are lurid, and 'actuality' is not an entirely redundant selling-point. Sometimes the directors have the temerity to assign their plots to an authentic country, *Blood Money* (Jerry Schatzberg, 1988) being set in Costa Rica because, like several other films, it involves gun-running and the Contras. Sometimes they are content to settle for regional anonymity, as in Michael Kennedy's *Caribe* (1988), which approaches southern climes with scarcely greater specificity or sophistication than did the producers of *Dallas* who, it will be remembered, contrived to have Ewing *père* die in an aircrash that took place in a zone no smaller than 'South America'.

Sometimes also the new wave of violent exploitation pictures manifests a probably justified but nevertheless abusive attitude towards its audience by packaging its product in a manner almost entirely unconnected to the contents of the plot. Thus, *Sandinista. War is Hell* (1989), also directed by Michael Kennedy – who is acquiring quite some experience in this field – bears absolutely no correspondence to any recorded events in Nicaragua over the last decade. There is a dictatorial (and entirely fictional) General González, some drug smuggling by a run-of-the-mill bunch of murderous mafiosi, an unsurprisingly careworn mercenary, and a glamorous female journalist who is very stupid even by the formidable standards of the genre. But no effort is made even to identify the country in which the action takes place, still less to tie the FSLN to drug-running, as had been done several years earlier by US government agencies. In all probability nobody on the set had the slightest idea of the film's eventual title.

On these grounds it is tempting to bracket such stuff alongside the antics of sundry sorcerers, dragon-slayers, space-travellers and avenging Amazons. Yet what is most striking about the corpus is the total absence of either humour or history as elements to temper threadbare plots, poor production values and a reliance on violence that is impressive even in the post-Peckinpah age of gore. These are not smirking, camp spoofs made for the chattering classes but straight-faced offerings for the readership of *Guns and Ammo* that pillage Corman, Peckinpah and Sturges without intelligence as well as without shame.

It is more than Central America's bad luck to have attracted an unusually high proportion of such an inevitable output, which threatens to infect more mainstream production although it is, in truth, rather hard to distinguish the upper and lower ends of this market. Perhaps, drawing one's limits around the Caribbean as a whole, one could identify a superior example in Abel Ferrara's *Cat Chaser* (1989), which is not only derived from an Elmore Leonard novel but also pays more than fleeting and less than spurious reference to the 1965 invasion of the Dominican Republic by the US marines. At the other end of the spectrum, but with a rather superior cast, stands Tony Scott's *Revenge* (1989), which is set in Mexico. This, as soon becomes clear, represents the limit for Latin mores and conduct, a significant part of the movie involving passage to and from the US border, which obviously represents the margin of civilisation.[2] Two aspects of this film attract attention. First, is the use of Anthony Quinn to portray the jealous and vengeful *caudillo* betrayed by his beautiful young wife. Already the screen personification *sans pareil* of 'Latin' temper, Quinn effortlessly hams his way through a series of extravagantly brutal scenes; it is clear to the viewer that what we have here is an exceptionally mean and calculating Zorba. Second, and more telling, is the contrast in the role of the female lead, Madeleine Stowe, with that in her previous film, John Badham's well-received *Stakeout* (1987).

In both films Stowe plays an apparently resourceful but powerless object of desire sought, in different ways, by two men. In *Stakeout* she is an Irish–Mexican waitress under observation by two Seattle cops lying in wait for her ex-boyfriend, a cop-killer who has recently broken out of jail. This involves no small amount of voyeurism, but beyond the predictable male-bonding between the policemen (and an audience blessed with a priori exculpation) as one of them succumbs to Stowe's charms lies the disturbing possibility that her past (and blood) will force her to prefer the evil killer. Badham, though, does not lead us for long down this

path; his denouement has the heroine unharmed (bar one casual back-
hander from the crook) and delivered into the arms of her new hero
after a textbook finale fight.[3]

In *Revenge* we are south of a different border and, although Stowe is
easily won away by a gringo (Kevin Costner) who is an old friend of
Quinn's, we know that no quarter may be expected. The level of violence
in this *ménage à trois* is not only much higher but also a significant
amount of it is visited directly upon the woman. The stabbings, rape and
intravenous administration of drugs undergone by Stowe's character are
at the centre of both the images and the narrative of a film that is as
small as its title. A bevy of worthless bit-parters expire as Costner battles
to retrieve his love, yet she survives to recover in a convent, where he
finds her having finally reached an *entente* with the resigned Quinn, who
mumbles some cod philosophy and wanders off, presumably back to
political fixing and generalised cow-raising activities. The point is not
that it would be impossible to contrive a less veiled 'Madonna and whore'
story. Rather, it is that what is merely imagined (in comic form) in
Seattle can be openly practised (and hugely exceeded) in Sonora.

The part of the cop smitten by Stowe in *Stakeout* is played by Richard
Dreyfuss, who the following year also took a leading role in a movie
'about' Latin America, albeit a comedy set in a fictional republic: *Moon
over Parador* (Paul Mazursky, 1988). This spoof is entirely predictable but
so amiably over the top that one is not completely convinced of the
artlessness of its advertising copy: 'Where else in the world would a
second-rate actor become president?' Yet whereas Reagan was elected
fair and square (with all that this entails in terms of 'political culture'),
Dreyfuss is dragooned by Raúl Julia's police chief into impersonating a
suddenly defunct dictator in a 'king for a day' romp that courts all sorts
of dangers but eventually parodies itself – and its venerable genre –
sufficiently to suggest that there is still space between PC (political correctness) piety and redneck philistinism in Hollywood's image of 'the
south'.

Parador is saved both as a film and from the fictional clutches of
Fascism in good measure by Sonia Braga's high-flying 'tart with a heart'.
Even if the audiences for this film would only know Braga from *The Kiss
of the Spider-woman* (Héctor Babenco, 1985) or, at a pinch, *The Milagro
Beanfield War* (Robert Redford, 1987), it is not difficult to grasp that her
'sultry temptress' part in *Parador* is so deftly played as to be typecast. In
fact, Braga here offers a sanitised pastiche of her earlier roles in Brazilian
cinema where on-camera fellatio and energetic couplings helped to raise
a reputation that is exploited but could never be properly reproduced in
Parador. While Dreyfuss plays an actor playing the *caudillo*, Braga simply
mimics her own screen persona.[4] The question of identity is not fully

triangulated, even courtesy of assistance from Raúl Julia and Fernando Rey. Yet neither is it so crassly handled as to give the impression that the latinos merely picked up Universal's cheque for lampooning their cultural birthright.

It is not simply the treatment of the core themes of sex and power that bracket the US vision of Central America, whether in comic or tragic voice. There is a wider sense of the relation between drama and the individual – one which, as Pauline Kael was quick to emphasise, is paradoxically but acutely evident in the progressive independent production *El Norte* (Gregorio Nava, 1983). Kael's criticism of this picture is that it reduces to simple emblems the Guatemalan couple who undergo the most bitter experiences in emigrating from their beloved homeland to an alien and aggressive USA; they lack discernible characteristics that might make them something more than the 'objects' of the rites of passage they are obliged to undergo.[5] Kael is also right to criticise the film's lack of attention as to why two young people should be forced to submit themselves to such indignity and severe risk. However, her criticism is sufficiently humane and informed to recognise that even if Nava's direction is wooden and derivative, the force of the movie lies precisely in its veracity. The often unspeakable experiences of illegal immigrants are in reality conducive to *both* melodrama and anonymity – a contradiction for which it is as hard to find a filmic formula as it is a place in the American Way of Life. It may be that Nava's artisanal production stumbled clumsily upon this by dint of empathy rather than technique; certainly the film has received a far warmer reception than might be expected on the basis of its purely cinematic qualities. In some respects it stands as the polar opposite of *Stand and Deliver*, which is a fluent and pugnacious celebration of individual self-help and resolution within the Hispanic 'underclass'.[6]

El Norte does indeed fail to address either the role of the US in Guatemala since the CIA-backed counter-revolution of June 1954 or the bloody regression of the 1980s that would have been the main cause for its protagonists to quit the largely spiritual protection of their sacred hills. Yet it will endure far longer as a commentary on the interface between North and Central America than two films – one of the right, the other firmly of the left – that treat the question of politics much more directly. It is perhaps stretching a point to include John Milius's *Red Dawn* (1984) in this context, but the fact that the 'Reds' who invade the USA in this risible reactionary piece include Nicaraguans as well as Cubans shows that Hollywood was by no means incapable of sharing Reagan's hyperventilated McCarthyite visions. The domino theory has always drawn its strength from the fact that it 'explains' why very distant events are far more dangerous than they seem to an American public that lacks experience of invasion or authentically dangerous neighbours. The unbending logic of the theory may be a grotesque distortion of events in post-war eastern Europe or Indo-China in the 1960s, but it bears more than passing similarity to the wilful projections of populist biblical exegesis that prevail so formidably in the USA today with their positively baroque depictions of heaven and hell. Heaven, of course, is home, and hell has always been its invasion, rather than the holocaust. Here, then, Milius simply reheats the essence of Alberto Cavalcanti's *Went the Day Well?* (1942), but whereas that film was shot within weeks of the Battle of Britain and a tangible threat of enemy occupation, *Red Dawn* was being shown at the same time as US advisers were directing an undeclared war inside the national frontiers of El Salvador and CIA agents were blowing up neutral ships in Nicaraguan harbours. This conflict was so demonstrably unequal that it is surely most interesting to ask why it had to be masked in utterly implausible inversions of reality. The notion that 'we are doing this to them before they do it to us' incubates a desperately threadbare *realpolitik* but also a rich seam of fearfulness that need by no means be open only to the left – as in *Dr Strangelove* (Stanley Kubrick, 1963) – to exploit. Milius, though, is content to serve up a paltry action movie.

Haskell Wexler's *Latino* (1985) is shot with all the technical accomplishment that one would expect from this outstanding cameraman, but the film is a bitter disappointment for it simply mirrors *Red Dawn* from the other side of the ideological spectrum. The denunciation of US crimes in Central America – in the form of support for the Nicaraguan Contras – is so insistent and unproblematic that its worthiness is distilled into a sermon for the already converted. It may be argued that this at least comforted an embattled progressive constituency within the USA and represented a retort to the likes of Milius's film in a genuine propaganda exchange. However, one cannot escape the feeling that such tasks would have been better achieved more directly through documentary form, and that a fictional approach needs to incorporate a much greater quotient of ambivalence and doubt in order to gain purchase on the imagination of precisely those in whom agnosticism imbricates with ignorance.

This is perhaps the central vindication of the two films dealing with Central America that have proved to be at least modest box-office successes – *Under Fire* (Roger Spottiswoode, 1983) and *Salvador* (Oliver Stone, 1986). Both films share the device of telling a Central American story (respectively, Nicaragua between September 1978 and July 1979 and El Salvador between January 1980 and January 1981) through the eyes and actions of US photo-journalists. This is justifiable both as a means to reach a broad American audience and as an authentic story source. Moreover, although both pictures significantly inflate the role of US journalists in those brutal days, the issue of media representation is both legitimate and sufficiently self-referencing as to uphold doubt – but not disbelief – about the story. In fact, both films share the attribute of incorporating a single, major lapse into an otherwise remarkably faithful rendition of the actual passage of historical events (although *Salvador* is much more closely tied to the lived experiences of an individual protagonist – the notorious Richard Boyle, beautifully played by James Woods – than is *Under Fire*, where a compellingly reticent Nick Nolte is a fictional amalgam of altogether more modest people). At first sight it is Spottiswoode's taking of liberties with history that seems the more objectionable since he introduces into the Nicaraguan Revolution an entirely fictional leader, known as Rafael, whose death Nolte's character eventually conspires to conceal in league with the rebels. In reality, as we know, the heroes of the Nicaraguan revolution – Sandino himself and Carlos Fonseca Amador – were already enshrined as martyrs for a movement that prided itself on its collective leadership and eschewing of personalism. By contrast, Oliver Stone appears to commit a minor infraction by depicting the uprising in El Salvador of January 1981 in the town of Santa Ana as a veritable cavalry charge by the FMLN guerrillas when, in fact, it began as a messy mutiny within the government garrison.

There is, however, some cause for reversing the importance of these 'tricks of the trade'. As Salman Rushdie has noted with respect to Sandino's hat, the politics of both pre- and post-revolutionary Nicaragua depended very heavily upon a pared-down symbolism; eventually, in the elections of February 1990, this was reduced to the two colours of two flags (red and black for the FSLN; turquoise and white for Violeta Chamorro's UNO).[7] Thus, although no Rafael ever existed, the use of this fictional motif does correspond to one critical feature of a lived experience. Moreover, it was precisely the issue of projection and concealment (particularly through the use of indigenous masks by the rebels) that caught the popular imagination within and outside Nicaragua in the first half of 1979. On the other hand, it is doubtful if this caused quite such a deep moral dilemma for the press as Spottiswoode would have us believe.

Stone ends *Salvador* with two twists. First he has the guerrillas ride on horseback into Santa Ana as heroic liberators in the true Western tradition, only – within a few frames – to begin executing government troops in cold blood once the revolt runs into difficulties. Then he has Boyle save his Salvadorean girlfriend by taking her to the USA, only for the immigration service to apprehend and expel her to an uncertain fate. This second twist explicitly draws a correspondence between the actions of the constitutional US and dictatorial Salvadorean states, most effectively exploding the liberal ambience created by the first. Yet Boyle is the only (and not hugely reliable) source for this denouement, and we know that the depiction of events in Santa Ana is a travesty of history. Thus, although these two Janus-like scenes provide both the dramatic apogee and political declension of the film, they rest on distinctly insecure foundations. Given that so much else in *Salvador* is scrupulously close to the record – the pacing of events is disarmingly accurate from the killing of Archbishop Romero to that of the US nuns – one wonders why such a final contrivance proved necessary.

Pauline Kael's answer to this question would almost certainly be that Stone's politics are too unbending to allow for anything but an absolute resolution. Indeed, it is interesting that Kael greatly prefers *Under Fire* to *Salvador* ('crude and profane'), not least because the former treats the female lead (Joanna Cassidy playing a gringa journalist) as an independent and authoritative figure whereas in *Salvador* Boyle's girlfriend María (played by the excellent Elpedia Carrillo, who takes a very similar role in *The Honorary Consul*) is passive and resigned.[8] Whatever Stone's intentions, this strikes me as an unusually superficial interpretation that corresponds to a wider misconception in 'the north' that caution, appreciation of the limited good and a reserved counsel are tantamount to fatalism. Nobody who has any experience of political terror would countenance such a brashly innocent reading. Stone's anger in *Salvador* may be disconcertingly direct but it is entirely justified. And while he and Spottiswoode predictably concentrate on the death of US citizens that took place in both countries, they, like Costa Gavras in *Missing* (1982), successfully impart the menace, fear and terror that so deeply pervaded these societies. At the end of the day it is the translation of that reality to audiences who have become so careworn in suspending their belief at the first sight of blood that constitutes the strongest achievement of these films.[9]

1993

The Study of Latin American History
and Politics in the United Kingdom:
An Interpretative Sketch

If, as Harold Wilson famously claimed, a week is a long time in politics, then thirty years should cover an epoch at least, and might even account for a substantial period in terms of history. In all events, it is worth opening even the most general review of Latin American studies over the last three decades by recalling that 1965 was the year of the Selma marches and Watts riots, when US civil rights workers were still being killed by the Ku-Klux-Klan, and even the formal exercise of citizenship was not yet assured to a significant minority of the inhabitants of the USA. At the same time, Washington was starting to accelerate the despatch of its troops to Vietnam, the existing garrison being augmented by 50,000 soldiers in September and October alone. By the end of the year over a million soldiers of various armies were deployed in that country, but no decisive battles had yet been fought in a war that would last another ten years.

On a broader front, 1965 witnessed the first practical test for the Second Vatican Council, the third session of which had concluded in October 1964 with the promulgation of a series of critical reforms and declarations of unprecedented radicalism for the Roman Catholic tradition. However, the fact that these included a (much disputed) commitment to religious liberty, condemnation of nuclear weapons and the arms race, and recognition of a conflict between the Church's ban on artificial birth control and 'the intimate drive of conjugal love' might, perhaps, diminish the sense of distance between that time and our own.

Certainly, there has been only modest progress in altering the balance of the Sacred College of Cardinals of that time, when it comprised 61 Europeans, with 33 members coming from the rest of the world (including 21 from all the Americas). Similarly, the resolute commitment of

General de Gaulle (who died 25 years ago) to France's nuclear *force de frappe*, and his steady progress towards breaking the original NATO compact – with the removal of its headquarters from Paris – may be seen as potent precedents for President Chirac, not least in terms of irritating the Anglo-Saxons.

On the other hand, the year that saw the deaths of Winston Churchill, T.S. Eliot and Albert Schweitzer also produced a Labour government National Plan that projected a 25 per cent increase in British output over five years, with a party defending a majority of just two votes preparing with understandable nervousness to nationalise the steel industry, striving without avail to stop a unilateral declaration of independence by Rhodesia's white minority, and graciously permitting Dr Beeching to return to his post at ICI after spending four years altering the British landscape – literally and metaphorically – by closing down large parts of the country's railway network.

Change of almost as radical a character was being touted by Soviet premier Nikolai Kosygin, who, having helped to remove Khrushchev the previous year, now felt able to criticise the most evident failings of the economic management of the USSR. Some were, in fact, rectified. In Spain Franco's rule remained comfortably unchallenged within and without whilst the rather tame Portuguese social democrats wearily withdrew from the elections scheduled for 7 November in recognition of Salazar's absolute stranglehold over that country's assembly. The Revolution and the independence of Portugal's colonies was nearly a decade in the future, and who, in 1965, could have sensibly foreseen their nature?

If we turn to the Latin America of thirty years ago, the impression is no less one of familiarity combined with historical distance and differentiation. Of those countries where events made the international headlines, the case of Brazil is plainly the most important. On 3 October 1965 the opposition had won 11 of the 22 gubernatorial elections called by General Castelo Branco, who, having led the overthrow of President Goulart in March 1964, was now seeking to establish a 'restricted democracy' or *dictablanda*. The election results effectively made this impossible, and on 27 October, under strong pressure from both civilian and military right-wingers, Castelo Branco introduced Institutional Act No. 2, which banned all parties for 18 months, allowed for the removal of constitutional guarantees from any individual for up to 10 years, and directed another 28 articles of a tightly restrictive nature against those whom the general called 'revanchistes, agitators of various hue, and counter-revolutionaries'.[1]

The privilege of hindsight enables us to identify the crackdown of 27 October 1965 as a key event in what would develop into a 21-year dictatorial regime of unparalleled institutional coherence. Yet at the time no precedent for this existed, no other large country in the region was ruled by dictatorship, and Castelo Branco remained publicly committed to stepping down in 1967. The severity of the Institutional Acts recalled the *Estado Novo*, but this government could still plausibly be viewed in its self-declared terms as both exceptional and temporary.

Late on the same day as the doomed Brazilian elections Fidel Castro had stunned a rally in Havana by reading out a letter written by Ernesto Che Guevara six months earlier in which he declared:

> I have fulfilled that part of my duty which bound me to the Revolution in your territory. I formally resign from my post as *comandante* and as a minister, and from my status as a Cuban citizen. In new battlefields I shall fulfill . . . the obligation to fight imperialism, wherever it might be.[2]

Apart from prompting speculation that Moscow had forced Castro to remove the 'pro-Chinese' Guevara, the publication of this document excited considerable comment and apprehension as to the precise whereabouts of the revolutionary leader, some very prosaic and peculiar locales being proposed. It was not, however, until early 1967 that it was known that Guevara was in Bolivia, undertaking a rural guerrilla campaign that would rapidly end in disaster. Yet neither this nor several similar experiences of abortive insurrectionary activity altered the heroic and strategic importance of guerrilla-ism for large sections of the regional and international left. For millions of people the example of Cuba remained exceptionally potent well into the 1970s as a model for the future rather than simply as the symbol of a valiant past.

If committed enterprises of the type led by Guevara do now appear as authentically 'historical' – perhaps for such a phenomenon we might identify the Chilean coup of 1973 as a watershed – it is worth recalling that a week before he disclosed Che's letter Castro had made another speech in which he announced that all Cubans with relations in the USA would be allowed to leave the country. In the last half of October some 3,000 people departed the island in what was considered an exodus by the standards of the day (perhaps predictably, this exodus included a 92-year old who claimed to be the inspiration for Hemingway's *The Old Man and the Sea*). The mass flights of 1980 and 1994 dwarfed this in terms of their size, but a pattern was being set and, of course, it has not yet been broken.

Brief mention should also be made of events in Argentina and Uruguay, where civilian governments were obliged to introduce states of siege and to deploy riot police in order to contain powerful mobilisation by the trade unions. In Uruguay, where output had not grown significantly since the mid-1950s, orthodox stabilisation policies designed to stem economic decline had produced a spate of strikes and demonstrations against a

Blanco administration that was divided within itself and lacked a parliamentary majority. Yet clear popular weariness with public disruption,
continued bipartisan collaboration in state administration, and the
country's exceptionally long-lived consensual customs could all be persuasively presented to support an optimistic scenario rather than one of
decomposition, polarisation and violence that we know eventually came
to pass but which not even the local forces of extreme reaction were then
predicting.

In Argentina the Illia government, weakened by two devaluations of
the peso in five months, was forced on 15 October 1965 to ban all trade
union activity and remove the 'visiting' Isabel Perón from Buenos Aires in
the wake of three days of demonstrations planned to celebrate the
twentieth anniversary of her husband's release in 1945. Having been
narrowly but clearly beaten by the Peronists in the parliamentary elections
of March, the incumbent Radicals faced not only defeat within the
democratic arena but also military intervention to halt what many in the
officer corps understood to be the noxious rising tide of Peronism. In the
event, the coup that might be said to match Castelo Branco's Institutional
Act came in 1966, under the aegis of General Onganía, whose regime was
to form the model for Guillermo O'Donnell's 'Bureaucratic Authoritarian' state. We should, though, recall that Onganía's government lasted
less than four years, did not inflict merciless violence on the Argentine
people – certainly nothing of the order visited upon them by Videla and
Co. a decade later – and was effectively removed by the same sort of
popular disruption and activism that so tested the Radicals in 1965.

Nobody looking back at 1965 can afford to ignore the Dominican
Republic, where the invasion by US troops under the public pretext of
halting another Communist takeover in the Caribbean had played no
little part in encouraging similar attitudes by armed forces in the southern
part of the continent. President Johnson's deployment of marines had the
effect of containing serious civil conflict within the country and it eventually secured a most obliging regime in Santo Domingo, but it was viewed
abroad as much more important in terms of a renewed US commitment
to international intervention by force when any suspicion of threatening
political activity might be harboured. The candour with which this disposition was expressed in the House of Representatives might have caused
shock in, for instance, 1979 or even 1992, but the experience of the two
Reagan governments and the Republican renaissance in Congress under
Messrs. Gingrich and Helms has probably dulled any liberal surprise at a
resolution, passed on 20 September, that stated: 'acts possessing characteristics of aggression and intervention carried out in one or more member-
states of the OAS may be responded to in either individual or collective
form, which could go as far as resort to armed force.'[3]

This motion was passed by 312 votes to 52 several months after US troops had been despatched without consultation, invitation or warning to another member-state of the OAS, the conference of which had to be postponed as a consequence of the outrage caused. There is no evidence of any public Latin American defence of the US congressional vote, and if southern reaction was met with nonchalance on Capitol Hill this might remind us how slight, short and shallow was the post-Cuban variant of hemispheric containment produced by John Kennedy.

Finally, and in a similar vein, we should register the considerable fuss caused on 12 October 1965 by the opening at Yale University of an exhibition of a Swiss-drawn *mappamundi* dating from 1440 in which Greenland is clearly shown, with the strong – not to say fierce – implication that 'America' had been first 'discovered' by Leif Ericson, not Cristóbal Colón. Although some, such as *Visión* columnist Alberto Lleras, produced requisite pieces entitled 'Otra vez nos descubren', it is clear that the real news-story for the Día de la Raza was the tussle between the Spaniards and the Italians over how to react to this putative Nordic upsetting of tradition. The US correspondent of Madrid's *ABC*, José María Massip, wrote:

> Italians will insist on the Italianist character of 1492, as if Spain had nothing to do with it and the discovery was an Italian achievement, which is just like saying that World War II was won by Germany because the Allied Commander, Dwight Eisenhower, is of German blood.[4]

On the other hand, Augusto Pedulla, Mayor of Genoa, declared: 'Each time somebody comes up with this old story of the Viking trip to the New World, but even if it happened it didn't represent anything for the history of humanity.'[5]

As spoken, such a statement is surely closer to the kinds of sentiments prevalent during the 500th anniversary of the conquest/discovery/ encounter, but the underlying attitude is a very great distance from the dominant attitude of 1992 in its unquestioning, unashamed eurocentrism.

Whether this produces a wry smile or tight-lipped irritation, it is surely useful in looking back thirty years to discard much of the knowledgeable cynicism subsequently accumulated as well as to respect the very unclear circumstances in which academic work was then being undertaken – almost always without strong intellectual antecedents or the comforts of a consolidated community of the type that obtains in the 1990s. At the same time, it is not just posterity in general that condescends – we should register great caution about academic fashion and modishness, which are certainly no less tyrannical than they are transient. Indeed, if today the most hyperventilated versions of hybridity lord it over the surpassed structuralism of some Stalinist lineage, who could evince surprise if social democrats of 1965 vintage felt compelled to extract some civilised revenge on the arrogant radicals of both right and left who alternately ignored or abused them for so much of the period under consideration? By the same token, of course, no anniversary is ever the end of the story.

History

In turning to the study of Latin American history I should emphasise that I am here primarily interested in how this has unfolded in Britain, even though such a trajectory is inevitably linked with the developments – not all of them readily comparable – elsewhere, particularly in the USA and Latin America itself.

Whilst some of the historical work published internationally in and around 1965 inevitably shows signs of age, the overriding impression is of continued usefulness, relevance and sometimes great influence. One notes the particular presence of religious themes – which would recede from fashion until the 1980s – in Mecham's still-cited *Church and State in Latin America*; the debate between Lewis Hanke and Juan Friede on the role of the Church in the conquest; the collection edited by Magnus Mörner on the expulsion of the Jesuits; the interest in the Inquisition taken by Richard Greenleaf and Lewis Tambs, amongst others; and Miguel León Portilla's edition of Torquemada's *Monarquía India*.[6] León Portilla's volume *La Visión de los Vencidos*, also produced at that time, is, of course, a core text in contemporary US teaching of the indigenous world in the sixteenth century, and as such it has entered the 'political correctness' debate as a rather elderly and respectable relation of Rigoberta Menchú's autobiography, the most prominent contemporary text.[7]

Amongst work that possessed a more modest public profile, but probably greater professional impact, we can cite Charles Hale's article on the Mexican Liberal Mora – an essay that opened a subtle, revisionist oeuvre on the nineteenth century, being characterised by a lack of iconoclastic 'show' despite the existence of a number of fat targets in the historiographical ranks; Carlos Sempat Assadourian's essay on the Angolan slave trade – a monographic work that was to presage more theoretical exploration on modes of production; and Barán and Nahúm's book on Uruguayan economics in the Independence period that again opened a prolonged investigative project, this time through a series of pointilliste case studies on rural society.[8]

The important debate on nineteenth century Argentine economic history that effectively began with Miron Burgin's book published in the immediate wake of World War II was significantly advanced not just by James Scobie's study of wheat but also by Tulio Halperín Donghi, whose research on beef exports in the early part of the century was subsequently developed into a complete 'national study' of the early republican period and then a synoptic survey of the subcontinent as a whole.[9] The latter text remains in print after 27 years and 13 editions, and, in addition to providing the sole historiographical foundation for the nineteenth century sections of Cardoso and Faletto's *Dependency and Development in Latin America*, is probably the most-read history book in the Latin American university system.[10]

Although Halperín's work brought him very briefly to the directorship of the Oxford Latin American Centre, British historiography at this stage was more focused on political and diplomatic issues. In 1965 Robin Humphreys and John Lynch, the first two Directors of the Institute of Latin American Studies (ILAS) and holders of the Chair in Latin American History at University College, London (UCL), jointly published in New York a textbook on the origins of Latin American independence.[11] The previous year, Humphreys's essays, which concentrated on the Independence period and nineteenth century diplomatic history, had been issued under the title *Tradition and Revolt in Latin America*.[12]

Lynch, some twenty years younger, had already opened a publishing career that is now nearly forty years long with a monograph on Spanish colonial administration in the Río de la Plata region and the first volume of his study of Spain under the Hapsburgs.[13] J.H. Parry, who was chairman of the committee that produced the report which heralded the establishment of Britain's five formal institutes or centres of Latin American studies, and who had in the 1940s written a monograph on sixteenth century New Galicia, published his popular *Spanish Seaborne Empire* a year after the report of his committee.[14] Also publishing in the field by this time, and so worthy of some kind of 'founding father' status, were David Joslin and John Street;[15] John Elliott; D.A.G. Waddell; Harry Ferns; Alistair Hennessy; and C.R. Boxer, the pioneer of Brazilian studies who has just had his *Golden Age of Brazil* reissued, when he is well into his tenth decade – something that one suspects will be a record although, I suppose, one rather hopes not.[16]

Institutional aspects

If one looks at the ILAS syllabus for the course 'Aspects of Latin American History', first taught in 1966, it is rather shorter and more focused on the nineteenth century than the corresponding course offered today, but also remarkably similar in its choice of topics (the influence of the enlightenment; the independence of Brazil; the social and economic basis of Spanish American independence; the formation of the Argentine state;

Mexican liberalism; Chile's 'aristocratic republic'; slavery and abolition in Brazil; *caudillismo* in the nineteenth century).[17] In fact, I would suggest that whilst the last thirty years have undoubtedly witnessed considerable expansion and innovation in the British historiography of Latin America, there is also a strong and perceptible continuity – not least compared with work in the USA.

The first feature of this is the emphasis on history-as-narrative, an approach which happens, thanks to Shama, Furet *et al.*, to be back in fashion at present – not least because of its testimonial possibilities – but which has certainly been treated as simple, superficial and reactionary for large tranches of the period under review. For Humphreys, 'History in my view is a branch of literature, and historians ought to try to write good English.'[18] I think this worthy sentiment rather less simple and innocent than it sounds, for Humphreys, speaking at the start of the 1980s, was undoubtedly faced with more than poor prose and bad punctuation. Indeed, I suspect that his main target was less syntactical insufficiency than the jargon of social science which we all know enjoys a pretty healthy existence, is normally evident in full-blown form rather than diligent proportion, and quite often succeeds in obscuring through quasi-scientism more than it reveals by challenging the dominion of common diction.

In making this observation I am revealing the sympathy I have for a second characteristic of what might be called the 'British school' (although if it is to be so, we should stress that it is all custom and no rules, more tradition than regulation). The characteristic might itself be termed 'empirical pragmatism', a term that should be taken to mean something quite distinct from its inversion. The essence of this is well captured in a recent essay on the study of the Mexican Revolution by Alan Knight:

> I admit to a certain impatience with analyses that begin with a lengthy 'naming of parts' peroration. Such an exercise – favoured by sociologists who have 'gotten history' like Michael Mann and Anthony Giddens – sometimes seems to involve the mass baptism of old ideas with abstract neologisms ... my own workaday belief is that the utility of such concepts becomes apparent only as – and to the extent that – they provide the machinery for making sense of concrete examples.[19]

I feel safe quoting Knight in this regard because he has worked in the USA, where this form of expression is almost mandatory in some disciplines, and because, although himself a 'document based' historian, he has a very good record of addressing new developments in the field, particularly with respect to comparative theory.[20] I also think that Knight is right when he identifies an advancing professionalisation in the history of Latin America over the last three decades.[21]

There can be little doubt that this development of skills, experience, resources and infrastructure was begun in 1965/6 with the establishment of the 'Parry Centres' at Cambridge, Glasgow, Liverpool, London and Oxford, three of which appointed historians as their first directors, all of which leaned heavily upon history as the 'core discipline' (although not all teach a 'core course' at master's level), and two of which already had established chairs in Latin American history (that at UCL has been 'frozen' for four years now). It is, of course, true that the University of London had a professor of Latin American history for a full 16 years before it had an Institute. It is also notable that J.H. Elliott, once Regius Professor of History at Oxford, is an expert in colonial Spanish America whilst Britain's 'best-selling' historian, Eric Hobsbawm, has taken a keen interest in the subcontinent and published on its politics and history since the late 1950s.[22] But it takes more than a professor – even one who is gifted, powerful or famous (three quite distinct attributes) – to enable significant numbers of young scholars to acquire specific expert skills within the discipline. In effect, the achievement of the Parry Centres was to make accessible what was in danger of becoming an obscure and elitist specialism.

Accessibility became popularity as a result of the mass expansion of higher UK education in the late 1960s and early 1970s, a simultaneous challenge to traditional disciplinary boundaries in the humanities and social sciences, and the particularly strong effect these developments exercised at taught postgraduate level – the natural locus of what we now call 'Latin American studies'. Of course, none of the Parry Centres was at a polytechnic (or 'new university' as they are now dubbed in a rather sad, Orwellian display of pseudo-democracy through euphemism; less false memory syndrome than false accounting, given the unfair terms inherited for research funding). Nonetheless, many of their students came from non-Oxbridge or metropolitan backgrounds or were influenced by the novel currents that managed to enter the collegiate fief. Both *Past and Present* and *History Workshop Journal*, for example, had strong representation of Oxbridge academics on their editorial boards, and if neither could be remotely described as a British *Annales*, they did provide a more congenial environment for work that took an international focus, was catholic in its methodology, and unphased by liberal custom. I think it fair to say that many of the elder generation of historians of Latin America found themselves in this new, hirsute company – between 1964 and 1992 full-time faculty in British universities rose from 19,000 to 46,000 – more by default than design, but the combination of their traditional formal training with the new perspectives and topics of interest was generally felicitous even if – as some of us recall – this occasionally involved moments of absolute mutual incomprehension.

In fact, the most emphatic inter-disciplinary pursuit of Latin American studies took place at two modern universities that did not receive Parry funds: Essex, which was founded on the institution and ethos of broad 'schools', and Warwick, which developed a Centre for Comparative American Studies within a rather more traditional framework. In both cases history was the 'lead discipline' and it arguably remains so within – it should be noted – programmes that are predominantly for undergraduates.[23] Both universities have also made recent appointments to lectureships in Latin American history – initiatives worthy of note when, to the best of my knowledge, there was no appointment of an historian of Latin America between 1975 and 1989.[24]

No less important a factor in professionalising and expanding Latin American history was the simple ability to travel to the subcontinent. If this seems obvious today, it should be pointed out that Humphreys did not go to South America until 1949, a year after he became a professor, and Harold Blakemore, the Academic Secretary of ILAS from its foundation until his retirement in 1987, only made the trip over a decade after he had completed his doctorate in 1955.[25] Even in the mid-1960s Malcolm Deas had to make his way to Bogotá by flying to New York and then taking a boat because those few flights that were available were also exceptionally expensive; at today's prices the (economy class) round-trip London to Buenos Aires in 1965 was nearly £4,000. It was the introduction of widebody aircraft (Boeing 747 in 1969; DC-10 in 1971), the advent of discount fares, and deregulation of air travel that really changed this position, Freddie Laker's Skytrain service coming into service between Tachito Somoza's heart attack in June 1977 and the first Sandinista attacks on provincial Nicaraguan garrisons in October of that year. The medium-term consequences of this were not only that the London–Buenos Aires airfare can now be bought for well under £1,000 but also that many – if not most – people visit Latin America before they study it.[26]

Until this state of affairs it was highly desirable, if not obligatory, to seek research material in Britain or Europe, which may explain the earlier concentration on diplomatic history, readily prepared through the Public Records Office (then wholly based at Chancery Lane and Portugal Street, less than 30 minutes' walk from ILAS) or company records, very often located in London (with several important firms' papers subsequently being housed at UCL). Equally, by the mid-1960s it was relatively cheap, if not politically pleasant, to travel to the Archivo de Indias in Seville – an indispensable source of colonial documentation, but one that required 'triangulation' based on papers reflecting the other end of the relationship (and housed, say, in Buenos Aires, Sucre or Mexico) if an excessively imperial focus was to be avoided.

By the same token, historical practice outside Latin America has become more professional because that within the region has undergone considerable advances. National and regional banks have in the last 15 years or so taken to funding state archive activity, so that at least at national level many of these can now protect and should be able to preserve their papers; some are even well catalogued. US universities and attendant enterprises have been microfilming Latin American newspapers and serials throughout the period with the result that regular runs may now be read thousands of miles from their place of origin – a two-edged sword in terms of certain research skills and experience, but surely a great advance in terms of preservation and propagation. Even trade union papers are being microfilmed with the support of international non-governmental organisations (NGOs).

The arrival of the personal computer revolutionised a publishing industry still inclined to an unedifying mix of mass sales and state contracts, thereby opening critical opportunities for scholarly journals and publications, which were in turn acceptable recipients of international support. When I first starting researching Bolivian history twenty years ago there were no historical journals there; now there are three well-established ones with a valiant pioneer having 'passed away' in the interim. Moreover, this small and poor country can sustain a publishing house dedicating to issuing history books, the overall quality of which in both theoretical and empirical terms is as high as that in Europe.[27] At the same time, advances in microchip technology have enabled a large part of the Chilean public library system to be put on to computer catalogue, with sections of those in Argentina, Brazil and Mexico not far behind. The national librarians and archivists of the subcontinent now meet and plan regularly – they may still preside over impoverished institutions but their ideas are no mere UNESCO hand-downs.

What takes you in can also take you out. Latin American scholars are learning more from abroad without having to travel so much – something, we should recall, that is an impossibility for the majority in any case without an international grant. Moreover, there are now regional post-graduate programmes in history, such as those run by FLACSO, that are often focused on research culture and methods, providing crucial training at master's level sufficient to start original investigative work – very often on a team basis – and, indeed, gain some teaching experience. It has, though, to be admitted that there are still very few professional historians in Latin America simply because there are insufficient funds to sustain them in university posts. If other inherited advantages of 'outsiders' are gradually being eroded, this critical one is not.

It seems logical that the British expression of such developments should be most telling in terms of 'output' or publication. After all, if most history 'originates' in the subcontinent, the great bulk of it is published, initially at least, in the UK. Here the record is clear and strong. Although there is no British journal corresponding to the *Hispanic American Historical Review* (HAHR, founded in 1918), the *Journal of Latin American Studies* (JLAS) was established by the five Parry Centres in 1969 with a marked historical bias – something that it has subsequently qualified without, I believe, sacrificing quality or character.[28]

The format maintained throughout by the *Journal* of full and finished articles together with extensive individual book reviews – as opposed, say, to the research reports and review articles characteristic of the *Latin American Research Review* (LARR) – may occasionally give it an air of stuffiness but is by the same token conducive to longevity, as exemplified (in one sense at least) by the special quincentenary issue of 1992. The *Bulletin of Latin American Research* (BLAR) was established by the Society of Latin American Studies (SLAS) in 1981 with a more marked multi-disciplinary mandate, emphasis on shorter pieces, and probably greater accessibility for younger academics. Both journals have provided a critical outlet for work that would most likely have been rejected by disciplinary journals as too esoteric, regardless of its quality, although it is, I suppose, a matter of conjecture as to whether the continued low profile of Latin America in general academic journals now results from the existence of area-specific publications.[29] It is, though, evident that neither of these 'house journals' sought to engage with those features of social history that might today be associated with 'cultural studies'. The JLAS explicitly abdicated responsibility for this area on grounds of competence and the existing alternatives for literary studies. The BLAR perforce engaged more fully because of its multi-disciplinary vocation and corporate responsibilities, but it has plainly felt more comfortable with mainstream history and social science. Partly as a result of this – and partly as a consequence of the enhanced popularity and confidence of cultural studies in recent years – a new publication based at the University of London and entitled first *Travesía* and then (on the cusp of odious respectability) *The Journal of Latin American Cultural Studies*, has established its presence.

The monographic study, usually based upon a doctoral dissertation, is still an essential part of an historian's apprenticeship. A series on Latin America has been published by the Cambridge University Press with various academic editors since the late 1960s.[30] To date over eighty titles have been issued and a few have been awarded a paperback edition.[31] The Cambridge series is independent of any institutional influence, and has never been restricted either to history or to authors of a given nationality, but I think it telling that by far the most substantial English language series on Latin American history should be edited mostly by British scholars.

This is even more the case with respect to the third major contribution to Latin American studies made by CUP: the multi–volume *Cambridge*

History of Latin America (CHLA), edited since 1974 by Leslie Bethell, Professor of Latin American History (now Emeritus) at UCL and Director of ILAS from 1987 to 1992. Of the 143 chapters published in the 10 substantive volumes (one is a collection of bibliographical essays) 53 have been wholly or partly written by Britons. Or perhaps one should say people of British birth since one might be thought to be beating the drum here and it is important to recognise that Latin American history has been the object (perhaps even disproportionately) of the delightfully termed 'brain-drain' for decades.[32] It is hard for somebody involved even tangentially in an enterprise such as the CHLA, which has multiple authors and a single editor, to pass brief and useful comment, but the overall structure and tone of this singular undertaking are an accurate reflection of Bethell's skills and interests, and although it has sometimes been criticised – most recently, I suppose, by Simon Collier for over-emphasis on the contemporary period – it undoubtedly remains the best synthetic expression of British historiography in the field.[33]

Intellectual developments

The main intellectual developments in the study of Latin American history over this period have inevitably interacted closely with the institutional processes at work. They have also displayed a mix of continuity and rupture, but in general there have been few sharp 'paradigmatic shifts', and even when the age-profile of the profession was markedly young - during the mid-1970s – the picture was less of iconoclasm than of hybridity. This is perhaps predictably the case with inter-disciplinary developments, where extra-mural borrowing was more tentative in method and modulated in style than in the USA. For example, 'cliometrics' (statistically led social history), which from the early 1970s seemed to be sweeping US departments (and which affected Latin American history directly through its controversial application to the study of slavery), did not really take off in the UK despite the strong presence of economic history as a sub-discipline and the pioneering work of Peter Laslett at Cambridge.[34] This is possibly due to the fact that the British generally feel less confident than do North Americans about the explanatory power of 'measurement' in social science. It may also have something to do with a suspicion that archival sources could be (and were being) purposefully ignored as a consequence of confident over-extrapolation from statistics. Most probably, however, it reflects a lack of resources sufficient to undertake strategic research and analysis of major primary documentation. Yet if there are few British equivalents to US research on, for instance, colonial finances of the type undertaken by TePaske and Klein,[35] there has been a notable contribution to the enduring and energetic debate over the demographic impact of European conquest from Linda Newson and George Lovell, both of whom are employed in departments of geography but work in archives and write as historians.[36]

A quite similar pattern can be discerned in the development of 'ethno-history' as anthropologists have increasingly made recourse to the archives. In some cases, such as that of Tristan Platt, contemporary observation has been almost completely displaced by use of documentary material in a critical reconstruction of the interplay between the Quechua and Hispanic worlds.[37] The work of Platt, and that of Olivia Harris, also reflects the influence of *Annales*, at least in part through their collabora-tion with French Andeanists and the importance of understanding precise market mechanisms and behaviour within the formidable ambit of colo-nial Potosí so as to move beyond the more base formulations of 'vertical-ism', 'capitalism' and 'feudalism' that prevailed twenty years ago. Britons have also made an important contribution to a different disciplinary mix of 'rural history', the work of Brian Roberts and Norman Long incorpo-rating strong sociological features, which are also evident in the substan-tial collection of essays edited by Kenneth Duncan and Ian Rutledge.[38]

By contrast, one of the richest texts in contemporary Latin American history – Peter Winn's *Weavers of Revolution* – derived from a formally trained historian making considerable use of oral sources to supplement the written record, and doing so in a manner that avoided the pitfalls of unqualified testimonialism as well as over-reliance on dessicated paper.[39] In general, though, history has not exploited oral sources as fully as might be expected, and certainly not as much as have students of sociology and politics. One reason can be inferred from the fact that Winn published his book some 13 years after he undertook the fieldwork upon which it is based – if all interviewing is highly vulnerable to political circumstance, then that which depends upon amalgamation with other sources is additionally subject to delay and analytical reconsideration.

Economic history has arguably exhibited less adventurous develop-ments in methodology, but it has undeniably retained its reputation over the last three decades and probably represents the strongest single area of British historical scholarship on Latin America. This is partly the consequence of the heated and protracted debate over 'dependency' and 'business imperialism' in which the British historian Christopher Platt took a prominent – some would say aggressive – role.[40] Platt's insistence upon precision in terminology and the interpretation of statistics often found a more attentive audience than did his invectives against *dependistas*, and it is notable that a 'second generation' of economic historians, some trained or directly influenced by him, has maintained a cool tone in work that ranges from detailed monographs to general surveys.[41] It is, of course, a mark of individual as well as generational maturity when polemical concern is transformed into (as well as out of) productive research, but few of those involved would deny that the controversy of the 1970s is now largely surpassed even if it occasionally resurfaces[42] or subsists as a device by which authors can 'locate' themselves (most often as 'revisionists').[43]

In all events, in the mid-1990s considerably less political capital is spun out of this issue, which twenty years previously provided ready ideological ammunition for those who could clearly see its relevance to debates over the political development and future of the region. Indeed, so tight did that entanglement become that it is necessary to insist upon the importance of research and analysis which was not so directly developed out of the dependency debate – whether this was the work of economic historians[44] or general historians who engaged with economic issues[45] or economists who adopted an historical approach.[46] The 'dependency debate' is perhaps unique in its impact across generations and disciplines, and one should stress that it was always a two-way street with historians gaining a challenge, object of study and sharp sense of relevance from analytical adventures undertaken in other disciplines.

In Great Britain the social and cultural history of Latin America has developed much more modestly. British scholars specialising in race, gender, the household and the family, for example, have tended to focus on contemporary issues. It has to be admitted that very few of the UK historians working on Latin America are women, and those that are – one thinks of Elizabeth Dore (a US citizen); Jean Stubbs (who spent many years in Cuba); Linda Newson (employed in a geography department); and Rebecca Earle (a US citizen) – cannot really be said to have benefited greatly from the British 'establishment' in the field (it might be germane in this regard to note that at the London ILAS women have comprised two-thirds of all master's students across the disciplines for the last five years). Unsurprisingly, there has been little published historical work on these themes of the quality produced by US and Latin American academics.[47]

By contrast, work on architecture by Valerie Fraser, art by Dawn Ades, and cultural journals and film by John King has established an international reputation as well as reflecting a substantive inter-disciplinary achievement, as opposed to that powerful current trading under the name of cultural studies that is apparently incapable of moving beyond the grandiloquent declaration of methodological platform and expression of heterodox vocation.[48] The issue here, surely, is that historians cannot plausibly halt their activity at the point of prospectus and allusion; they must engage substantively and court all the risks that this involves, not least in attention to matters that some deem 'middle-brow', pedantic and uninspiring.

One attribute of the inter-disciplinary movement of the last quarter-century is that it has tended to privilege analytical texts derived from secondary sources over those rooted in direct research. And yet it is hard to conceive of some of the flightier work on 'the baroque' subsisting without somebody having undertaken painstaking research on, say, cathedral architecture in Cuzco. Likewise, one notes today a fearless popularisation of the work of artists such as Kahlo, or the incorporation of directors such as Sanjinés into mainstream communications courses. All of which is laudable and uplifting, but also unimaginable had there not previously been rigorous investigation unworried by vanity. What to some seems merely artisanal is often the triumph of content over form.

This is, I suspect, nowhere more difficult to reconcile than at the interface of history and literary studies, perhaps because of the particularly fluid notion of 'discovery' – and so of 'research' – in and between these fields. Amongst the few who have achieved a consistently creative tension here the example of Gerald Martin stands out. This is not only for producing an analytically controversial literary history, but also for moving directly from a British polytechnic (Portsmouth) to a US university (Pittsburgh) without any intermediate stage at a UK university – a trajectory that some might deem as healthy as it was necessary.[49]

It is noteworthy that the most accessible general history book in the UK – *The Penguin History of Latin America* – is not written by a professional historian at all but by a professor of Spanish literature, Edwin Williamson of the University of Edinburgh, whose cautious and conservative approach makes him rather rare in the field. As expressed in R.A. Humphreys's conviction quoted earlier, many liberal historians are inclined to view themselves as part-time students of literature – just as many contemporary students of literature are wont to see themselves as exiles from an oppressive golden age regime. Yet, paradoxically, both groups today place a premium on the 'text' – whatever degree of authority they are disposed to confer upon its writers and readers and however 'sovereign' such subjects might be deemed to be – in a manner that should enhance archival work no less than analytical dexterity. The most distinguished examples of this genre in epistolary and novelesque form, such as Stephen Greenblatt's *Marvelous Possessions* and Doris Sommer's *Foundational Fictions*, are North American.[50] However, a British presence is registered by Peter Hulme for the Caribbean, and, of course, by Benedict Anderson, the original instigator of 'imagined communities'.[51] Moreover, when the cultural voice shifts to a register more recognisable for political ideas senior British scholars have made impressive contributions: Gordon Brotherston; Anthony Pagden; Malcolm Deas; David Brading.[52]

Within the history of political ideas and institutions there has been a marked concentration on the late colonial and early republican period of

Spanish America. Whilst in the 1960s this might be explained by the interests of Humphreys, Lynch and Street, their influence cannot alone account for the enduring salience of the epoch for historians, especially since the British record was of a piece with that elsewhere. Whether it be the intrinsic fascination of changing political order, enticing comparisons with North America, the role of ideas in 'transitional societies', the evident influence of British interests and intromission, or simply the need to subject the existing historiography to a cool reappraisal, there has never been a lack of attraction to this period, which is likely to maintain its popularity in the post-Cold War climate.

The direct question of political power that dominated earlier studies of the nineteenth century – one thinks of Lynch's essay 'Bolívar and the Caudillos'[53] – has tended to be displaced by a concern about the exigencies and experiences of forming, managing and living in new nation states, and the experience of the post-independence period (c.1830–60), which had hitherto attracted less attention, perhaps because it was seen to exhibit a retrograde rather than complex character. Michael Costeloe, in particular, has focused on this period for Mexico,[54] but it also features strongly in the work of Brian Hamnett, Malcolm Deas and John Lynch himself, whose general survey on caudillos excited much discussion. Just as the debate over economic history served to open up new areas of study for younger academics on 'economic liberalism' in the mid- and late nineteenth century, so is the burgeoning interest in the second and third quarters of the century producing a new wave of research, this time more political in character, as evident in the work of Rebecca Earle, Will Fowler, Mattias Röhrig Assunção, and Adolfo Bonilla, where one can espy a preoccupation with 'liberalism' as a more complicated and constrained phenomenon than had perhaps been recognised hitherto.[55]

Indeed, such has been the interest that it now sustains a vibrant annual workshop on nineteenth century themes held at the London Institute under the aegis of Eduardo Posada-Carbó, a scholar of Colombian political history.[56] The fact that Posada can feel that Colombian history is neglected in Britain when he has as colleagues in this field Christopher Abel,[57] Deas, Earle, and Anthony McFarlane should surely be taken as a positive sign. One hears similar objections from students of Mexico and Peru, although these are arguably better covered than Colombia and Chile – another country that received early attention and that predictably lost it during the 1970s. The thinness of coverage elsewhere is unsurprising except in the case of Argentina, still scantily studied by British academics for the period between Rosas and Roca.

In terms of regional concentration two other trends deserve brief note. The first is the upsurge of interest in Central America following the Nicaraguan Revolution of 1979. This placed a premium on the rare existing work in the field, such as that by Murdo MacLeod and David Browning[58] as well as providing a much wider audience for scholars such as Victor Bulmer-Thomas, who were about to publish the results of a prolonged (and hitherto quite lonely) research programme, and encouraging interest from both young scholars and those working on other areas.[59] This tendency fortified the contribution made by historians to the wider debate over revolutions, their origins, experience and consequences, wherein Mexico is the best covered and Bolivia probably the least attended of the Latin American examples.[60]

The second trend is much less positive – the persistently low level of work on Brazil, notwithstanding the early research of Leslie Bethell, his editorships of the CHLA and JLAS, and his supervision of many doctoral students (as these were mainly Latin American). This state of affairs, it should be stressed, stands in marked contrast to the pattern in the USA, where there is extensive work on Brazil. Explanations of structure rather than agency are evidently called for, and at least one institutional and one intellectual factor can be proposed as a contributory cause. Portuguese is not, of course, widely taught either at school or at university level. As a result, the critical first steps by which a student would come to the subject are not readily provided, even at second-hand via Portugal. Equally, the motivation to transfer across from Spanish studies is appreciably less for pre-1930s Brazil than for the later period, more readily subsumed into politics. As already noted, over the last twenty years the study of Brazilian slavery and its abolition has not featured large in the UK (Robin Blackburn's book ends in 1848), and few have been able or willing to follow the lead of Colin Lewis in exploring the rich possibilities in comparative entrepreneurial history and economic policy.[61] Brazilian studies in Britain are nowhere as strong as they might be – one reason why ILAS instituted (in 1996) an MA in Brazilian Studies – but they are weaker in history than in either literary studies or economics.

Two final observations may strike the reader as less obvious, even perverse. The first is to note the resilience of the 'gentleman (for they are all men) scholar', outside the academy with all its bureaucratic demands and weight of teaching as well as its nervous attention to fashion and career. The work of Hugh Thomas has ranged from Spain to Cuba to Mexico (with an occasional intermezzo on the world as a whole) and is no less characterised by the length of the studies than by the controversy they spark.[62] The late David Nicholl's work on Haiti manifests a sensitivity to cultural and social detail that is particularly impressive given the scope of his other area of expertise – the relationship between political theory and theology from the sixteenth to the twentieth century.[63] And John Hemming's work on Peru and Brazil stands as potent illustration of the capacity of human geographers to produce incisive writing on historical themes.[64]

My last point is more general and contestable. It is that the British historiography on Latin America, whilst it exhibits a strong interest in the study of ideas (Brading, Pagden, Cervantes), is quite distinct from that in the USA in that it displays no profound concern with cultural differentiation and the 'otherness' of the subcontinent with respect to that elusive familiar – 'the Anglo-Saxon, Protestant tradition'. It could be argued that such a preoccupation has driven US history of the regions of the continent since the days of Bancroft, Parkman and Prescott, perhaps finding its most eloquent contemporary exponent in Richard Morse.[65] Today this strand sometimes takes the form of an intellectual anxiety, as in the writing of Glen Dealy, or of polymathic illustration of dichotomy, as in the work of Claudio Véliz,[66] but whatever the nuance, it retains a pertinence to North American political attitudes and debate that does not apply in the British case and which would not, I feel, find a receptive audience for its 'totalising' ambition. As this (tellingly protracted) extract from Howard Wiarda's widely used textbook shows, US notions of 'civilisation' extend beyond the headlines generated by Fukuyama and Huntington, and they derive directly from an interpretation of history that academic specialists cannot ignore even if they find these notions misconceived, clumsy and politically manipulative:

> Our biases and ethnocentrism have helped . . . to perpetrate some fundamental misunderstandings of Latin America . . . (which) has its own social and political institutions and its own ways of achieving change, and it is both presumptuous of us and detrimental to a proper understanding of the area to look at it exclusively through the prism of the USA or Western Europe developmental experience . . . Latin American systems have their roots in the ancient Greek notion of organic solidarity; in the Roman system of a hierarchy of laws and institutions; in historic Catholic concepts of the corporate, sectoral, and compartmentalised organisation of society based on each person's acceptance of his or her station in life; in the similarly corporate organisation (army, church, town, nobility) of Iberian society during the late medieval era; in the warrior mentality and the walled enclave cities of the period of the reconquest of the Iberian peninsular from the Moors; in the centralised bureaucratic systems of the early modern Spanish and Portuguese states; and in the absolutist, scholastic Catholic political culture and institutions of the Inquisition and the Counter-Reformation.[67]

Such assurance has elicited a response from British 'empirical pragmatism' that might best be described as one of calm interest. Perhaps the most telling remark in this connection is made by J.H. Elliott in an exchange with Claudio Véliz:

> In his last published book, *L'Identité de la France*, Fernand Braudel urged the claims of comparative history, 'a history that seeks to compare like with like –

the condition of all social science if the truth be told'. But what constitutes 'like'? Every historian who sets out to compare two or more societies is liable to discover very quickly that the like, on closer inspection, turns out to be unlike. While differences may in fact prove to be more illuminating than similarities, all such comparisons . . . tend to be elusive.[68]

By contrast, the reaction to Wiarda and Véliz from a British social scientist such as Ian Roxborough exhibits a more direct and energetic reservation:

> As an explanatory device, tradition is only of interest to the extent that its continuity, embodied in institutionalized practices of socialization and cultural transmission, acts as an effective cause of system stability. Judged entirely in its own terms and on the basis of its own interpretation of the historical record, the theory of centralist tradition must be found seriously wanting.[69]

The main thrust of Roxborough's piece, which was a controversial and important contribution to the study of modern Latin America, was to emphasise the value of comparison and the interpretative need to employ a series of variables for explanation that avoids both uni-causality – Roxborough's main target, with *dependistas* as well as 'traditionalists' in his sights – and empiricist abdication from all but the most filigree of analysis. If in the early 1980s his attention was legitimately directed at the merchants of meta-narrative, over a decade later there would appear to be a case for reviewing no less stringently the disingenuous disclaimers made by the radical relativists. However, the impact of 'post-modernism' on the practice of history has hitherto been quite slight since it has little or nothing to add to traditional empirical procedures, and has only marginally affected the subject matter of a scholarly community already predisposed to take micro-activity seriously.

Politics

The study of Latin American politics in Great Britain has not generally sought to resolve or evade the modern 'problem' of the discipline – the explicitly complex interaction of normative and objective enquiries – by resorting to 'science'. There are in the UK more departments of 'politics', 'government' or 'political studies' than there are of 'political science', and few of the approximately thirty Latin Americanists working in those departments attempt to overcome analytical difficulties and dilemmas by means of mathematics. Even within a discipline which tends to find consolation in definition, which is inclined to "understanding through tidiness", and therefore more open than is history to the merits of abstraction, Latin American 'specialists' (those with detailed knowledge in a certain field) clearly outnumber the 'generalists' (those who concentrate on comparative and 'strategic' issues).

This, of course, is again more a comparison with scholarship in the USA than with that in Latin America itself. Indeed, it may be that, in addition to general cultural differentiation, British 'political scientists' are intellectually and temperamentally distinguishable from their North American counterparts by virtue of a much greater geographical distance from their object of study. Moreover, whatever their personal ideological predilection, the actions of the UK government in the region are so slight in comparison with those of the USA that they are free of most of the personal and political pressures that confront US scholars. Equally, nobody (not of Latin American background) who works in a British university has had to endure the demanding and dangerous conditions prevailing in the subcontinent over the last thirty years, and it is worth recalling that the confident, expansionary 'golden years' of British academic social science – say, 1967 to 1979 – coincided with the spread of dictatorship across Latin America.

In some sense, then, European students of regional politics were uncommonly privileged, and in certain cases such privilege expressed itself in the form of hubris, presumption and myopia beyond that required for any form of public statement about public affairs. But this was neither unusual for such a period of engagement nor particularly widespread, notwithstanding the fact that most British students of Latin American politics have been on the left of the ideological spectrum, with very few representatives of the traditional right to be found. It is possible that the coincidence of an ageing profession and a widely acknowledged crisis of socialism has altered this picture somewhat, undermining many of the unsupported assumptions of the 1970s. Yet the prevailing outlook remains sufficiently associated with redistributionism, welfare and social justice to recall the aspirations of the Attlee government (1945–51), even if many of those who were brought up through the institutions that it had created subsequently assailed these as suffocating and hegemonic (the new left minority) or corporatist and inefficient (the liberal–right minority).

Plenty has, of course, been said about the apparent similarities between 'Thatcherism' (always a keenly contested category) and the Latin American neo-liberal regimes of the 1980s, but more work could usefully be done on how the course of British politics has affected the study as well as the practice of that in Latin America. Perhaps such analysis might reveal the trajectory famously followed by Fernando Henrique Cardoso to be less singular in its ideological underpinnings and more so in its honesty? At the very least, Cardoso's shifting intellectual concerns offer a fair reflection of those of a majority of European as well as Latin American academics, even if they exclude the game-theory and 'rational-choice Marxism' interpretative currents so popular in the USA.[70]

Cardoso is undoubtedly exceptional in the influence wrought by his writing and his general ability – Perry Anderson has described him as 'arguably the most intellectually sophisticated head of any contemporary state' – but he is decidedly not unique in moving from an intellectual to a political career.[71] This is a quite familiar Latin American phenomenon, highlighting a greater 'real-world interest' than obtains in many academic disciplines, and which requires an extra element of analytical caution.[72] However, it should also serve to remind us that students of Latin American politics from outside the region are themselves sometimes at only one remove from power by dint of the journalism, consultancy and advisory work available to them outside the academy. As suggested above, this may only be of genuine consequence (remuneration aside) in the USA – one thinks of Professor Roett's misjudged words on the Zapatista uprising – but even in Britain the nature and openness of one's audience can certainly affect the balance between imaginative and reactive realism.[73]

In practice, academics working on Latin American politics are no more likely to be consulted by governments, banks or firms than are economists or even historians, since they undertake very similar tasks to the research departments of these organisations – often with inferior resources – and 'current awareness' in the age of the fibre-optic cable lacks the edge of that in the telegraphic epoch, even if the Zapatistas of the 1990s can conduct a 'post-modern' guerrilla politics through it. There is a plausible argument that readers of the British broadsheet press are less well served in the 1990s than they were in the 1960s in terms of Latin American coverage – that in the tabloids remains magnificently unchanged – but this is now of secondary importance. With very few exceptions, the public requirement of expertise has shifted from the esoteric knowledge of the explorer to sound-bite synthesis of a suitably rehearsed smoothness. For some the corresponding loss of mystique may be bittersweet since Latin American politics has been deprived of much of that exoticism which attached itself even to those who decried extremism, fulminated against dictators or issued stern admonitions on points of factual detail.

There is, however, scant evidence that such shifts have diminished student demand. In 1988 there were 21 university and polytechnic undergraduate courses on Latin American politics in some recognisable format, over a dozen such at master's level, 27 academics listed as teaching the subject, and 26 doctoral theses under preparation. In 1995–6 the concentration is – very much as twenty years earlier – in Essex, Liverpool, London and Oxford.[74] At ILAS politics and international relations courses were taught from the start of the MA in 1966, political sociology from 1976, and indian and peasant politics from 1991 – all of which, together with a number of smaller, specialist options, have been amongst the most subscribed courses on the programme.[75] Partly as a result of this, an MSc in Latin American Politics was established in 1994. Obvious though it may be, it is worth reiterating that Latin America is generally of interest to students of politics (for reasons of both deviance and conformity) whilst politics is often attractive to those who have engaged with the region from other disciplines or experience.

Democracy

The debate over democracy has altered considerably over the last three decades, but in the 1990s as in the 1960s it was rarely off the top of the academic agenda. Although the Parry Committee owed its existence in more than small measure to declining British economic influence and London's concern at the Cuban Revolution (not least in terms of its consequences for the decolonising British Caribbean), this was in the context of growing interest in the question of third world forms of government beyond the 'Westminster model', which had already collapsed in Pakistan, Burma and most of Britain's ex-colonies in Africa.

As we have seen, in 1965 the Latin American scene was not so readily definable in terms of either where it stood or where it was going. It could still be argued that a majority of the states possessed constitutional and significantly competitive forms of government (Argentina, Chile, Colombia, Costa Rica, Peru, Uruguay and Venezuela) or regimes of a partially pliable and occasionally reformist record, albeit erratically institutionalised and often at variance with liberal democratic procedures (Dominican Republic, Ecuador, El Salvador, Mexico, Nicaragua). Even where there did exist open dictatorship of a military (Bolivia, Brazil, Guatemala, Honduras, Paraguay) or civilian (Haiti) or combined (Cuba) character, this was generally young and sufficiently qualified by populist rhetoric, satellite parties or vestigial personalism to allow for a possible permutation to a 'mixed' or 'intermediate' regime without major rupture. Although the next few years in fact witnessed a widening and hardening distinction between these types of government – with a corresponding consolidation of opinion behind Juan Linz's rejection of 'a continuum from democracy to totalitarianism' – such an evolution was not yet evident.[76]

In 1996, when one could argue that Cuba alone fails to adhere to the formal protocols of liberal democracy, only four of the region's twenty republics have constitutions dating from the 1960s (and these four are currently quite liable to extensive reform).[77] Yet, just as it might be said that the 1960s experienced an underlying movement towards autocracy in

Argentina, Bolivia, Brazil, Peru and Uruguay, so it could be maintained that that decade consolidated competitive forms in Colombia, Costa Rica and Venezuela, and did both simultaneously in the extraordinary instance of Chile. Even if the rather distinctive geopolitical arena of the Caribbean is included, precise academic analysis and public punditry remained insecure, placing something of a premium on predisposition and long-range interpretation.

In this regard both Marxists and liberals in Britain shared an approach rooted in political economy and privileging the role of the bourgeoisie in a manner already well rehearsed for the England of the nineteenth century and, as suggested above, modified for the post-war neo-Keynesian welfare state. However, this was patently inapplicable to most of Latin America, where both interpretative strains lacked persuasive analytical alternatives to their clumsily teleological 'big cousins' – orthodox Marxism–Leninism (ultimately immutable procession of modes of production) and modernisation theory (inherently and decisively progressive vocation of the middle classes). Nonetheless, the recent experience of the Cuban Revolution did provide an important safety-valve for the left, not just in terms of absconding from a univocal and implausible determinism but also through association with the Revolution's early idealism, which promoted agency and initiative in a theoretically awkward but politically enticing manner.[78] Indeed, at least until the 'Prague Spring' of 1968 and probably up to the 'Ten Million Ton Harvest' disaster of 1970 (or maybe the Padilla affair the next year) most strains of radicalism bar the most spartacised Trotskyists encountered in Cuba some relief from arid Stalinist formulae.

The main discussion on the radical left with respect to liberal democracy during this period, then, was whether it could offer some alternative to the 'classical' or Cuban insurgent paths to power – a seemingly marginal consideration that was eventually tested in Chile under *Unidad Popular* with such a tragic outcome that few in the region seriously debated the merits of the 'peaceful road to socialism' for at least a decade after the 1973 coup, however seriously this was taken by some (southern) European radicals.[79] The Chilean coup – probably the single most decisive political event in the thirty years under review – was, therefore, doubly retrograde. Not only did it physically open an exceptionally severe regime but it also seemed to many to provide absolute justification for repudiating all the claims of 'bourgeois democracy'. Just as, in the shadow of reactionary despotism, most European radicals effectively jilted 'pluralism' between 1940 and 1950, so throughout the 1970s the left of Latin America and its international sympathisers tended to see liberal democracy as lacking in both heroism and intellectual respectability. As a consequence, the debate was, for well over a decade, virtually monopolised by conservative and liberal writers – positively bursting at the seams in North America, but thin on the ground in northern Europe.

None of this should be taken to mean that mainstream or liberal debate on democracy was ever sophisticated, undivided or uncontested. Even before the onset of the dictatorships there was a marked reaction against the presumptions underlying the approach led by John Johnson, perhaps the most prolific and renowned US commentator on Latin American politics in the 1950s and 1960s. This is Johnson on the Latin American middle class at the end of the 1950s:

> They are overwhelmingly urban. They not only have well above average educations themselves but they also believe in universal public education. They are convinced that the future of their countries is inextricably linked to industrialisation. They are nationalistic. They believe that the State should actively intrude in the social and economic areas while it carries out the normal functions of government. They recognise that the family has weakened as a political unit in the urban centres, and they have consequently lent their support to the development of organised political parties.[80]

Such a viewpoint was criticised not only by the 'culturalists' but also by liberals, such as David Apter, who were far less sanguine about the overall character and development of the political economy of regions like Latin America: 'the experience of the modernizing nations indicates that democracy, as we understand it, is not appropriate to their stage of development.'[81] In the USA this critique would be taken forward into the 1970s and 1980s by Samuel Huntington and, in a much more pugnaciously political fashion, Jeane Kirkpatrick.[82] However, from a British (and Latin American) standpoint the progressively weaker claims for a democratisation of Latin America during the 1960s elicited a mix of cultural, institutional and economic explanations, best represented by two volumes edited for the Royal Institute of International Affairs (Chatham House) by Claudio Véliz: *Obstacles to Change in Latin America* (1965) and *The Politics of Conformity in Latin America* (1967):

> The Nineteenth Century European pattern of political ideologies is not relevant to contemporary Latin American conditions, and this partly explains the failure of the traditional groupings – including socialist, radical, liberal and conservative parties – and the relative success of the grass-roots 'populist' movements with their confusing mixture of nationalism, social reformism and authoritarian centralism . . . self-interested and determined political activity of a forward-looking, reformist, anti-aristocratic, and generally progressive and modernizing middle-class should have been sufficient to solve the problem. But the problem has not been solved.
>
> In this book scepticism gains ground . . . far from showing profound alterations, the traditional structure has suffered fewer changes than is usually thought . . . In fits and starts since 1929, the countries of Latin America have been returning

to their own Hispanic, hierarchical, and more or less authoritarian political tradition. If both the USA and the Soviet Union may justly be regarded as nations with great social mobility and a generalized aspiration to become egalitarian societies, precisely the converse would apply to Latin America . . . it is now possible for countries like Brazil, Mexico, Chile or Argentina to develop impressive industrial sectors incorporating the latest available technology and even modes of consumption without all this resulting in fundamental changes in the traditional social structure.[83]

Here, of course, we see the burgeoning of Véliz's 'centralism' thesis, but many of the contributors to these volumes and the debates around them shied away from this, preferring closer empirical exploration. Amongst the British academics this has probably been strongest in the spheres of institutions and ideas, both in the work of the 'first wave', such as Alan Angell,[84] Ken Medhurst[85] and Peter Flynn,[86] directly affected by the experience of the 1960s, and also in that of their doctoral students – such as Celia Szusterman, D'Alva Kinzo, Carol Graham, Anita Isaacs, Jenny Pearce[87] – which focused on other periods and exhibited a clear 'post-authoritarian' sensibility. It is, I believe, quite telling that no British academic has attempted a major survey of political attitudes of the type produced in the early 1960s by Almond and Verba, who included Mexico in their highly influential *Civic Culture* volume.[88] (A second generation of research students – principally geographers undertaking fieldwork in the 1970s and 1980s – made greater recourse to survey techniques, largely for the purpose of analysing sectoral structure and behaviour.)

The question of democracy was revived from the early 1980s with the varying erosion and collapse of the Southern Cone dictatorships, the debate now exhibiting a richer combination of political economy, institutional and behavioural factors. For the first years discussion was less concerned with the Schumpeterian structural preconditions for democracy that had dominated the 1960s than with the behavioural factors pertinent to 'regime transition'. Here the influential trajectory of the Argentine social scientist Guillermo O'Donnell was most telling in its shift from the long-range and predominantly structural explanations applied to the dictatorships to a more tactical, empirically nuanced and short-term assessment pertinent to the new conjuncture.[89] Whereas O'Donnell's earlier concerns had overlapped significantly with those of the British new left (see below), he was now quite widely viewed by that current as propounding *realpolitik* and seriously overselling liberal procedure. Moreover, many British academics found the debate around this new, fluid reality closer to the functionalist and game-theory approaches of the US and European traditions than a malleable, narrative-led account could readily accommodate.[90] Yet one of O'Donnell's leading collaborators at that time was Laurence Whitehead, the Oxford social scientist who has maintained a high trans-Atlantic profile and energetically evaded narrow country specialisation.[91] Moreover, the expanded research experience acquired in the 1970s and 1980s provided British scholars with far greater empirical confidence in receiving the theory traversing the Atlantic, both north and south. As twenty years earlier, analytical caution prevailed.

In the early 1990s the question of democratic 'consolidation' in the Southern Cone combined with that of 'transition' in Central America, throwing up some illuminating contrasts. With a few exceptions – notably the work of the British ex-patriate Charles Gillespie on Uruguay[92] – UK academics desisted from full-scale theoretical applications to national experiences. Certainly there was no wholesale embracing of the work of Giovanni Sartori, who exercised considerable influence over Latin American and US scholars moving rapidly into institutional debates to do with electoral systems, legislative powers and presidentialist arrangements.[93] Instead, we find both monographical and comparative treatment of the leading post-authoritarian issues – human rights policy and impunity; constitutional reform and corruption; local government – by a younger 'third generation' which did its fieldwork in the early years of the decade (Lowden, De Brito, Sieder, Domingo)[94] and the 'second generation' that had come of intellectual age at the start of the authoritarian cycle (Nickson, Little, Munck, Pollack).[95]

Umberto Eco has mischievously remarked that freedom of speech should include freedom from rhetoric, and at times over the last decade there has prevailed a strong sense that the study of Latin American politics is really about perfecting the operation of liberal democratic institutions.[96] For some, like Fernando Rojas, such a scenario reflects little more than a change in administrative form of domination:

> Geographical and theoretical reductionism, inspired by the failures of the dictatorships of the Southern Cone, have established the basis for another form of reductionism, engaged in mainly by the US government and the international media. This new over-simplification consists in identifying democracy with only two features of 'normal' political regimes: multiple political parties and formal elections to parliament and government posts. Other essential or important conditions for the existence and operation of capitalist democracies are then either greatly discounted or entirely forgotten.[97]

One might expect one set of simplifications to beget another in response, but in practice the reaction of British academics has been to suspend the theoretical constructs that remained largely unchallenged in the dictatorial epoch, and to engage with a tighter testing of the claims of the new dispensation. One could protest, in fact, that this has been 'under-theorised', but an approach that is not clouded by culturalist predeterminism, institutional triumphalism or presumption of a quasi-conspiratorial 'capitalist logic' stands a fair chance of producing analysis of enduring value. By 1995 most of the states of the region had become – to borrow Alex Wilde's term – 'dangerous democracies' quite similar to those of 1965 not only in terms of their practical mutability but also in their resistance to the ideal-types preferred by ideologues.

The interest of British commentators in this experience of change might, I think, have something to do with its lack of precise precedents and the awkwardness of its timing in terms of global patterns. There were few, if any, European instances of – or models for – the type of regime transition witnessed after 1982, even if the Moncloa Pact in Spain offered some attitudinal pointers. Democracy by conquest, rather than by default, was the principal European experience at mid-century, and thereafter the main transition, aside from Spain, Portugal and Greece, was from the Fourth to the Fifth French Republic – in almost the opposite direction.[98] Equally, the emergence of the Southern Cone civilian regimes in the early and mid-1980s, under Reagan and before the collapse of the USSR, was somewhat anomalous with 'northern political time' even if the initial transitions in Central America from 1987 to 1991 might be seen as more directly an 'effect' of super-power shifts in policy and confidence. Whatever the case, there were throughout Latin America few and inexact parallels with eastern Europe, enhancing a general sense of political diversity within the broader context of neo-liberal economics which were, following the Mexican debacle, themselves losing the kind of essentialism so associated in Britain with Margaret Thatcher in her – relatively short-lived – prime.

Revolution, dictatorship and the changing boundaries of politics

The question of democracy has not, of course, always been at the top of the analytical agenda over the last thirty years. Sometimes it was treated as a derivative or subset of political revolution and autocracy, and sometimes it was entirely displaced by these phenomena. In fact, until quite recently one could plausibly periodise the study of Latin American politics in terms of revolutionary and counter-revolutionary cycles – from Cuba to Chile (1960–73); from Chile to Nicaragua (1974–79); from Nicaragua to the pacification of Central America (1980–91) – with little less relevance to the right than to the left in terms of both pessimism of the intelligence and optimism of the will. It is, after all, notable that both poles of the ideological spectrum sought in their own manner to abolish or severely curtail the state, and within both communities the essential fault-lines corresponded to the timing and means for this.

The British literature on the modern revolutionary experiences is broad-ranging, which might be expected not only from the consistent interest in Mexico, but also from engagement with all phases of Peronist Argentina.[99] Much of the earlier work on and around Cuba was no less interesting in scholarly terms because of its openly committed nature: Blackburn's 1963 essay and his polemic with the sceptic wing of Trotskyism best represented throughout our period by Mike Gonzalez; Richard Gott's detailed and vivid study of the guerrillas of the 1960s.[100] There is, understandably, greater distance by the 1980s, when Toni Kapcia and Jean Stubbs were writing, first in the wake of the Chilean coup and then after the collapse of the Soviet Union.[101]

A similar trajectory can be discerned with regard to Chile and Central America. In the first instance the steely new-leftism evident in the collaborative work of Ian Roxborough, Jackie Roddick and Phil O'Brien, written shortly after the 1973 coup, yields less to 'told-you-so' polemic than to their own, sober consideration of the consequences of dictatorship,[102] the notably precise work of David Hojman,[103] and to more elegiac studies, such as that based on exile interviews by Colin Henfrey and Bernardo Sorj.[104] From the right there were the non-academic, populist but incisive surveys of Alistair Horne and Robert Moss, whose approach closely resembled that of Paul Johnson, a high-profile visitor to Pinochet's Chile.[105] In the case of Nicaragua the triumphalist timbre on the left in the early years, perhaps best represented by George Black, gave way to a period of 'critical support' that was decidedly more open and contested than that for Cuba, and then, after the Sandinista electoral defeat in 1990, a renewed polemic that quite accurately reflected the divisions between radicals and fellow-travellers at home and abroad.[106] At the same time, however, the prolonged conflicts elsewhere in Central America progressively induced caution, sharper interest in institutions, and consideration of both the social costs and the political gains of civil war.[107]

Throughout one perceives some hesitation with respect to theories of revolutionary causation – a tendency here, perhaps, to borrow from the general approach of Miliband rather than that of Poulantzas – but Ian Roxborough at least engaged positively as well as critically with that, predominantly North American, literature.[108] One finds the role of ideas and organisation just as prominent as structural context in the studies of Harding and Taylor on Sendero Luminoso, Harvey on the Zapatistas, and Gillespie on the Montoneros.[109] There is certainly some methodological overlap and continuity here with a longstanding British interest in the labour movements of the region.[110]

By contrast, academic analysis of the dictatorships of the 1970s was extensively underpinned by theoretical consideration. As suggested above, this was partly a conjunctural matter, the middle years of the decade witnessing considerable receptivity in UK universities to the ideas of

Althusser, Poulantzas and other proponents of what might be termed 'structuralist Marxism'. Moreover, the traditional British appetite for political economy was at this point attracted to the later, more sophisticated variants of dependency theory, with the consequence that for a while these three currents dominated debate. The result was a rather stylised voice that frequently fell back on abstraction, but which at the same time posed a sharp challenge to the analytical indolence of local empirical custom and practice, responding to a situation of unprecedented rupture in Latin America with genuine intellectual curiosity. Guillermo O'Donnell and Fernando Henrique Cardoso were the two main Latin American points of reference, both men attending a conference at Cambridge in December 1976 – strongly influenced by the March coup in Argentina – on 'The State and Economic Development in Latin America'.[111] In many ways that conference marked the high-point of the exploration for a new international political economy of Latin America, but only an Occasional Paper, rather than a commercial publication, resulted from it.

Subsequently Ernesto Laclau, who had been a speaker at Cambridge and who had begun his research career in economic history, engaged in a major and highly influential theoretical reconsideration of Marxist politics, leaving Latin America behind (although one can sometimes sense its presence in his later writings).[112] On the other hand, David Lehmann, a leading organiser of the conference,[113] Colin Henfrey,[114] Paul Cammack,[115] Cristóbal Kay[116] and Christian Anglade[117] went on to publish inter-disciplinary work that both focused on Latin America and was dedicated to a critical reconsideration of political analysis, albeit more firmly within the Marxist idiom than that of Laclau. This current recognised the importance of political institutions but was not, ultimately, very interested in them, producing a rather strange complementarity with the work of those, like George Philip, who justifiably treated the armed forces as a key object of analysis.[118] It is probable that there would have been more of this latter type of study were it not for the obvious fact that the military is exceptionally difficult to study at close quarter to high scholarly standard.

The British literature on the international relations of Latin America forms part of one of the longest-standing traditions of political analysis in this country, and it has reflected quite closely the two principal interpretative declensions of recent years – 'realism' and international political economy – but generally at second-hand rather than through open theoretical elaboration. The older scholars, such as Fred Parkinson, Gordon Connell-Smith and Peter Calvert,[119] broadly worked in a political science application of international or diplomatic history, well-established at the LSE in the post-war period and particularly prominent for this region in terms of its relations with Britain in the nineteenth century. However, the twentieth century has, of course, been dominated by relations with the USA, upon which UK scholars have, as a rule, not concentrated – although on occasion, such as Whitehead's essay on Washington's Central American policy, the 'outside view' has proved distinctly advantageous.[120] It is possible, but unlikely, that more attention to the Falklands/Malvinas issue prior to 1982 might have exercised some influence on policy. Subsequently the case has been treated in appreciable detail, bringing Latin Americanists into unusual limelight with respect to policy-making in London.[121]

The evidently limited scope, in a distant and crowded field, for developing innovative research on Latin American relations with the USA has predictably focused attention elsewhere. The inter-American system itself has been an object of study although, until recently, one could find relatively few issues of real consequence there. Amongst the exceptions are Mexican and Brazilian foreign policy, and regional agreements on nuclear matters, studied by Edward Best, Joe Smith and Mónica Serrano respectively.[122] The possible development of regional trade zones and markets into a process of genuine political integration – as suggested by both NAFTA and Mercosur – offers another area of interest, as does the apparently lacklustre but still consequential issue of regional relations with the EC/EU.[123] Here also, one finds some of the surprisingly few instances of collaborative work between Latin Americanists and Caribbeanists specialising in the Anglophone and Francophone societies.[124]

This analysis of international relations and politics is probably more vulnerable than most strands of the discipline to the impact of change. If there is for Latin America no group akin to the 'Kremlinologists', so recently and comprehensively displaced from the centre of the academic stage, the ending of the Cold War and the advent of 'globalisation' – sometimes (and surely wrongly) known as 'multi-polarity' – has required extensive reconsideration of received beliefs, 'mindsets' and research agendas. Published before the collapse of the USSR, Nicola Miller's book on Soviet relations with the region is likely to remain a core survey on that topic.[125] Andrew Hurrell's work both on the environment and broader questions of international power reflects a new agenda, substantively and in terms of theoretical exploration.[126]

Post-war custom in the British academy has been to subdivide the study of politics into government and institutions; international relations; theory (sometimes known as political thought); and public policy. Such divisions are usually imperfect – where does one put political sociology? – and sometimes crude, but they do provide some assistance in surveying a particularly broad discipline. For our purposes it is worthy of note that British work on public policy – broadly understood to be the 'systems and management' side of public administration – has been very slight indeed except where this is directly related to economic and foreign policy. The treatment of state and government operations has tended to focus on these as arenas of conflict and channels for power rather than on the purely technical issues.[127] However, as the explicitly ideological component of Latin American politics has diminished – by dint of shifting, generally from the left, to the 'centre' – there has also been some analytical convergence. This, combined with the increasing 'market-orientation' of UK universities over the last decade (involving the recruitment of high-fee-paying overseas students) is likely to increase interest, as suggested by the recent establishment of an MSc in the Public Policy of Latin America at the University of Oxford.

It is more difficult to identify a distinctive 'political theory' from the interpretation of substantive issues, aside from those relatively rare cases of open philosophical exploration – Laclau, Larraín, Merquior, Unger.[128] Nonetheless, the last ten years have witnessed an exceptionally rich experience in the reconsideration of the traditional boundaries of the discipline. At times, of course, this has never risen above an indolent iconoclasm, and it has yielded some extremely ugly prose. Yet the polemics over structure and agency, the influence of Foucault, the claims of 'identity politics' and 'subaltern studies', and the general collapse of ideological custom and practice have contributed – often in combination – to a much deeper and variegated debate. In the case of Latin America there is a good argument to be made that the practice plainly preceded the theory, the emergence of 'new social movements' in the 1970s and the virtual evacuation of the traditional conservative and radical motifs from the stage in the 1980s compelling fresh approaches and pluralist methodology.

In one sense it is understandable that the analytical deconstruction which attended this process should have favoured the specific study over the general survey. David Slater is one of the few to have taken a broad compass, from the standpoint of political geography[129] although one notes a similar, revisionist perspective in the work of two anthropologists – John Gledhill and Richard Wilson.[130] Joe Foweraker, however, is unique in addressing sub- and post-dictatorial political sociology with books on both theory and detailed case studies.[131]

Although issues such as popular religion and human rights have retained a salience well into the civilian period, it could be argued that the political analysis of race and, particularly, gender, have been even more comprehensively recomposed because important changes were taking place outside Latin America as well as within it. The upsurge in testimonial literature and greater attention paid to 'subjectivity' was mirrored by significant developments in theory. In the UK, Maxine

Molyneux's role has been as prominent in this general debate as in its application to Latin America, whilst the work of Jo Fisher, Sarah Radcliffe and Georgina Waylen has contributed to its empirical and analytical depth.[132] However, for race, Peter Wade's work on Colombia is a rare instance of British scholarship on this vital subject in mainland Latin America.[133]

In all cases the notion of 'what is politics' has undergone more than marginal elasticity – in some instances it has almost been effaced completely – but few of those named above so doubt the existence of power with perceptible social origins and consequences that the question 'who governs?' is rendered redundant.

Very little of the academic work on politics mentioned above ever was or remains uninfluenced by the small but particularly vital group of people who work on Latin America outside of higher education. I am not here thinking solely of the stringers and correspondents of the press and electronic media although many of these have written or edited valuable book-length texts on and around politics – Richard Bourne, Sue Branford, Eduardo Crawley, Richard Gott, Phil Gunson, Colin Harding, Hugh O'Shaughnessy, James Painter, Simon Strong.[134] Richard Gott valiantly endeavoured to maintain an engaged series of original, edited and translated books for Penguin in the 1970s.[135]

In addition to the influential reporting and commentary of the Latin American Newsletters (LANL) since 1967 (involving at some stage Harding, O'Shaughnessy and Crawley from the above), there has been a quieter but vibrant input from the staff of non-governmental organisations working in and on the region. Whilst LANL shifted from a broadly radical to a market-oriented stance in the early 1980s, the NGOs have proved less ideologically mobile. Pure 'solidarity' work was mostly restricted to denunciation, particularly in the Southern Cone in the 1970s and Central America in the 1980s, but it was often highly informative and frequently resulted from a much closer knowledge of the day-to-day business of countries than that possessed by academics. Moreover, most NGOs working in Latin America (Amnesty International, Oxfam, Christian Aid, Cafod, Catholic Institute for International Relations, UNAIS, amongst others) have to operate programmes based as much on technical expertise and diplomatic manoeuvre as on altruistic resolution, which is far more evident in the outreach aspect of their work. The Latin America Bureau (LAB), a small independent body established largely to bridge these gaps between popular development education, academic study, and support for an anti-dictatorial, 'social justice' political platform, has published a range of book-length studies over nearly twenty years. LAB lacks the resources available to its North American counterparts – Washington Office on Latin America (WOLA) and North American Congress on Latin

America (NACLA) – but it has been able to resist the absolute tyranny of the market, commissioning and issuing studies that many mainstream publishers would find commercially unattractive, even had they thought of them in the first place.[136]

If there has been some tendency over the last thirty years for academics to view the development agencies as rather narrow and simplistic in their political understanding, and for these agencies themselves to feel exasperation at ivory-tower evasion of brutish realities, this differentiation has become much less stark. Indeed, both groups appear to share the perception of a highly mobile, complex reality, in which it is, for instance, no more easy to devise the criteria for 'fair trade' than to resolve the judicial dilemmas created by the ex-dictators. The certainties on either side are palpably eroded. Yet the human condition in Latin America in the mid-1990s is not, in many important ways, any improvement upon that in the mid-1960s. The same, of course, could be said of Britain itself – governed for over half the period under review by the same political party under the shade of a single individual. Perhaps, then, it is unsurprising that one finds in the academic work the underlying sentiment less of a jeremiad than of admiration of resilience in the face of unfeeling change.

1996

The United States and Latin America
in the Long Run (1800–1945)

The principal object of your mission is to cultivate the most friendly relations with Bolivia. The enemies of free Government throughout the world point with satisfaction to the perpetual revolutions in the South American Republics. They hence argue that man is not fit for Self Government; and it is greatly to be deplored that the instability of those Republics and in many instances their disregard for private rights have afforded a pretext for such an unfortunate assumption. Liberty cannot be preserved without order; and this can only spring from a sacred observance of the law. So long as it shall be in the power of successive military chieftains to subvert the Governments of the Republics by the sword, their people cannot expect to enjoy the blessings of liberty. Anarchy, confusion, and civil war must be the result. In your intercourse with the Bolivian authorities you will omit no opportunity of pressing these truths upon them, and of presenting to them the example of our own country, where all controversies are decided at the ballot box . . . Instead of weakening themselves by domestic dissensions, the Spanish race in these Republics have every motive for union and harmony. They nearly all have an enemy within their own bosoms burning for vengeance on account of the supposed wrongs of centuries, and ever ready, when a favourable opportunity may offer, to expel or exterminate the descendants of their conquerors.

James Buchanan, Secretary of State, 1848[1]

We must have Cuba. We can't do without Cuba, and above all we must not suffer its transfer to Great Britain. We shall acquire it by a *coup d'état* at some propitious moment, which from the present state of Europe may not be far distant. How delighted, then, am I to feel that you have selected a diplomatist and fit for the work – one who, possessing no vanity himself and knowing when to speak and when

to be silent, is so well calculated to flatter the pride of the Dons –
who by the gentle arts of insinuation and persuasion can gradually
prepare the queen mother, the ministers and courtiers for the great
surrender – and who above all is a perfect master both of the
language of Louis le Grand and of the knight of rueful countenance.
Cuba is already ours. I can feel it in my finger ends.

James Buchanan, 1849[2]

Consideration of relations between the USA and Latin America over the
long range must necessarily be a broad and speculative undertaking, but
it does offer a number of interpretative opportunities. Perhaps the most
important of these is simply to review the current, brief post-Cold War
scenario in an extended pre-Cold War context, which might modulate
some of the claims of conclusive 'newness' that have understandably
proliferated within a generation of academics and policy-makers mostly
born and entirely educated after 1945. Equally, there is merit in taking
stock not only of developments within the USA over the long run, but
also in relations between the hemisphere and Europe – if only to test the
standard view of a constantly burgeoning and unchallenged inequality
within the Americas.

In a recent, polemical textbook Peter Smith[3] has emphatically restated
what might be characterised as the 'imperialist thesis', at the end of which
he presents a very suggestive table of 'strategic options' (see Table 6.1).

Smith's depiction here registers the different levels of interaction,

Table 6.1 **Peter Smith's 'strategic options' for Latin America**

Strategy	Imperial era 1790–1930s	Cold War 1940s-80s	1990s–
Collective unity (political integration)	attempted (economic integration)	attempted	unlikely
Extra-hemispheric protection	attempted (Europe)	attempted (USSR)	—
Subregional hegemony	attempted (Brazil / Argentina)	—	possible (Brazil)
International law/organisation	success	attempted	—
Non-socialist revolution	Mexico	Bolivia	—
Socialist revolution	—	Cuba/Nicaragua	—
Third world solidarity	—	attempted (NAM/G77)[5]	—
Alignment with USA	attempted (Brazil / client states)	success (authoritarians)	attempted (Mexico + ?)

Source: Peter H. Smith, *Talons of the Eagle. Dynamics of US–Latin American Relations* (Oxford
University Press, New York and Oxford, 1996) p. 331.

policy and response as well as respecting the external dimensions of a relationship that is frequently assumed to be hermetically hemispheric and univocal. Although it is evident more in the table than in the main body of the book, this variegated picture suggests that Latin America has not always followed in craven fashion the kind of advice offered to Sheridan senior by Swift in 1725 about the importance of openly supplicant form:

> Take the Oaths heartily to the powers that be, and remember that Party was not made for depending Puppies . . . take care of going regularly through all the forms of Oaths and Inductions, for the least wrong step will put you to the trouble of repassing your patent, or voiding your Living.

That is what Ronald Reagan called 'saying uncle', and it is what, from an opposite point of view, Rodolfo Cerdas Cruz exhorted the Sandinistas to do in order to avoid a rhetorically accelerated conflict in the 1980s.[4] Yet even in 1945 communications were far less developed than today, a more general and distended pattern of decision-making, formulation and implementation of policy giving the vocal aspect of inter-American relations less immediately acute consequences – if not always a less urgent timbre – than has been the case in recent, televisual decades. Whereas it is possible to measure – albeit imperfectly – industrial production, trade flows and the concentration of weaponry, this more cultural aspect of foreign relations is quite elusive and vulnerable to anachronistic interpretation. In fact, it is probably the feature most misunderstood if viewed exclusively with the sensibilities of the 'historical present' of the late twentieth century.

The eras or epochs identified in Table 6.1 are not, of course, determined by the bilateral relations of the USA with the rest of the American colonies/republics. In those terms, and from the perspective of the USA, one could propose a sub-periodisation of the 'imperial era':

1780–1820   Acquisition and consolidation of continental US territory from Europe
            (Louisiana purchase; war of 1812; Florida purchase)

1823–1860   Doctrinal rejection of Europe from political intervention; consolidation of continental US territory from Mexico; operational parity with Britain achieved in Caribbean
            (Monroe Doctrine; war of 1846–8; Clayton–Bulwer treaty)

1860–1880   Vacuum of power; temporary loss of ideological confidence; momentary European resurgence
            (Civil War; French occupation of Mexico)

1880–1898   Hemispheric ambitions openly expressed
            (Pan-Americanism)

1898–1930   Hemispheric ambitions aggressively pursued
             (Roosevelt Corollary; dollar diplomacy)

1933–1940   Diplomatic relations modulated; economic reconsolidation
             (Good Neighbour policy)

1941–1945   Wartime acceleration of continental integration and political
             fault-lines; full emergence of Pacific theatre; full ideologisa-
             tion of external powers and rearticulation of international
             politics.

A chronology seen from the Latin American perspective would not be radically different although there are, of course, quite distinct crises and ruptures for each country (Paraguay, for instance, was at war in the 1860s and 1930s, when US influence in the region was at a relatively low level). The key challenge, though, is to discern a balance between the long-run processes and the discrete events/ruptures which lie behind any set of dates like these. Of course, some, such as Richard Morse or Claudio Véliz, would reject this chronology as being a distraction from the deeper, historiocultural differentiation between the Anglo and Iberian societies transplanted across the Atlantic.[6] Others, such as Samuel Flagg Bemis, find a more compelling matrix of distinction in physical conditions, particularly the climate, which opens and dominates Bemis's 1943 study of US Latin American policy:

> It is a scientific fact of political, economic and social geography, that the areas of best and of second best climatic energy coincide geographically with the more impressive evidence of human civilization, such as maximum wheat production, maximum of professional occupations, maximum of industrial production, greatest numbers of schools, of colleges, of automobiles . . . favourable climate is a necessary basis of modern civilization.[7]

When measured against such maxims – written in the midst of a world war fought between states with eminently 'temperate' climates – the observations made in 1787 by Thomas Jefferson strike one as almost postmodern in their fluid, pluralist approach to the latitudes:

> The glimmerings which reach us from South America enable us only to see that its inhabitants are held under the accumulated pressure of slavery, superstition and ignorance. Whereas they shall be able to rise under this weight, and to shew themselves to the rest of the world, they will probably shew they are like the rest of the world . . . (those) going from a country in the old world remarkably dry in its soil and climate fancied there [to be] more lakes and fogs in South America than in Europe. An inhabitant of Ireland, Sweden, or Finland, would have formed the contrary opinion.[8]

Jefferson's (controversial and risky if not, at $15 million, inordinately expensive) decision to press ahead with the Louisiana purchase in 1803 both gained control of the Mississippi and effectively committed the states – I use the term deliberately in the plural – to a westward, continental and federal expansion. Even at the start this had sharp implications for Mexico (which some, such as Vice-President Aaron Burr, wanted to annex from Spain into a separate slave-holding confederacy) and Cuba (where the whites of Saint-Domingue abandoned by Bonaparte fled in greater numbers than to New Orleans). In the short term the purchase enabled the USA to exploit Spain's weakness by raiding and then annexing-through-purchase Florida in 1819, at the height of the independence wars in the south. In the medium term it led – through the creation of the republic of Texas – to the Mexican war of 1846–8, the treaty of Guadalupe Hidalgo and the payment of another $15 million for all the remaining territory up to the Pacific between present-day Canada and Baja California (the Oregon limits had previously been settled with Britain). The traditional longer-term projection is of a vocational expansionism supported throughout by the ideology of 'manifest destiny' (a term first used in 1845) and revived by the needs of corporate capitalism from the reconstruction era into the twentieth century. This lineage stretches, then, directly from Jefferson's pragmatism in exploiting European conflicts through Monroe's opposition to new European intervention in the hemisphere in defence of its new republics, and through Polk's clumsy appropriation of that doctrine to justify the violent acquisition of American lands, to Roosevelt's corollary, fashioned for the correction of domestic affairs of other continental states regardless of the European factor. It is, however, a problematic and challenged inheritance which can too readily be rendered 'natural' and uncontradictory. I shall here give some emphasis to these problems and moments of indeterminacy because the literature on the left from Thoreau to Chomsky has glossed over them whereas that on the right merely dismisses them as operational infelicities or products of a naïve idealism.

Cuba

The exception to my qualification-through-complication approach is Cuba. The island has evidently been problematic to the USA from the first years of the republic in a relationship that is only partially comprehensible through the lens of international political economy. Buchanan's opening declaration is illustrative of a sentiment towards Cuba within the US political class that alternates between attraction and frustration, for which any adequate explanation must rely in part on psychology. Jefferson was privileged in that during his presidency the issue was so little developed. Yet even he declared that he would place at the southern tip of the

island a notice – *nec plus ultra* (nothing beyond here) – exhibiting a
confidence expressed rather more explicitly by John Quincy Adams,
secretary of state to Monroe, as Spain was losing the military struggle to
retain its mainland colonies:

> It may be taken for granted that the dominion of Spain upon the American
> continent, north and south, is irrevocably gone. But the islands of Cuba and
> Puerto Rico still remain nominally, and so far really, dependent upon her ...
> Cuba, almost in sight of our shores, from a multitude of considerations has
> become an object of transcendent importance to the commercial and political
> interests of our Union ... there are laws of political as well as physical
> gravitation; and if an apple severed by the tempest from its native tree cannot
> choose but to fall to the ground, Cuba, forcibly disjoined from its own
> unnatural connection with Spain, and incapable of self-support, can gravitate
> only towards the North American Union.[9]

Nearly thirty years later Buchanan, himself on the cusp of the presidency, was no less confident. After the Civil War Grant prepared a serious
financial offer, and was only one of four presidents so to do. Theodore
Roosevelt felt that he had participated in the act fulfilled – an island
penetrated is as metaphorically available as an apple, fallen by grace of
gravity or proffered by the hands of Eve – and today Messrs Helms and
Burton chafe so because their law forbidding Europe (or anyone else) to
have intercourse with Cuba is not fully upheld. As much as one resists
recourse to the analysis of Lacan (because of its frenzied germination and
dullard propagation) the energy that charges between the real, the
symbolic and the imaginary orders in this respect is compelling.[10] Jefferson was fond of quoting the phrase with which Cato the Elder ended all
his speeches to the Roman senate – '*Delenda est Cartago*' (Carthage must
be destroyed) – and he habitually dubbed Britain as Carthage for its lack
of republican asceticism. He would surely despond if he knew that this
ritualistic incantation has since 1959 remained an integral part of US
public rhetoric as applied to the Caribbean island administered by Fidel
Castro. Prospero watches amazed as he is called Caliban by Caliban
himself.[11] The temptation to pathologise is exceptionally strong.

What Jefferson anticipated and most of his successors insisted upon in
the case of Cuba was the 'non-transferability' thesis, derived from the
Monroe Doctrine and initially intended to preserve as American and
independent all Europe's ex-colonies in the hemisphere. For Buchanan,
as for Edward Everett, who was secretary of state seven years after him, the
objective of this policy was to retain Cuba as either a formal colony of
Spain or a US protectorate or direct possession but decidedly nothing
else. This aim was upheld from 1823 to 1960 by quite widely differing
measures and under very distinct circumstances: the replacement of the

Platt Amendment by sugar quotas in 1934, for example, is certainly a far from inconsequential matter and relates – as do the events of 1895–1902 – to the emphatic agency of the Cuban people. Equally, the period after 1960 is not homogeneous. Up to the collapse of the USSR this loss was overwhelmingly approached as a modern, ideological issue. After 1990 it becomes possible to reinterpret US policy towards Cuba in terms of 'non-transferability', albeit still within the rhetorical guise of democratic anti-Communism, which was too familiar and reassuring to ditch.

Monroe

The Monroe Doctrine has been widely viewed as a charter for expansionism and intervention, but it is best seen as a declaration of containment. Although in 1823 those identified as its targets were the European states ruled by monarchies and possessed of colonies, the Doctrine was always available for self-application at the service of isolationism – a current that has its domestic roots far closer to those of 'manifest destiny'/expansionism than is normally recognised:

> We have here no concern with South America; we have no sympathy, we can have no well founded sympathy with them. We are sprung from different stocks, we speak different languages, we have been brought up in different social and moral schools, we have been governed by different codes of law, we profess radically different forms of religion . . . How can our mild and merciful peoples, who went through their revolution without shedding a drop of civil blood, sympathise with a people that are hanging and shooting each other in their streets, with every fluctuation of their ill-organised and exasperated fractions? . . . We are told it to be a maxim clearly established in the history of the world that none but the temperate climates, and the climates which produce and retain the European complexion of skin in its various shades, admit of the highest degrees of national civilization.[12]

This attitude would endure through quite different political conditions, but on the brink of Latin American independence Monroe had no need to make open recourse to it because the principle of non-intervention could be stated directly and plausibly in terms of the balance of international power:

> It is impossible that the allied powers should extend their political system to any portion of either continent without endangering our peace and happiness; nor can anyone believe that our southern brethren, if left to themselves, would adopt it of their own accord. It is equally impossible, therefore, that we should behold such interposition, in any form, with indifference. If we look to the comparative strength and resources of Spain and those new governments, and their distance from each other, it must be obvious that she can never subdue

them. It is still the true policy of the United States to leave the parties to themselves, in the hope that other powers will pursue the same course.[13]

I stress this element of containment because, of course, Spain did contrive to retain Cuba and Puerto Rico until the very end of the nineteenth century, much of the Caribbean remains under direct colonial rule from Europe beyond 1945 – some is still part of France – and there was little domestic consensus within the USA over how to respond to major extra-hemispheric powers. Furthermore, in his diary Secretary of State Adams gives an account of the cabinet debate over the presidential message that was to contain the Doctrine that underscores the possibility of self-application, as both a mark of virtue and a prophylactic against tempting alliances and adventures:

> After much discussion, I said I thought we should bring the whole answer to Mr Canning's proposal to a test of right and wrong. Considering the South Americans as independent nations, they themselves, and no other nation, had the *right* to dispose of their condition. *We* have no right to dispose of them, either alone or in conjunction with other nations. Neither have any other nations the right of disposing of them without their consent.[14]

It is worth recalling that this statement was written three years before Canning made his celebrated boast: 'Contemplating Spain such as our ancestors had known her, I resolved that if France had Spain, it should not be Spain with the Indies. I called the New World into existence to redress the balance of the Old.'

On the other hand, the argument that the Monroe Doctrine effectively 'called the Old World into existence to redress the balance in the New' has always been fortified by the examples of Polk in the Mexican war and Roosevelt in the occupation of Cuba, where high-minded rhetoric was deployed in support of military aggression. By explicitly extending the exclusionist component of the Doctrine to the USA itself, and by asserting the rights of 'other peoples' to join the Union, Polk simultaneously warned London against interference in the case of Texas in 1845 and provided himself with a formal – if flimsy – *casus belli* against Mexico the next year.[15] Some fifty years later Roosevelt, by explicitly introducing as new considerations for the application of the Doctrine the internal condition and political behaviour of the states of the hemisphere, made the truly qualitative jump from the avowal of principle to the assertion of conditionality:

> All that we desire is to see all neighboring countries stable, orderly and prosperous. Any country whose people conduct themselves well can count upon our hearty friendliness. If a nation shows that it knows how to act with decency in industrial and political matters, if it keeps order and pays its obligations, then it need fear no interference from the United States. Brutal wrongdoing,

or an impotence which results in the general loosening of the ties of civilized society, may finally require intervention by some civilized nation, and in the Western Hemisphere the United States cannot ignore this duty; but it remains true that our interests, and those of our southern neighbors, are in reality identical.[16]

If the Monroe Doctrine has widely been understood in the light of these sentiments – so readily applicable to the 1990s – this is because Roosevelt is seen to have made public and plain those attributes of 'manifest destiny' that were ever present and yet seldom enunciated so bluntly. But, as already suggested, it is one thing to assert superiority and quite another to engage in political expansionism, especially that requiring military intervention. Although Polk's war completed the process begun by Jefferson in 1803 and transformed the USA into a truly continental power in the space of a few months through the actions of a mixed regular and volunteer army, the president – never a popular figure – did not face opposition simply from figures on the 'left', such as Emerson, Greeley and Thoreau.[17] The position of Calhoun was characteristically blunt:

> I know . . . that we have never dreamt of incorporating into our Union any but the Caucasian race – the free, white race . . . I protest against such a union as that [with Mexico]. Ours, sir, is the Government of a white race [with which the Mexicans are not fit to be connected].[18]

Calhoun had been secretary of state in the previous administration, and he might be thought here to be maximising his pro-slavery position in opposition to the government, but even a Democrat expansionist like Lewis Cass was clear about the social restrictions on annexation:

> We do not want the people of Mexico either as citizens or subjects. All we want is a portion of territory which they nominally hold, uninhabited, or, where inhabited at all sparsely so, and with a population which would soon recede, or identify itself with ours.[19]

These are, of course, elite views, but the evidence suggests that they conformed to an important body of popular opinion within the white male constituency of Jacksonian America. This was a population, the humorists had it, for whom, 'Thet Mexicans worn't human beans – an orange outing nation. A sort o'folks a chap could kill an never dream on't arter.'[20] At this level the distinction between conquest, annexation and dismemberment could readily be confused or lost. Of the 73,000 volunteers enlisted in the USA for the war with Mexico, 25,000 came from the free north-eastern states, but many of these, like Thomas Tennery arriving in Matamoros from Illinois, held convictions that were comparable to those of Calhoun in their origin, if not in their virulent application:

Everything appears dull, the houses, the inhabitants little above savages and without energy or business of any importance going on. This appears to be caused by the want of commerce, with the indolence of the inhabitants and perhaps the want of a settled government that will secure some property. But to bring about this change the country must be inhabited by a different race of people. The Spaniards and the Indians do not make a race of people with patriotism and candor enough to support a republic, much less to form, sustain and establish one out of the present deranged fabric called the Republic of Mexico.[21]

A racially based pessimism of this type was shared by many in the Latin American elite, but for such an ardent advocate of European immigration as Juan Bautista Alberdi the whole thrust of the Monroe Doctrine was to reimpose isolation from a vital source of civilisation, both north and south of the Rio Grande (where the US border with Mexico had been newly fixed). Furthermore, Alberdi saw the defence of the political form of republicanism – which could uphold the institution of slavery as well as any other – as spurious in the extreme:

We do not dissent from the republic in itself, in the abstract and ideal, but from the republic deformed and monstrous, which we see in practice; from the republic with tyranny and misery, with disorders, with revolutions; we dissent in a word from the governments of Bolivia, Peru, New Granada, La Plata, which only by sarcasm can be called republics . . . to isolate oneself from Civilised Europe is to recolonise oneself.[22]

By the time Teddy Roosevelt was making a similar contrast between form and content (or procedure and substance), the USA was strenuously exercising its claims to represent an alternative source of civilisation. However, until the 1890s there existed a palpable gap between US claims and capacities – a gap made all the more obvious by the extravagance of the claims. Few Latin American presidents could ever plausibly strike the tone adopted by Polk in his address to Congress in December 1847:

No country has been so much favoured, or should acknowledge with deeper reverence the manifestations of Divine protection. An all-wise Creator directed and guarded us in an infant struggle for freedom, and has constantly watched over our surprising progress, until we have become one of the great nations of the earth.[23]

At the time of the Mexican war most heads of state in Central and South America could point to some recovery from the wars of independence and growing commercial ties with Britain, but usually in the context of political behaviour that Alberdi so scorned and which President Carlos Soublette, regaling the Venezuelan Congress, listed as part of a litany with equally providential or natural qualities as that presented by Polk:

Unfortunately, evils of every description have occurred during the last year, and all kinds of misfortunes have assailed us: floods, failures of the harvest, disease and contagious epidemics, discontent and disquietude in the public mind, mobs and tumultuous assemblies, and sometimes even the necessity of employing force to suppress seditious practices; all of which, together with their consequences so fatal to commercial and industrial transactions, have contributed to increase the losses and difficulties which have been experienced . . .[24]

This is a familiar image, and nowhere is it more acutely drawn than in the comparison between the USA and Mexico in 1848. It is, however, worth noting that the campaign ended by the treaty of Guadalupe Hidalgo was conducted with ordnance still dominated by muskets and muzzle-loading weaponry, that on its eve the total enlistment of the US army numbered less than 9,000, and that after the termination of hostilities this returned to only 11,000. The eventual logistical undertaking was indeed formidable, and it relied critically upon a capacity to raise troops and taxes in a manner quite beyond the divided and disoriented authorities in Mexico. Yet the USA fought the war in terms comparable to Mexico, sometimes needing more than a natural incidence of good luck – Taylor's 'victory' at Buena Vista, for instance. Their troops were still raised with the promise of land grants, and most volunteers lacked uniforms; Polk's law partner Gideon Pillow had himself appointed major-general, and at the end of the war the navy of what Polk was describing as a great world power possessed just 21 ships of all types built after 1840.[25]

The activity and influence of the Department of State is usefully reconsidered in this same light. In 1833 it employed in diplomatic posts a total of 152 personnel, served by six clerks in Washington. By 1856 the total establishment in Washington had risen to 57, including a single librarian and a solitary translator (of Spanish and French); there were 10 full embassies abroad (by contrast, at the end of World War II, the Department itself employed 3,767 personnel and the Foreign Service 7,000 with a budget of $50 million).[26]

Economics and ambition

For the broader development of the economies of north and south Table 6.2 suggests that it would be mistaken to identify any clear US supremacy before the 1890s. Even in 1912, had the Latin American states followed the advice offered them today by Peter Smith and dealt with the USA as a united bloc, they would have possessed appreciable bargaining power. Of course, by that stage the USA had experienced qualitatively greater development of its industrial production and infrastructure, and before

Table 6.2 **USA and Latin America: population and exports, 1850–1912**

Year	Exports ($000)	Population (000)	Exports per capita (US$)
Latin America			
1850	159,484	30,381	5.2
1870	344,123	38,628	8.9
1890	602,147	51,662	11.7
1912	1,580,534	77,456	20.4
USA			
1850	162,000	23,192	7.0
1870	400,000	39,818	10.0
1890	859,607	62,948	13.7
1912	2,307,000	94,569	24.4

Source: Derived from Victor Bulmer-Thomas, *The Economic History of Latin America since Independence* (Cambridge University Press, Cambridge, 1994), pp. 38; 69; 432–3.

World War I she was far less dependent upon overseas trade – 13 per cent of GDP in 1850; 12 per cent in 1910 – than were the European powers to which Latin America was still largely oriented at the start of the twentieth century: Great Britain 51 per cent; France 33 per cent; and Germany 36 per cent (all in 1910).[27] As can be seen from Table 6.3, the levels of US–Latin American trade are decidedly modest throughout the nineteenth century, and, indeed, only Cuba and Brazil are partners of any conse-

Table 6.3 **US trade, 1830–1900 ($ million)**

	1830	1840	1850	1860	1870	1880	1890	1900
Total								
Exports	72	124	144	334	471	836	858	1,394
Imports	63	98	174	354	436	668	789	850
Canada								
Exports	3	6	10	23	25	29	40	106
Imports	—	1	5	24	36	33	39	39
Cuba								
Exports	5	6	5	12	14	11	13	26
Imports	5	9	10	32	54	65	54	31
Mexico								
Exports	5	3	2	5	6	8	13	36
Imports	1	1	1	2	3	7	23	29
Brazil								
Exports	2	2	3	6	6	9	12	12
Imports	2	5	9	21	25	55	59	58

Source: US Department of Commerce (1975), pp. 904–6.

quence for the decades after the Civil War (when they retained the slavery abolished in the USA).

From a Latin American viewpoint the explicit or implicit maintenance of the Monroe Doctrine up to World War I had to be assessed in the light of the military and commercial capacity of *both* the USA *and* the European powers. In this regard the Civil War (1861–65) represented a short but very severe interruption of the developing balance of power. For Thomas Schoonover the war not only offered France, Spain (and Great Britain) a rich opportunity to pursue their interests by force in Mexico and elsewhere – as the hapless Secretary of State William Seward, an expansionist if ever there was one, looked the other way – but it also stymied the political possibility of an unprecedented ideological convergence between Washington and Mexico based on liberalism and republicanism that he finds incarnated in the meeting between Lincoln and Romero in January 1860. It is, though, difficult to see the ideological issue as greater than that of the international balance of power when, in July 1862 – nearly sixty years after the Louisiana purchase and following the withdrawal of British and Spanish forces from Mexico – Napoleon III declared:

> The prosperity of America is not a matter of indifference to Europe, for it is that country which feeds our manufactories and gives an impulse to our commerce. We have an interest in the republic of the United States being powerful and prosperous but not that she should take possession of the whole of the Gulf of Mexico, thence command the Antilles as well as South America, and be the only dispenser of products of the New World.[28]

Porous though it proved, Lincoln's naval blockade relieved Latin American governments of any severe choice over recognition between the belligerent parties in North America, but, particularly in Central America, the recourse of the Confederacy to privateers as well as the fear of slavery recently reawakened by William Walker and other filibusters required discretion in statements and activity (there was also the reasonable analogy with the break-up of the isthmian union 25 years earlier that had not been reversed by force and that had important international consequences for the concept of sovereignty.)[29] Clearly, the fact that the USA was plunged into an internecine slaughter without parallel elsewhere in the continent did more than interrupt trade and reduce prior claims of unity and internal stability to competitive sectional ideology. Beyond the conflict itself, reconstruction and the attendant caution in foreign affairs slackened the immediate pressure on Cuba (itself at war from 1868) and, arguably, offered Latin America a unique window of opportunity at a time of expanding trans-Atlantic commerce.

On the other hand, Walter LaFeber has long argued that it is precisely at this stage (1860–98) that the United States came to pose a profound threat to the rest of the region by transforming itself into a 'new empire':

> Two important features distinguished it from the old. First, with the completion of the continental conquest Americans moved with increasing authority into such extracontinental areas as Hawaii, Latin America, Asia and Africa. Second, the form of expansion changed. Instead of searching for farming, mineral or grazing lands, Americans sought markets for agricultural staples or industrial goods.[30]

For LaFeber, Seward is the man of vision who when, in May 1864, he is urged to face down Napoleon in Mexico, responds, 'Five years, ten years, twenty years hence, Mexico will be opening herself as cheerfully to American immigration as Montana and Idaho are now.'[31] This was after Gettysburg, with immigration to the USA exceeding 250,000 a year for the previous 15 years, contributing to an unparalleled acceleration of what would a century later be termed the 'military–industrial complex' (it is only in 1865 that the US currency was standardised). It might be thought justified confidence. Seward, though, saw still longer cycles at play, claiming that his vision derived from

> a political law – and when I say political law, I mean a higher law, a law of Providence – that empire has, for the last three thousand years . . . made its way constantly westward, and that it must continue to move on westward until the tides of the renewed and of the decaying civilizations of the world meet on the shores of the Pacific Ocean.[32]

Such assurance about underlying movements could, of course, encourage resistance to intervention, as in the case of Calhoun, for whom 'manifest destiny' had twenty years earlier needed little or no executive encouragement: '*Time* is acting for us; and if we have the wisdom to trust its operation, it will assert and maintain our rights with restless force, without costing a cent of money or a drop of blood.'[33]

LaFeber argues that the myth of the frontier was widely believed, and that mass apprehension at its imminent 'closure' in the 1880s had critical consequences for economic planning, international strategy and the popular imagination. His first book might certainly be deemed a child of its teleological times in that he identified a Rostow-like 'take-off' period in 1843–57 and assumes patterns of causation that are rather unsophisticated by today's standards.[34] Yet the last third of the nineteenth century is evidently a watershed of critical importance, not least, of course, because Seward was able to buy Alaska from the Tsar at a price of $7.2 million ($5 billion in today's prices) within two years of the end of the Civil War, thereby reducing European-administered territory on the American continental mainland to British Honduras and the Guyanas (Canada gained self-government in the same year). Moreover, Seward was far from extraordinary in his emphasis upon the burgeoning Pacific dimension and the emergence of a tri-continental theatre, with its considerable consequences for naval strategy and inter-oceanic communication. The 1882 Exclusion Act, which banned all immigrant labour from China for a period of 10 years, was just as important a point of closure – of free inter-continental migration – as was the previous year's proposal by Washington of a Pan-American Congress to secure intracontinental cooperation in the context of a fully global theatre.[35]

The 1881 Pan-American Congress failed to take place because Secretary of State Blaine was removed from office (as a result of the assassination of President Garfield), and replaced by Freylinghuysen, who agreed with him on the essential issues but was not convinced of the value of a summit – a quite rare initiative for that epoch. The fact that one was only eventually held in 1889–90 is a reminder of the importance to US foreign policy of domestic political actions and individual initiative. The original objective had been to seek a means of averting regional conflicts in the wake of the prolonged Paraguayan War (1865–70) and the War of the Pacific (1879–83). The congress finally held in Washington followed this through with a proposal for compulsory arbitration that was fiercely resisted by Chile, which had annexed large and rich portions of Peruvian and Bolivian territory. However, the agenda in 1890 also included extra-dition and citizenship, monetary and exchange controls, uniform customs and commercial regulations, health and sanitation issues and, perhaps most important of all, a draft convention for the settlement of financial claims. From Washington's perspective this last issue was not restricted to the growing interests of US companies and investors. Between the French intervention in Mexico and the 1890 congress the failure to repay debts had led to the threat or use of force by seven European countries (Denmark; France; Germany; Great Britain; Italy; Russia; Spain) against five Latin American states (Colombia; Haiti; Nicaragua; Santo Domingo [now Dominican Republic]; Venezuela). The next year Washington and London found themselves supporting different sides in the Chilean civil war, and, in the wake of the economic crisis of 1893, they clashed over British claims to the Orinoco for which Venezuela sought international arbitration.

In short, at the start of the last decade of the nineteenth century the Monroe Doctrine seemed both to have been fully revived and to have been given an expression that was at least tolerable to many Latin American governments. In 1902 this would take the form of the Drago Doctrine, designed to prohibit the use of European force to collect debts – an initiative that itself inspired the Roosevelt Corollary. That, in turn, did not elicit universal repudiation. In 1906 the veteran Brazilian states-man Rio Branco embraced both Monroe and Roosevelt with a racial

stereotyping typical of its day but deployed with unusual emphasis at the
service of a strategy of 'cohabitation' between Brazil and the USA. This
was a strategy that 75 years earlier Bolívar had come to fear as a serious
threat to Latin American union, just as it is one that Peter Smith today
sees as a potential option for the 'age of uncertainty':

> Latin America has nothing to fear from Anglo-Saxon America. The United
> States is a nation of English origin and principles and therefore beneficial for
> the civilization of other peoples because the sentiment of individualism is so
> much part of their race that English or North American imperialism, if it
> should manifest itself, would never be of the same type as German or Latin
> imperialism, which seek to destroy or annihilate everything, contorting every-
> thing in order to create from the incompatibilities and irreconcilables the same
> kind of country in all regions of the world. Nothing, absolutely nothing, in the
> policies of the United States would be able to cause uneasiness to the national
> sensitivity of the other American countries. Just the opposite, these nations find
> in the preponderance of the first nation of the continent support for their
> causes and aspirations.[36]

It is, though, not the case that prior to the renewed use of military
intervention by the USA itself in 1898, Pan-Americanism was viewed in a
universally favourable and instrumental manner in the south. Over previous decades relations with the USA had taken on increasing importance
as an issue within the domestic political life of the Latin American states,
generating a degree of division and controversy. This was particularly true
in the Caribbean Basin, and within it especially true of Cuba. Further
afield, as in Argentina, with relatively weak economic and cultural ties
with the USA, matters could appear less urgent. Hence, on the eve of the
First Pan-American Congress José Martí, a Cuban émigré based in New
York, wrote his dispatch for *La Nación* of Buenos Aires with an energy that
impresses almost as much as does the continued relevance of his theme:

> The customs union proposal that would permit free entrance of the products
> of every nation to all countries of the union should be no cause for alarm;
> merely announcing it would make the proposal collapse ... Taking United
> States products duty free – because its cosmopolitan factories produce all that
> is known or can be suggested by the entire world – would be like tossing the
> principal customs revenues into the sea ... Why go as allies, at the height of
> youth, into the battle the United States is able to launch upon the rest of the
> world? Why must it fight its battles with Europe in the American republics, and
> rehearse its system of colonization on the territory of the free nations? ... Why
> in the halls of this Congress arrange projects of reciprocity with all the
> American nations when one such project, that of Mexico, has for years been
> waiting in vain for congressional sanction, because the special interests affected
> by that project, to the detriment of the national interests, oppose it?[37]

World power in local context

Six years later, when Martí was killed in the Cuban independence struggle, Great Britain had backed down over Venezuela, accepted the US-sponsored dismantling of the Moskito 'kingdom' in Nicaragua, and was visibly withdrawing her longstanding support for Spain over Cuba (scarcely, though, on a point of anti-colonial principle – what San Juan del Norte in Nicaragua had ceased to promise now needed resolute defence in Mafeking in South Africa). Nonetheless, as can be seen from Table 6.4, the US military apparatus could not yet match that of Great Britain, even if generous allowance is made for the skills of the veterans of the Indian wars or the widespread deployment of British troops. Moreover, from a Latin American perspective, the maintenance of British naval bases at Halifax, Bermuda, Jamaica, St Lucia, the Falklands and Ascension Island was, prior to the construction of the Panama canal, a consideration of greater gravity than it might appear today, when the canal itself has lost much of its direct strategic importance and we have become accustomed to aviation-directed military operations.

Table 6.4: **Military personnel and warship tonnage, 1880–1914**

		1880	1900	1914
USA	Troops	34,000	96,000	164,000
	Tonnage	169,000	333,000	985,000
Britain	Troops	367,000	624,000	582,000
	Tonnage	650,000	1,065,000	2,714,000
Germany	Troops	426,000	524,000	891,000
	Tonnage	88,000	285,000	1,305,000
Russia	Troops	791,000	1,162,000	1,352,000
	Tonnage	200,000	383,000	679,000

Source: Paul Kennedy, *The Rise and Fall of the Great Powers* (Fontan, London, 1989), p. 261.

So familiar are the interventionist images conjured up by Table 6.5 that it is worth reminding ourselves that the Liberal dictator of Nicaragua, José Santos Zelaya, sought a European alliance to play off the USA a full decade after the invasion of Cuba, and that another decade later the Tinoco brothers thought that they could manage without Washington's imprimatur in Costa Rica. There are, nevertheless, slim pickings for revisionists in this area after 1898, and the main interest lies in the different temporal and spatial distribution of US authority in both its own terms and in those of European decline.

In this regard, let us revert briefly to the global context before picking

Table 6.5 **USA and Latin America, 1898–1932**

Year	Non-recognition	Loan manipulation	Supervision elections	Support rebels	Troops deployed
1898					Cuba / Puerto Rico
1899					
1900			Cuba		
1901					
1902					
1903				Panama	Dominican Republic / Panama / Honduras
1904					
1905					
1906					Cuba / Nicaragua
1907		Honduras / Dominican Republic		Honduras	Honduras
1908			Cuba		
1909				Nicaragua	
1910	Nicaragua				
1911		Nicaragua			
1912	Central America / Mexico				Cuba / Nicaragua
1913	Peru	Dominican Republic			
1914			Dominican Republic	Mexico	Mexico
1915	Haiti		Haiti		Haiti
1916	Dominican Republic / Central America	Nicaragua	Nicaragua		Dominican Republic
1917	Costa Rica	Costa Rica	Haiti		
1918			Panama / Haiti		
1919					
1920	Mexico / Bolivia		Cuba		
1921					
1922					
1923	Honduras	Honduras			
1924			Dominican Republic		Honduras
1925	Ecuador / Nicaragua	Ecuador			
1926					Nicaragua
1927					
1928			Nicaragua		
1929					
1930	Guatemala / Bolivia / Peru / Argentina / Brazil				
1931	El Salvador / Peru				
1932	Chile	Chile	Nicaragua		

Source: Derived and expanded from Paul Drake, 'From Good Man to Good Neighbor, 1912–1932', in A. Lowenthal (ed.), *Exporting Democracy. The United States and Latin America* (John Hopkins University Press, Baltimore, 1991), p. 4.

Table 6.6 **Comparative economic strength, 1914**

	Population (million)	National income ($ billion)	Per capita income ($)
USA	98	37	337
UK	45	11	244
Germany	65	12	184

Source: Paul Kennedy, *The Rise and Fall of the Great Powers* (Fontana, London, 1989), p. 314.

up the hemispheric story. As can be see from Table 6.6, by the time war had erupted in Europe, the US economy had overtaken those of its principal competitors.

However, over the next 25 years the performance of US industry was markedly superior, creating the kind of parallax in the inter-war era (Table 6.7) depicted by Ian Clark:

> The incipient global system at the turn of the century seemed [between 1918 and 1940] to have reverted to an earlier European one in which Britain and France appeared as centres of world politics. Much of this was, of course, illusory, contingent upon the introversions of the United States and the Soviet Union and the mirage of a Europe fully restored.[38]

This, it should be recalled, is the productive backdrop of an international scenario wherein the USA refuses to join the League of Nations, the USSR is born and remains a pariah, and Japan becomes mired in an imperialist war in Manchuria.

To what degree were US–Latin American commercial ties affected by the activity signalled in Table 6.5 – known popularly as 'the big stick' and 'dollar diplomacy' – and the impact of World War I?

Table 6.8 suggests that during the war, which the USA entered in April 1917, the US share of Latin American commerce rose from around a

Table 6.7 **Indices of manufacturing production, 1913–38**

	1913	1920	1925	1930	1938	(% share) 1938
World	100	93.2	120.7	137.5	182.7	100.0
USA	100	122.2	148.0	148.0	143.0	28.7
UK	100	92.6	86.3	91.3	117.6	9.2
Germany	100	59.0	94.9	101.6	149.3	13.2
Japan	100	176.0	221.8	294.9	552.0	3.8
USSR	100	12.8	70.2	235.5	857.3	17.6

Source: Paul Kennedy, *The Rise and Fall of the Great Powers* (Fontana, London, 1989), pp. 386; 426.

Table 6.8 **Latin American trade with the USA, 1913–29 (%)**

	1913		1918		1929	
	Exports	Imports	Exports	Imports	Exports	Imports
Latin America	29.7	24.5	45.4	41.8	34.0	38.6
Mexico/Central						
America/Panama	67.2	53.5	83.5	78.1	57.4	65.7
Cuba/Dominican						
Republic/Haiti	73.9	55.2	66.1	76.8	68.9	59.6
South America	16.7	16.9	34.9	25.9	25.1	31.4
Argentina	4.9	14.7	29.3	21.6	8.3	23.2
Brazil	32.3	15.7	34.0	22.7	45.5	26.7
Chile	21.3	16.7	56.8	41.5	33.1	30.8
Peru	33.2	28.2	39.1	46.8	28.8	41.4
Uruguay	4.0	12.7	25.9	13.2	10.7	30.2
Venezuela	28.3	32.8	60.0	46.7	26.5	57.5

Source: Victor Bulmer-Thomas, *The Economic History of Latin America Since Independence* (Cambridge University Press, Cambridge, 1994), p. 159.

quarter to just under a half, falling back to a third on the eve of the 1929 depression. But within the region the pattern varied, the already very high levels of trade with the Caribbean Basin proving less flexible whilst the shift in South America is more towards buying from the USA than selling to it. Table 6.9 shows this development in the cases of Brazil and Argentina, the two largest economies in the south, in terms of US and UK market share – the key variable, after all, in LaFeber's thesis – the swing during the war years being more marked in terms of imports than exports. Table 6.10 follows the pattern through the period covering both world

Table 6.9 **Argentina and Brazil: trade with UK and USA, 1913–19 (%)**

		1913	1915	1917	1919
Brazil					
Exports	- USA	32.7	41.8	46.1	41.4
	- UK	13.3	12.1	12.6	7.2
Imports	- USA	15.7	32.2	47.1	48.0
	- UK	24.5	21.9	18.0	16.2
Argentina					
Exports	- USA	4.7	13.0	29.3	18.3
	- UK	24.9	24.4	29.2	28.5
Imports	- USA	14.7	19.2	36.3	35.5
	- UK	31.1	35.6	21.8	23.5

Source: Bill Albert, *South America and the First World War: The Impact of the War on Brazil, Agentina, Peru and Chile* (Cambridge University Press, Cambridge, 1988), pp. 76–94.

Table 6.10 **Latin American trade partners, 1913–48 (%)**

		1913	1938	1941	1945	1948
USA	- Exports	29.7	31.5	54.0	49.2	32.8
	- Imports	25.5	35.8	62.4	58.5	52.0
UK	- Exports	20.7	15.9	13.1	11.8	13.3
	- Imports	24.8	12.2	7.8	3.6	8.1
Germany	- Exports	12.4	10.3	0.3	—	2.1
	- Imports	16.5	17.1	0.5	—	0.7
France	- Exports	8.0	4.0	0.1	—	2.3
	- Imports	8.3	4.0	0.1	—	1.9
Japan	- Exports	—	1.3	2.7	—	0.9
	- Imports	—	2.7	2.6	—	0.1

Source: Victor Bulmer-Thomas, *The Economic History of Latin America Since Independence* (Cambridge University Press, Cambridge, 1994), pp. 74; 76; 240.

wars and the depression because it is the sequential and compound impact of these global crises that really accounts for the state of play in 1945. Seen from this perspective, the picture bears out Clark's observation about the inter-war period upholding merely an illusion of European resurgence. At the Armistice in 1918 the USA had captured almost half of the hemispheric trade. By 1929 this had fallen back appreciably, being further but more modestly eroded through the depression. Over the critical 25-year period of 1913–38 the UK, which was at the start the main competitor of the USA in the region, saw its share of the Latin American market halved, falling well behind Nazi Germany in 1938. This, it should be recalled, is a year before Europe goes to war, but three more years were to elapse before the USA entered a conflict in which the collapse of trans-Atlantic trade was only the most severe of a number of disruptive factors (the figures for 1948 indicate the weak demand for Latin American goods from all the conquered states – Allied and Axis alike).

It was, however, investment and loans rather than trade shares that agitated the public profile of US–Latin American relations in the years up to the Good Neighbour policy depicted in Table 6.5. In this respect the pattern shifts in a manner that might help explain the lessened pretension and lower overall incidence of US military intervention – Nicaragua excepted – in the 1920s compared with the previous two decades. Investment both moves south from the Caribbean Basin into less directly 'manageable' South America and it diversifies, arguably away from more labour-intensive and so more politically sensitive sectors. Table 6.11 aggregates direct and portfolio investment, and while direct investment more than doubles to account for two-thirds of the total, portfolio investment increases more than fourfold over this period – something

Table 6.11 **US direct and portfolio investment in Latin America, 1914 and 1929**

	1914	1929
Latin America ($ million)	1,614.0	5,369.0
By region (%)		
Mexico / Central America / Panama	57.7	23.5
Cuba / Dominican Republic / Haiti	20.0	20.4
South America	22.3	56.1
By sector (%)		
Agriculture	18.7	24.1
Mining / Smelting	43.3	22.0
Oil	10.2	20.1
Railways	13.8	6.3
Public utilities	7.7	15.8
Manufacturing	2.9	6.3
Trade	2.6	3.3
Other	0.8	2.2

Source: Victor Bulmer-Thomas, *The Economic History of Latin America Since Independence* (Cambridge University Press, Cambridge, 1994), p. 161.

that might be thought consistent with expansion out of 'enclave' agricultural and mining operations.

In this sphere Rio Branco was surely mistaken in his analysis of US ambitions, which increasingly required precisely a uniform approach to property and particularly to capital. This could be no mere issue of disposition. If Theodore Roosevelt had been educated at Harvard, his ranching days in North Dakota provided the basis for macho 'rough-riderdom', redolent of the frontier. Yet he was no more emphatic upon this matter than was Woodrow Wilson, political scientist, progressive president of Princeton, and ardent advocate of social justice, who gave vent to the characteristic 'Anglo' complaint to an audience at Mobile in October 1913:

> There is one peculiarity about the history of the Latin American states which I am sure they are keenly aware of. You hear of 'concessions' to foreign capitalists in Latin America. You do not hear of concessions to foreign capitalists in the United States. They are not granted concessions. They are invited to make investments. The work is ours, though they are welcome to invest in it. We do not ask them to supply the capital and do the work. It is an invitation, not a privilege.[39]

This cultural gap was one that, a dozen years later, José Carlos Mariátegui identified as the distinction between Pan-Americanism, 'based upon economic interest and business', and Ibero-Americanism, 'founded upon sentiment and tradition'. For Mariátegui these were both ideals and irreconcilable. And yet – as so often in his writing – the analysis captures with a sedulous logic an image that transcends these common lines, proposing new contradictions:

> The economy is . . . more powerful than space . . . Ibero-America appears for all practical purposes to be at odds, divided and balkanized. However, her unity is no utopia; it is not an abstraction. The men who make history in Ibero-America are not so different from one another . . . The Argentine is more optimistic, more assured than the Peruvian, but the two are equally irreligious and sensual . . . Is it the fault of the USA if we the Ibero-Americans know more of the thought of Theodore Roosevelt than that of Henry Thoreau? . . . The country which has produced the greatest captains of industry has at the same time produced the most powerful masters of idealism.[40]

This was written in the wake of the presidency of Warren Harding, whose name is these days only dimly remembered, who made knowledge of Spanish obligatory for US diplomats posted to the region, and who, according to Kenneth Grieb, had a 'low-key, practical' approach to hemispheric relations. Harding withdrew troops from the Dominican Republic and eastern Cuba, wanted to do the same in Nicaragua, mediated the Tacna–Arica dispute, and refused to countenance military options in seeking to overcome the challenge posed by article 27 of the Mexican constitution.[41] Yet, like all his successors down to Bill Clinton, he had perforce to confront the problem of public property in Mexico, which in the early 1920s was still enmeshed with the question of political disorder. Following the Bolshevik revolution this had been transformed from an issue of cultural recalcitrance into an ideological perversion of the law of nations:

> Intercourse, from the standpoint of business, consists in the making of contracts and the acquisition of property rights . . . and the most important principle to be maintained at this time with respect to international relations is that no State is entitled to a place within the family of nations if it destroys the foundations of honorable intercourse by resort to confiscation and repudiation.[42]

Whatever the tactical preference of the White House, and no matter how propitious the conjuncture, it seemed that the USA was now so 'integrated' with Latin America, and particularly with Mexico, that Washington could no longer conduct foreign policy towards these states without automatically interfering in their domestic affairs. And yet the anti-colonial political culture of the USA would no more countenance deviation from the norms of separate sovereignties than could its logistical resources keep even small and local protectorates, such as Nicaragua, Haiti and Cuba, peacefully compliant. Moreover, as both the Mexican Revolution and the peculiar insurgency brewing in Nicaragua indicated, direct intervention was far from cheap, created diplomatic embarrassment elsewhere, and seemed to compound bad relations in the region itself. Most importantly, of course, it could not be guaranteed to achieve even short-term objectives.

There were few more lucid expressions of the resentment caused in Latin America by this experience than that voiced by Honorio Pueyrredón, the Argentine delegate at the Sixth Pan-American Conference early in 1928. Although David Sheinin dissents from the common interpretation that this broadside was representative of an Argentine tradition of critical independence of the USA – a tradition that might be argued to have endured down to Menem – it was keenly remembered by Cordell Hull as he set about designing an alternative policy in 1933:

> I retained a vivid, uncomfortable memory from reading the pyrotechnic clash between our Government and Argentina at the Pan-American Conference at Havana in 1928. The United States Delegation, headed by former Secretary of State Hughes, sustained repeated attacks from the Argentine Delegation, largely over our intervention . . . A powder magazine was built at Havana which could easily explode into numerous discordant factions among the 21 American nations.[43]

Hull was, of course, defending his own political record as well as that of F.D. Roosevelt when, in retirement, he wrote,

> Over a long period until almost 1933 the United States had pursued policies towards Latin America of so arbitrary – and what some of those countries considered so overbearing – a nature that prejudice and feeling throughout Central and South America against our country was sharp indeed.[44]

But he had at least registered that the diplomatic response to this lay in the realm of temper, form and recognition of difference – while Frank Kellogg, his predecessor in the Coolidge administration, saw these as simply exasperating problems to be overcome:

> If I had the time, I could justify every act we have performed; in fact, we have been patient beyond any degree to which we would ordinarily be with a more responsible government [than Mexico]. The same is true as to Central America countries. The United States has no desire to dominate them, as you know, but it is hard to make these countries realise that we are not imperialistic and ambitious.[45]

The limits of neighbourliness

If the outward features of the Good Neighbour policy may be traced to the diminishing returns to be had from close invigilation of Latin American political life, its foundations may be found behind Hull's tantalising 'almost'. Not, perhaps, in 1929 itself, but in the chaos stemming from the 1929 crash and the need for a radical review of economic policy in the context of fierce isolationist sentiment in the USA and what appeared to be the spread of the 'Mexican scenario' to the rest of the subcontinent as governments identified with the pursuit of economic liberalism and obeisance to its political forms were swept away.

Equally, during the depression political conflict had quickened mark-edly in Europe, further reducing the competition faced by the USA in Latin America. Neither a trans-Atlantic nor a hemispheric audience needed the 'demonstration effect' of an interventionism that was increas-ingly controversial at home and – especially after the Japanese invasion of Manchuria – at open odds with US policy elsewhere in the world. On the commercial front, Roosevelt and Hull possessed a strong card in the ability to bargain reductions in the 1930 Smoot-Hawley tariff in order to restore some of the 70 per cent fall in imports from Latin America between 1929 and 1932 (against which the duty had not been primarily aimed). As with the Morill tariff of 1861, once a protectionist measure had served its initial purpose, it was overtaken by eulogies to freer – even free – trade, a practice in which the British had diligently instructed the USA after the abolition of the corn laws.[46] Nevertheless, the economies of the south so badly needed restoration of the US market that it must have been an enticement as well as a balm to hear Roosevelt announce his new policy to the Pan-American Union just five weeks after taking office:

> The essential qualities of a true Pan-Americanism must be the same as those which constitute a good neighbor, namely, mutual understanding, and through such understanding, a sympathetic appreciation of the other's view . . . We all of us have peculiar problems, and, to speak frankly, the interest of our citizens must, in each instance, come first. But it is equally true that it is of vital importance to every nation of this continent that the American governments, individually, take, without delay, such action as may be possible to abolish all unnecessary and artificial barriers and restrictions which now hamper the healthy flow of trade . . .[47]

Within weeks the overthrow of the Machado regime in Cuba put these worthy sentiments to the test, the mediation of Sumner Welles replacing the despatch of troops, and the abrogation of the Platt Amendment by the US Congress in May 1934 being underpinned – as already suggested – by the introduction of sugar quotas. Early in 1936 Welles reminded an audience in Baltimore that Roosevelt had formally declared, 'that armed intervention by the United States in any other American republic was a thing of the past', and he presented the removal of Platt, the new quotas, negotiations with Panama over the canal and mediation in the Chaco War as just as much a replacement of 'dollar diplomacy' as was the evacuation of troops from Haiti and Nicaragua. Yet Walter LaFeber argues that,

> Between 1933 and 1939, Franklin D. Roosevelt's Good Neighbor policy did not change the Central American policy it inherited, but built on it. The Good Neighbor carried on interventionism in Central America and tightened the system far beyond anything Theodore Roosevelt or Woodrow Wilson probably imagined.[48]

LaFeber may here be overstating an important point precisely because of the success of the proponents of the Good Neighbour in presenting their policy as a radical shift in both the form and the content of US–Latin American relations (a success often reflected in subsequent academic literature critical of Cold War inflexibilities and in search of some prior virtue). It is also a moot point whether recognition of dictatorships, a replacement of private by public US loans, and the negotiation of trade agreements constituted something beyond the imagination of Theodore Roosevelt and Wilson (it is certainly difficult to conceive of Washington's response to the nationalisation of oil companies in Bolivia and Mexico in the late 1930s without the wider parameters of the Good Neighbour policy.) What LaFeber misses as he strains simultaneously to recognise and deny change is that the new policy was not primarily about the domestic political condition of the Latin American states – this part of the Roosevelt Corollary had been relegated beneath economic considerations – and that it was far more concerned than previously about the internal US and extra-hemispheric impact of the use of military force. Indeed, if we survey the Latin America of March 1933, when Franklin Roosevelt came to office – a month after the 44-year old Adolf Hitler became Chancellor of Germany – there are exceptionally few elected governments upholding the full rule of law; arguably, only Colombia. (In the light of their political reputations, it is worth recalling that in 1932 the US ambassador to San José had to arbitrate forcefully to stave off crisis following the re-election of Cleto Jiménez in Costa Rica, whilst in Uruguay, the new Terra regime was the country's first dictatorship since 1904.) Had the institution and maintenance of a liberal democratic regime in Latin America been a priority for the Roosevelt administration, it would have been engaged in intervention to a far greater degree than its predecessors – even in Central America, where the Good Neighbour policy was under sharpest scrutiny because of the small and vulnerable nature of the isthmian states.

The key shift in this respect comes not early in 1933 but late in 1941, with the US entry into the war and the full embracing of the anti-dictatorial ideology that was at the heart of the Allied cause and propaganda. This naturally made more acute the contradictions inherent in support for (or even recognition of) figures such as Somoza and Trujillo, but those difficulties were still deemed subordinate to the need for Latin American governments – of every type – to toe the US line on foreign policy. Sufficient compliance on that front would make it easier to explain away the anomalies of authoritarian regimes supporting a democratic cause through reference to war-time exigencies.

In World War I the late entry of the USA had meant that the issue of diplomatic recognition and declarations of neutrality or war never became a critical issue in hemispheric relations (and Washington's lead was fully followed only by Brazil and the smaller states of the Caribbean Basin).[49] The fact that the second global war drew political ideology so much more tightly into the weave of international relations meant that those governments that did not follow Washington's example needed strong arguments of expediency – such as Chile's fear of a coastal attack from the Pacific – to avoid being tarnished as worse than a fair-weather Pan-American, from which it was but a small step to being a crypto-fascist. Yet the pattern was again far from one of uniform acquiescence.[50]

This story has been exhaustively explored and debated – in good part because it forms an essential preamble to the Cold War cycle in hemispheric relations – particularly in terms of the hostile relations between the USA and the Argentine military dictatorship that would mutate into the Peronist government less than a year after the war. It is, though, worth recalling the concern expressed by Washington at the state of play prevailing in June 1942, that is, under the civilian Ortiz government, before the presidency of the much more pro-Axis Castillo, and a full 18 months before the military coup that brought Perón to power. Again, one must make allowance for the fact that Cordell Hull was writing in self-vindication as well as at a time when relations between Buenos Aires and Washington remained very tense, but in a sense it is precisely the image – rather than the more prosaic reality – that counted, both at the time and in the late 1940s (Hull refers to US protest at Argentina's agreement to accept a new ambassador from Japan):

> Our note recited numerous instances of Argentine territory being used as a base for Axis operations. The Argentine Government had failed to prevent group or individual activities detrimental to the security and welfare of the American republics. Axis agents were openly engaged in espionage and other work to defeat our war effort. Other agents of the Axis were working to undermine democratic institutions. Newspapers, radio stations, and publishing houses were disseminating totalitarian propaganda. Argentina had become a communications center for the Axis nations. Each message and even each word we said, that the Argentine Government permitted to be transmitted to the Axis nations, either directly or indirectly, might mean the loss of valuable material needed for the prosecution of the war, and, what was more, the loss of

precious lives of citizens of the American republics now engaged in defending the hemisphere.[51]

Here the issue of communication is certainly prominent, and it is presented in a tone of accusatory anxiety fully resonant with that of the post-war years, when US policy was designed and directed by men who had become accustomed to the culture and logic of war. Henceforth, the existence of a nuclear arsenal as well as the IMF qualitatively altered the context and repertoire of 'intervention' and 'deterrence'. This did not, however, immediately affect Latin America, which – Argentina included – signed up to the unambiguous celebration of democratic liberty and economic cooperation in the Act of Chapultepec of 6 April 1945 – three weeks before the death of Hitler – in understandable expectation of hemispheric as well as global renewal.

1999

The Third Man:
Francisco Burdett O'Connor and the
Emancipation of the Americas

What's in a name?

For the last five hundred years most people in Europe have been given at
least two names. In a few countries, such as Spain, they hold three,
retaining the surname of the mother after the patronymic, and some

married women add that of their husband to their maiden name. With the exception of native North Americans, this pattern has generally been followed in the colonies established by the European powers, so that a name normally indicates a family as well as a personal history.

Parents face a constrained choice in bestowing one or more forenames on their expected or recently-born child insofar as subsequent usage will bear only partly on the aesthetic or allusive routes to nomination. In childhood the rhyming and rhythmical potential of a name can be positively tyrannical, and even for adults the degree of formality used in address does not fit any common threshold of familiarity. It is a banal fact of life that we address many people with whom we have but the slightest acquaintance by their forenames in the same way as do those who know them with the greatest intimacy. A name is only a starting-point, and it can obscure as much as it reveals. Besides, names can be changed.

This is what happened in the case of my subject in this chapter. After September 1819, when he arrived in Venezuela from Dublin to join the independence campaign for Spain's colonies in the Americas, Francis – or, as his family and friends called him, Frank – O'Connor became Francisco Burdett O'Connor. This might seem to be an unremarkable Hispanisation of a forename. However, I think it telling that this process would restore to O'Connor the qualities precisely of a Christian name, and it may well be that such an early translation helped to ensure that over the rest of his life – some 52 years – he would never return to the British Isles.

At the same time, O'Connor proudly provided himself with a new surname, placing 'Burdett' in the position of the patronymic – that is, where Hispanic custom locates paternity – and so causing open and subliminal confusion as to his inheritance or, in the demotic of our own day, his identity.

Those inclined to the Viennese school of analysis will discern a rich and deep motivational field here, but none of us can quiz O'Connor on that now, and the fact is that until his death he continued to be known by his original surname. Burdett loitered as a quasi-forename. It was, though, no mere embellishment. When he signed his will, O'Connor simply included the initial 'B', but the first article of that document of 1866 studiously indicates that his father was Roger O'Connor, his mother Wilhamena Charlotte Caroline Bowen, and his godfather Sir Francis Burdett. Moreover, when Frank had been a teen-ager Burdett had acted *in loco parentis* in a serious and practical fashion. His godchild might well have had political or psychological reason to promote him and adopt his name, but he had been a genuine *padrino*, as it is put in Spanish.

Today one of the provinces of the Bolivian department of Tarija carries the name of O'Connor – it includes the farm Francisco built up near the town of San Luis – and in the 1830s the division he commanded as a general of the Bolivian army was also named after him. O'Connor was personally associated with the establishment of a third of the units that comprised the armed forces in the first century of the republic, and he is the only man to have served three times as their chief of staff.[1] In 1826 the Congress of the new state awarded him 5,000 pesos as a 'liberator', but he himself never used that title despite the rare honour it bestowed, and all these institutional vestiges have now been lost outside the mustiest of books.

Only one of O'Connor's children survived – a daughter, Hercilia.[2] So, if tradition had been followed his name should also have disappeared from the family within a generation. However, his grandsons adopted his own voluntarist attitude to nomenclature: they not only retained their matronymic but also converted it into a patronymic.

Hercilia had married one Adhemar d'Arlach, which in the valleys of Tarija had no less exotic an echo to it than did O'Connor – which may explain why, even though they traded places, these two possessive surnames have stuck together over the generations as a composite, O'Connor d'Arlach today being a single surname in southern Bolivia. Indeed, the origins of this paper lie partly in a request from the deputy foreign minister of the country, Eduardo Trigo O'Connor d'Arlach, for an explanation of the appearance of Burdett in the name of his forebear.

The name Burdett appears in most textbooks on modern British history as an opponent of the Pitt and Liverpool governments, a forceful advocate of civil liberties – particularly *habeas corpus* – and an architect of parliamentary reform. The name of O'Connor is usually associated with the Chartist leader Feargus, also an MP but more widely known for his ability to mobilise the masses and his frequent arrests in the campaigns of the 1830s and 1840s for political change. This O'Connor was born three years after Frank and was, indeed, his younger brother.

In the simple sense of localised public knowledge Francisco Burdett O'Connor is a 'third man' in that the owner of a forename stands behind two famous surnames that in historical memory belong to other people before they do to him. In some respects, then, the earliest parts of the present story are the most important.

This is particularly so because we have the interesting challenge of the relationship between siblings – not just between Frank and Feargus but also between their ebullient father Roger, a sportsman and spectacular spendthrift who exercised his charm equally upon the greatest of Whig grandees and the most humble of countrymen, and Roger's brother Arthur, renegade MP, hardline leader of the United Irishmen and convicted traitor to the British crown, who was idolised by his nephews as a persecuted and heroic patriot.

The imbalance between their father and uncle in terms of public profile and achievement possibly helps to explain why both Frank and Feargus maintained throughout their lives that the family descended from the kings of Connaught, thereby providing some dynastic compensation – perhaps even excuse – for the fact that Roger was, in the words of Graham Wallas, 'a semi-lunatic'.[3]

Of course, a romance like ours begins bereft of both innocence and rigour. It is bad form even in Whig and Freudian terms to put the *craich* in place of the deconstruction. Blood-ties provide structuralists with the most numerous, and least stimulating, linkages. Karl Marx himself thought Feargus 'patriarchal and petty-bourgeois' – the ultimate put-down, even coming from the accused in the second biggest ideological paternity suit in two millenia.

I'm not myself sure if any publicly practising post-modernists really exist east of Gander and north of Calais, but if so the chances are that they see biography less as fragmented irony than the meta-narrative of solipsism. And for many sophisticated people in receipt of funds from the public purse for purveying to the young ideas ancient and modern the notion of an improving tale is utterly primitive – a veritable Chernobyl of the mind.

Nevertheless, as that great historian Johan Huizinga reminds us, 'sophistry, technically regarded as a form of expression, has all the associations with primitive play . . . The sophism proper is closely related to the riddle. It is a fencer's trick.'[4] Jules Michelet, a contemporary of the O'Connor boys, is no less persuasive of the pleasures and profit in managing the affairs of the dead in our day – when he is celebrated for his treatment of sex and magic – than he was in his own – when he was famous for democratic demands and dates.

The central date for our purposes is 12 June 1791, when Francis, or Frank, was born in the city of Cork to Wilhamena Bowen, second wife of Roger O'Connor, who had previously been married to Louisa Strachan. The son of that earlier union, Roderick, was the elder brother to whom Frank and Feargus both looked for a lead and who later established the Commonwealth branch of the family by settling in Tasmania in 1824. Today his descendent Roderic has preserved a family tradition by occupying in Cressy a house called 'Connorville' after the original family estate in County Cork. Feargus would establish a settlement with the same name in the 1840s, when he sought to establish a yeoman based land company in England as part of a political vision of self-sufficiency and the citizen-as-producer which he shared with Frank, which they both inherited from Arthur, and which Arthur in turn derived from a close reading of Adam Smith.

That notion of the farm and the home as the basis of a republican civilization has strong roots in the family experience, and the first six years of Frank's life were comfortably set within it. His grandfather had bequeathed a considerable income of £10,000 a year to his four sons, and the eldest of these, Daniel, had already sold his inheritance to Roger in order to fund his elopement to Bristol with a Mrs Gibbons. For a child, life on the Connorville estate at Bandon must have been exciting enough in a family so devoted to the chase that when the season for foxes closed they took to hunting hares. After 1795, when Frank's Uncle Arthur made an arresting speech in the House of Commons in favour of Catholic emancipation, the comings and goings increased further still.

One central reason for Arthur's unexpected initiative was the suicide by drowning of his sister, Anne, who had been prohibited from marrying her Catholic love. A family that for three generations had combined political conservatism, commercial success and social stability was plunged into such a fierce conflict that the second son, Robert, who was the local sheriff, tried to have Roger executed as editor of the nationalist *Harp of Erin* – well before both Roger and Arthur were accused of treason for their part in the French invasion plans of 1796 and 1798 and their role in the failed uprising of the latter year.

When, on the eve of his own detention, Arthur published an article in the radical Dublin paper *The Press* praising the Gracchi brothers – the reformers of late republican Rome murdered by conservatives – he was surely displaying more than knowledge of the classical tradition, offering an autobiographical reflection, if not a hostage to fortune.

Arthur took the lead in this shift to what we would now call the left. Roger organised clandestine meetings in Cork and occasionally visited London to frequent those Whig salons where it was fashionable to cherry-pick policies and attitudes from revolutionary France, but it was Arthur who actually went to France to negotiate an alliance with the Directory, who did deals with the real radicals of the London Corresponding Society, and who was followed by Pitt's spies in both London and Ulster. According to Marianne Elliott, Arthur's 'confidence, his informed loqaciousness and oratorical abilities won more support for the movement than it might otherwise have attracted', but 'his obvious desire to run the show' also split a fractious and underprepared organisation.[5]

Today names such as Horne Tooke, Wolf Tone and Napper Tandy sound quaint and antique – almost as if they were penned by Tolkien – but two hundred years ago their ideas about freedom of the press and association and the claims of popular and national sovereignty made them dangerous enemies of the state, which – especially in times of war – sought to have them hanged, drawn and quartered. In none of these cases did Pitt succeed – Theobald Wolfe Tone came closest but killed himself on the eve of execution. Nonetheless, in the 1790s Britain had a regime that so combined the rule of law with the apparatus of dictatorship that opponents were generally given enough rope with which to hang themselves. Ireland was still a different polity and jurisdiction, but it was ruled by the same monarch and cabinet; and there the frontier between privileged security and outlaw status was much more readily crossed.

Frank O'Connor's innocence ended before his seventh birthday, in February 1798, when his uncle trespassed across that fateful line. Roger followed Arthur into prison almost immediately, and the boys were left with their younger sisters in the care of their mother and their godfather Burdett.

Arthur had been arrested at the King's Head, Margate, the day before he was due to flee to France in the company of the radical priest Reverend James Coigley. O'Connor's life was saved by some good luck – the state was reluctant to produce as evidence papers its agents had intercepted in the mail, and his servant succeeded in flushing other incriminating material down the privy in the hotel before the Bow Street Runners broke down the door. However, Arthur also owed much to the fact that before Roger was arrested he had persuaded Arthur's Whig friends to testify to his good character and innocence at the trial held in May – the subject of one of Gilray's most laconic and telling cartoons.[6]

Father Coigley benefited from neither such oligarchic solidarity nor Arthur's emphatically selfish defence strategy, which even moved the judge to remark,'Mr O'Connor, do you not see how much this is to the prejudice of the other prisoner?' However, Mr Justice Buller did not hesitate to pass the death sentence on the priest, whose guilt seemed to be sought at any cost by all other parties and was sealed by the papers found on his person.

Arthur was acquitted in what Thomas Packenham describes as:

one of the strangest scenes in a British court of justice. O'Connor could be re-tried under Irish law on exactly the same charge of which he had been acquitted under British law. Accordingly, two Bow Street Runners were waiting by the dock ready to re-arrest him. But no sooner had the death sentence been passed on the unfortunate Coigley than O'Connor rushed from the dock to the bar, and from the bar into the body of the court, with the police in hot pursuit. The court was plunged into confusion. Outraged Whigs, including O'Connor's council and Lord Thanet, tried to snatch him to safety. Swords were drawn – the swords that were lying as evidence on the table. Furniture was smashed and heads broken. O'Connor might have got clean away, but for the quick-wittedness of the judge's coachman, who brought him crashing to the floor.[7]

Although Arthur was duly dispatched to Kilmainham jail with some 80 other United Irishmen facing charges of high treason, the state was almost as tarnished by the trial as was the embattled republican movement. Pitt eventually won the day, although he had to execute four more people before the rest of the convicts agreed to a trade of their confessions for life. In the process Roger joined Arthur in the Scottish prison of Fort George, and it was only in 1803 that he was permitted to return to Ireland on condition that he settled within 30 miles of Dublin. Arthur took the logical step of exile in France, where, at the age of 44, he married Condorcet's daughter Eliza, who was just 17, buying Mirabeau's estate at Le Bignon and being gazetted by Napoleon as a divisional general.[8]

Arthur O'Connor rather misjudged the balance of forces in 1814–15, but he never came close to a real battle and was able to draw a military pension from the French taxpayer for a full 47 years. This was probably just as well since Roger soon either squandered or stole his brother's share of the family inheritance, and Eliza, who until the Whigs came to power was alone permitted to enter Ireland, proved to be no match for her brother-in-law.

In 1848, at the age of 85, Athur published a sprawling three-volume work – *Monopoly – the Cause of All Evil* – the ill-discipline of which he compounded by styling himself Arthur Condorcet O'Connor. That work added little or nothing to his 110-page pamphlet, *The State of Ireland*, published in February 1798, where one finds a fluid and compelling mix of Smithian logic, the scepticism of Hume, and a Kantian appetite for freedom, equality and independence. The piece, although over-stretched, still constitutes a major document of a republican movement striving to escape the stain of Jacobin excess.[9]

Perhaps Arthur's most practical legacy to his nephews was an insistence upon the power and importance of the press to a democratic politics.[10] Feargus took the injunction seriously enough to found a new *Northern Star* in the 1830s as a mouthpiece for Chartism, and although there would be no newspaper in Tarija until the early 1850s, Frank wrote in *El Condor* of Chuquisaca within six months of its establishment in 1825, and his grandson Tomás, to whom we owe the publication of the general's memoirs, was editor of *La Estrella de Tarija* for 27 years.

The O'Connors shared a healthy appetite for expression; Francisco alone published no book in his lifetime and positively shied away from speechifying – on Bolivian social outings he would often accompany the ladies so as to avoid the elaborate and inebriated toasting that was the masculine order of the day. Yet, in addition to the published memoirs,

which had been written up until 1839 when he died, we have five volumes
of diaries dating from 1849, in a varied state of repair but their sparse
Spanish – never English, not even Spanglish – is generally readable even
for those untrained in palaeography. The two inalterable features of each
day's entry are the weather and O'Connor's location. We are usually also
given the state of his health and transactions. Sometimes we get a
reflection on the wider world, very much less often an inner thought.
There is very little mention of Francisca Ruyloba, the 17-year old
daughter of a family of clerks and priests whom he – twice her age –
married in 1827. O'Connor unfailingly refers to Francisca, of whom we
have a firm and attractive photographic portrait, as 'La Señora', and he
sometimes has the good grace to allude to advice she has given and he
accepted.[11]

As he grew old in Tarija O'Connor imbibed more of the ethos of the
Franciscan brothers whose monastery dominated the centre of the small
Andean town and, with 5,000 books, possessed the best library of the
region. In his will he ordained that every school in the department should
be donated a copy of his favourite book, Marmontel's *Belisaire*, but also
that – following the example of the censors of pre-revolutionary France –
its mildly deist chapter 15 should first be excised. Perhaps predictably, his
legacy came to nought, saving *Tarijeño* youth from some rather tiresome
ruminations on Byzantine affairs as well as the risk of passing on to
Procopius's *Secret History*, a text which, by virtue of its references to the
more intimate forms of animal husbandry, was unlikely to appear even in
an O'Connor syllabus for the history of the book.

Francisco's sympathy for the Catholic Church was not so evident early
on – as military governor of Tarija in 1826 he closed all the monasteries
except that of the Franciscans (who numbered then, as they do today, just
three friars) – although it may well have been a reaction against his father,
who habitually declared that Voltaire was his only God.

Frank and Feargus had spent much of their youth and early adulthood
coming to grips with Roger's behaviour, which, following his release from
jail in 1802, became increasingly extravagant. On one occasion the boys
fled his house, stole two horses belonging to their brother Roderick, sold
them in Dublin to fund the trip to London, doorstepped Burdett at his
home in Stratton Street, off Piccadilly, and asked to move in.[12]

At the time Burdett, whose marriage to Sophia Coutts, daughter of the
banker, had provided him with more than enough cash to fund his
political campaigns, was serving as an MP and publishing incendiary
material – much of it on the sale of parliamentary seats – in Cobbett's
Register. Whilst he was happy to subsidize the boys, show them the town
and the radical *demi-monde*, he was not prepared to test further domestic
arrangements made very fragile by his affair with Lady Oxford and his

frequent clashes over parliamentary privilege with the Speaker and the magistrates. Frank and Feargus returned to Dangan Castle, County Westmeath, which Roger had bought from the Wellesley family in 1803 for £40,000, declaring the mansion to be of a grandeur sufficient for receiving Napoleon when Ireland was finally liberated. And, indeed, a few months later the Emperor sent Arthur an undertaking that he would not conclude a peace with England until Ireland was free.[13]

When, five years after its purchase, part of the Dangan building burned down with only a portion of the price paid in cash, it was widely believed that Roger had planned an insurance fiddle. However, writing his memoirs 60 years later General O'Connor records that he had started the fire by accidentally spilling molten lead on the floorboards when casting bullets for his target pistols.[14] Whether he thought so at the time is unclear, but in his old age O'Connor ruefully presents the blaze as the main reason for his mother's early death, which left the children even more exposed to Roger's antics even as he ran off with a Mrs Smith, took up with her maid Dora Reynolds, and then, in 1817, settled down with a woman uniformly described by the distinctly secondary sources as 'a young peasant girl' at Ballincollig.

By that stage Frank was 26, physically and fiscally independent, having completed his military training; Burdett had already been obliged to talk him out of joining Napoleon's comeback campaign. It is unlikely that he was still lodged at Dangan, but the evidence suggests that he had been around in October 1812, at the time of the infamous robbery of the Galway mail, which was carrying a large sum of cash for the purchase of cattle at the annual fair of Ballinasloe.

Roger was immediately suspected of organising the 10 highwaymen who staged the assault, in which the coach's guard was killed. The day after the robbery it was he who informed the police that much – but by no means all – of the loot had been found in the grounds of his home. It is just possible, but unlikely, that Frank and Feargus were aware of the plot, which understandably appears nowhere in their memoirs even though five years later Roger was formally charged with the crime as the result of a plea-bargain struck by a criminal in another trial.

The case was heard before Mr Justice St George Daly at Trim Assizes in August 1817. Burdett, recently re-elected MP for Middlesex, rushed across to give evidence on behalf of the father of his godchildren. On the day of the trial the heat was so intense that Roger fainted into Burdett's arms, but his friend provided an even more critical form of support in convincing the jury that he had no need to rob the mail in order to secure funds. Under examination Burdett was as studiously reliable in an uncertain cause as had been Sheridan some twenty years before in order to save Arthur's neck:

If Mr O'Connor had occasion for a particular sum in 1812, would you have
advanced it for his accommodation?

Undoubtedly, and I can hardly mention the sum to which I would not go to
accommodate him.

You were surprised at such a charge as this being made against him?

I felt ready to sink to the ground.[15]

Roger, who was now 55, proved unable to accept his acquittal as a
salutary warning. Later that year he enraged his saviour by preferring
charges of perjury against the main prosecution witness in the case,
putting it about that the aim of the heist had been to recover Burdett's
letters to Lady Oxford now that she had transferred her affections to Lord
Byron. Henceforth Burdett stayed with Roderick on his visits to Ireland
despite the fact that Roger dedicated to him a book published in 1822
under the title *The Chronicles of Erin*, with the purport of being the only
true account of Ireland 'translated from the original manuscripts in the
Phoenician dialect of the Scythian language'. Described in the *Dictionary
of National Biography* as 'mainly, if not entirely, the fruit of O'Connor's
imagination', this text contains a great many grammatical errors, as did
Feargus's later writings, opening him to the lampoons of enemies who in
their youth had been obliged to undertake classical studies.

In tracing this trajectory, I am deliberately tripping around a caricature –
the etching of the pantomime Irishman that is the engine of English
condescension – for the purpose of asking a second question: Why does a
person cross the Atlantic? I should also reassure the reader that I do not
propose to survey the rest of Frank O'Connor's life at a pace proportional
to that struck hitherto; this has been undertaken with a view to establish-
ing a distinct perspective on our subject's private emancipation in the
Americas even as he participated in their public liberation.

Today, of course, people cross the Atlantic to and fro the whole time,
but until at least 1945 – and maybe until the days of Freddy Laker – most
made the trip from east to west with much greater thought of arriving
and staying than of returning. It was, historically, a journey of escape, and
there were usually strong push as well as pull factors.

Roger O'Connor had provided his children with a superabundance of
the exotic which is so frequently hung on Latin America and popularly
associated with the 'magical realist' school represented by Gabriel García
Márquez's *One Hundred Years of Solitude*.[16] Yet at close quarter and within
familiar distance such 'otherness', as it is now dubbed by dowdy Anglo-

Saxon scholars, could be distinctly disturbing, far from alluring, and conducive less to associational admiration than to the living grief of embarrassment at a life conducted on the very margins of its own ambition.

Terry Eagleton has commented that,'if Ireland is raw, turbulent, destructive, it is also a locus of play, pleasure, fantasy, a blessed release from the tyranny of the English reality principle.'[17] Elsewhere I have argued that Ireland is usefully looked upon as an American country unaccountably located in the wrong continent, but here I certainly do not want to postulate some kind of ectopian utopia.[18]

Rather, I should like to suggest that while the English bayonets were forever the avowed cause of Francisco Burdett O'Connor's voluntary exile from his homeland, the 'collateral damage' wreaked by an eccentricity raised in response to them is an additional factor. We are here, in a sense, dealing with an inversion of the picaresque.

O'Connor was not escaping metropolitan drudgery simply for adventure although this he would experience to intense and dangerous measure; over the rest of his life I estimate that he spent some 24 hours in direct combat, three weeks within an hour's ride of enemy forces, seven years in military campaigning and 45 years farming. His life was transformed by no luxuriant apparitions of butterflies, no wondrous ice-making machines, and no dusky seductions – well, just the one – but, instead, by a land of regularity and modesty, naturalism and the rigours of the real. It was a life dedicated more to construction than creativity, and, of course, such a path can be transcendental in a wider philosophical sense as well as within subjective fulfilment.

What is of particular interest to us here is how this trajectory passed through and beyond the paraphenalia of heroism. Francisco Burdett O'Connor was no representative man in the Emersonian sense, and just as Carlyle could write the 70 pages of *Chartism* without once mentioning Feargus, so would he have encountered problems, had he known of Frank's existence, slotting him into *Heroes and Hero-Worship*. In saying this I do not mean to infer that O'Connor was resistant to fame and adulation; he certainly bridled at lack of recognition. But he treated the heroic with an affectation so light as to suggest that it was almost wholly attributable to an inescapable genetic endowment.

We need less to promote O'Connor or rehabilitate him to some overdue iconic status than to go back behind the superficial surrealism that still infects the image of Latin America and interrogate a deep culture of heroism which remains so resiliently attached to the origins of its independence.

Here I simply note that the heroic version derives from the needs as well as the condescension of posterity. It is not easy to resist the crisp, sub-

Bonapartist iconography populated with handsome, focused and beautifully attired young generals. Of those who led the struggles few survived
long enough to have their photo taken, and such portraits generally
reflect the weight of exhaustion and pain visible in the picture we have of
O'Connor (although I persist in the conviction that there is gentleness in
those fair eyes).

The telescope given to him by Bolívar has disappeared, as have the
many artefacts that most families lose through carelessness and pilfering
and that we know from his will were still held in his final years. In that
final testament O'Connor claims,

> I entered marriage with capital of 26,000 pesos, without counting the value of
> my silver service, shotguns, firearms, horses, mules, books, etcetera, etcetera,
> about which I say nothing more here because my wife denies it, saying that she
> has never seen any of it, but in the distribution of my possessions she will
> receive one half of everything.

Even if we believe Francisca here, we can be sure that Frank did not
leave for the Americas in order to make a fortune. When, in July 1819, he
boarded the *Hannah* with 200 other members of the Irish Legion he
carried Burdett's letter of credit for £500 drawn on the Bank of England.
Two years later when stationed in Panama he would issue a bill for £1,000
to be drawn on Coutts, and just as during the campaign he often kitted
out his men from his own purse, so as a landlord was he accustomed to
pay small fines and forgive the debts of his tenants and workers, even if in
every case he kept a detailed record and in most instances registered a
careworn complaint.

Most of all, O'Connor went to America for political reasons. There is
no sign that he wished to practise politics himself – and he never did so
in Bolivia – but we should not underestimate the extent to which people
left Europe, including Great Britain, in the early nineteenth century
because it was an unfree and counter-revolutionary place. In 1801 Ireland
lost those vestiges of self-government that were still in place when Arthur
had tried to drive through to full independence. This, of course, would
only be obtained 120 years later, under the aegis of Eamon de Valera,
born in the USA of a Spanish father.

A fortnight after the Irish Legion set sail for Venezuela in 1819 11
people were killed and more wounded when the militia charged with
sabres upon a political reform meeting held not in Caracas but in
Manchester. It was not until 10 years after that 'Peterloo Massacre' that
any Catholic was allowed to vote or hold public office, and it was three
more years before there took place a British parliamentary election in
which a large number of seats were not effectively bought and sold; even
then the franchise was restricted to propertied men. There was no World

Bank, IMF or other multilateral agency to tutor the Westminster and Whitehall of the day in the manners of good governance.

Of course, a popular vote for the presidency of the USA was not held until 1824, but it is today easy to forget how, compared to a reactionary post-Waterloo Europe, the Americas offered the only real prospect for a democratic, republican politics. Nowadays that is accepted almost by default in the celebration of Anglo-American 'exceptionalism' and in the lamentations over the collapsed promises in the south of the continent – a disappointment which is explained with depressing frequency in terms of some cultural blindness or mimetic clumsiness, without any sense of the wider world which posed such a political challenge.

O'Connor could not but recognise that dual feature of Independence. Soon after it was achieved – probably in 1827 – he began drafting an essay on the political economy of Bolivia that is strikingly similar to his uncle's *State of Ireland*.[19] In June of that year he published a proclamation encouraging 'Men of Ireland' to settle in the 'New Erin' of Tarija,'where the poor of my flesh and blood will be received with open arms and provided with a good cow, a horse, a pig and some farmyard fowl . . . They will be absolute masters of their own destiny.'[20] This now familiar motif of liberty residing in an industrious rural community averse to luxury and extravagance also lies behind O'Connor's consistent advocacy of protectionism against British textiles – an anti–imperialism that was kept alight by the daily sight of even the most humble of Bolivians wearing clothes of foreign-made fabric.[21] The image we have of him as a patriarch decked out in Palmerstonian check and English cashmire was one most reluctantly assumed.

Feargus would likewise inveigh against free trade as just 'a substitute for landed monopoly at home'.[22] He, however, did not take the critique as far as his spartan elder brother, who on 28 January 1850 noted in his diary,

Upon my arrival [at Tarija] I paid to Don Antonio Cortés 43 pesos and one *real*, which I owed him from last week for the clothes . . . I bought in his shop, and this is the first expenditure of this size that I have made for the purpose of clothing my person in 13 years, but I had nothing left to wear . . . It would have pleased me much to have spent this money on a product of national manufacture, but all the money leaves the country for Europe, where it maintains the industries of those countries, and I am caused great discomfort by the idea of contributing to the ruin of my *patria*, where I eat my daily bread.

Naturally, neither that *patria* nor any other aside from Spain existed when Frank O'Connor set out from Dublin, and it is, above all, as a soldier who fought to make their existence a possibility that history recalls

him. In 1999, with the outbreak of the first major armed conflict in
Europe for over fifty years, more than one generation is acquiring for the
first time a sharp sensibility as to the physical and mental consequences
of warfare. Even those predisposed to accept claims made for modern
weaponry on the basis of scream-free and bloodless videos know that the
exercise is not, and cannot be, free of butchery, cruelty, privation and
that volunteered madness which is required to kill and court death.

In a campaign fought with the ordnance of Waterloo the scale of
damage inflicted was certainly different. Not a single shot was fired at the
Battle of Junín in August 1824, when O'Connor was chief of staff of a
Patriot army of 1,5000 ranged against the viceroy's 7,000 troops and nine
artillery pieces; an engagement confined to cavalry charges ended within
an hour. Four months later at the Battle of Ayacucho, the last set-piece of
a 15-year conflict, the Patriots fielded just one cannon, and the Royalists
only managed to fire ranging shots with theirs.

On the other hand, the Patriot cavalry won at Junín largely because the
Royalists had cut down their lances to six feet in order to lessen the stress
on the backs of horse and rider ('lumbago' was a complaint common to
all soldiers but experienced especially by lancers, and O'Connor suffered
it all his adult life). The fact that the Patriots had not done the same
meant that they had a three-foot advantage with which to impale their
enemy or his horse. The wounds suffered were not neat bullet-holes but
dismemberment and evisceration. When treatment could be administered
it was undertaken with anaesthetic comprising the same liquor served up
in slightly more modest quantities before the start of the battle. At
Ayacucho over 1,500 men were killed and more than 1,000 wounded in a
couple of hours.[23]

Moreover, at Junín and Ayacucho prisoners were taken. When
O'Connor first arrived in Venezuela in 1819 this was not the case, the war
being formally and practically 'to the death'. Even for a professional
soldier whose father had twice escaped capital punishment this was a nasty
shock. O'Connor reports that after the Battle of Ciénaga de Santa Marta
in November 1820:

> there were two badly wounded Spaniards, unable to move, lying on the field.
> An adjutant to the commander approached him when I was sat beside him and
> asked permission to slit the throats of the Spaniards. It was in vain that I
> opposed such barbarism . . . and the next day the officer told me that he had
> hung the prisoners upside down over the river before decapitating them with
> his sword.[24]

It is not surprising that almost the entire Irish Legion had deserted or
died within six months of its arrival in Isla Margarita. No amount of

promotions and promises could compensate for such experiences, although it was disease that was the main fear and the principal cause of death. Yellow fever and cholera were the two greatest killers in the lowlands, into which the commanders tried to hem their enemy. Tuberculosis, of course, kept mortality rates generally high, but although he frequently coughed up black blood, O'Connor seems to have been resistant to it. He also escaped the attacks of diarrhoea that ravaged troops and officers alike. However, as the army moved south through the territories that would become Colombia, Ecuador and Peru he became increasingly concerned about his 'terciana' – a less virulent strain of malaria – and 'Peruvian wart', also caused by insect bites and with the unpleasant symptom of discoloured tumours on the face.

These ailments meant that he was constantly compelled to experiment with remedies, from the familiar 'Dover salts' based on magnesium sulphate and opium to local potions of chocolate, celery and *chicha*, often prepared by his orderly, to whom he attributed the saving of his life on two occasions. Years after the campaign the general – who was often in pain, usually on the farm and seldom mentions a doctor or dentist – would administer himself formidably powerful purges, usually with an opiate base of 'English salts' drenched in Jalapa pepper, honey and calomel or mercurious chloride.[25]

There is a second sense in which I see Francisco Burdett O'Connor as a third man. Some seven years ago I gave my first inaugural lecture in the University of London, at Queen Mary and Westfield College. In that earlier lecture I placed between two historical stereotypes – a warrior felled in his prime and a scribe spared to ruminate – the figure of a third man representing those who died in defeat, the disappeared forgotten as individuals by all bar family and friends.

In this chapter I seek a much less tragic shadow, but I cannot fail first to notice that in 1992 my exemplar for it was a man – Jorge Ríos Dalenz – who had been executed in Santiago de Chile on 15 September 1973, following the coup led by General, now Senator, Augusto Pinochet. I do recognise that there are in this hall today distinguished persons convinced that Pinochet's detention last October in London at the behest of the kingdom of Spain was a denial precisely of the kind of republican sovereignty fought for at such cost by O'Connor and the other founding fathers.

England and Spain have, indeed, been the villains of my piece this evening. Nonetheless, I am of the firm, if inexpert, view that the arrest of the former dictator on such charges, whilst it undeniably further alters the ever-mutable condition of national sovereignty, provides welcome support precisely for those rights of man – that we today call human rights – and that individual sovereignty without which no civil society – let alone a nation – may flourish in freedom. Many of the claims for an increasing internationalisation of society in the post-Cold War world are both exaggerated and misconceived, but the evolution of law in this field clearly does promise progress beyond both property based ideologies and Westphalian frontiers.

As I have already intimated, the third man I discern today is both warrior and scribe, and he is a victor who survives, but he is a technician, planner and strategist, not the heroic leader. This is the O'Connor who stands behind Bolívar and Sucre in the campaign of 1824 in Peru, and this is the same man who stands behind Sucre and Santa Cruz in the construction of Bolivia until the late 1830s.

In his own account O'Connor was told by Bolívar that after the campaign for independence he would lend a regiment of Hussars to help the Irish cause. The offer was, of course, even less serious than that made twenty years earlier by Bonaparte to Arthur.[26] However, Bolívar had quickly gained a high regard for the young Irish colonel, whom he appointed chief of staff of the United Army of Liberation within six months of his joining it from Panama early in 1824. It was O'Connor who kept the Patriot forces coordinated and supplied as they manoeuvred under Sucre's command in distinctly hostile territory to bring the last Spanish viceroy in mainland America to battle and defeat.[27]

This was a far more demanding task than it might appear today. Even the modest rebel army required a cattle train of some 6,000 head, which had to be kept close enough to afford regular supply but sufficiently distant to avoid enemy raids. A horse is more primitive than an armoured car, but it still needs considerable upkeep – not only in terms of forage but also shoes, and nails for those shoes, and farriers to fix them, and forges to melt down the requisitioned iron, which was so precious that even carbines were converted in order that the chargers might be shod on all four hooves, uncommon at that time.[28]

Moreover, for every horse the army needed several mules, not just to carry the stores across the Andean fastnesses – 300 mules were required for the reserve depot alone – but also to provide fresh mounts for marches and counter-marches at altitudes which sickened beasts as well as men. O'Connor's equestrian youth underpinned his aptitude for logistics of this type, but his assiduous quartermastership reflected a far less natural-istic factor, and sometimes his liking for dispatch and detail drove other members of the command to distraction.[29]

In his will O'Connor scrupulously notes that he was not chief of staff on the day of the Battle of Ayacucho but chosen by Sucre to determine where the Royalists should be engaged. The disgrace of being replaced by a Peruvian – General Agustín Gamarra – for political reasons when the engagement was imminent was felt most deeply, even bitterly. O'Connor sourly notes that no unit of the Patriots' Peruvian Division was actually commanded by a Peruvian, and all the officers who had been born outside the Americas must have taken some umbrage at the fact that only one of their number – the Irishman Colonel Arthur Sandes – was mentioned in Sucre's official despatch after the battle.

Otto Braun, the commander of the Grenadiers already denied proper recognition for his action at Junín, adopted a Germanic brown study. William Miller, who led the Hussars in the charge that swung the battle, remarked that the last cannonade of the day had signalled the moment for all foreigners to get out. By contrast, O'Connor, who showed no sign of leaving, protested to Sucre, who then withdrew his promotion to general – he would have to wait six years to receive the rank.[30]

However, it is telling that following this very public difference of opinion Sucre put O'Connor in command of the operation to hunt down the remaining Royalist forces under General Pedro Olañeta, whose escape into Alto Peru would lead the angry but disciplined colonel into his new *patria*, shortly to be renamed Bolivia.

This was a command entailing considerable confidence, and indeed it would seem to revindicate O'Connor's achievement at Ayacucho, where the Royalist army of over 9,000 troops had been nearly twice as large as that commanded by Sucre. O'Connor knew that a battle could only be won by choosing terrain which permitted an attack to be pressed home before the enemy could collect all his forces, and that this would most likely happen as a result of surprise, when LaSerna's troops were descending rather than climbing the steep gorges of the zone.

After an initial encounter in which the Patriots lost most of their baggage train and so many of their rearguard that the veteran Sandes wept as he reported their deaths, the two armies manoeuvred for nearly a week. In the eyes of his former chief of staff, Sucre began to lose his nerve, and O'Connor, who now formally held only a regimental position, had difficulty in persuading him not to make a defiant stand but to continue marching the exhausted and demoralised force to Hauicho and then engage the Royalists as they confidently approached from the heights of Condorcunca. Despite his many years of attachment to the turf, Francisco Burdett O'Connor was not a betting man, but on 9 December he wagered his pay on the result.[31]

Something similar is discernable almost 15 years later when O'Connor, then in his late 40s and much more familiar with the terrain, rejoined forces with Otto Braun to inflict a defeat on the invading Argentine army at the Battle of Montenegro. That victory was also obtained by a series of flanking manoeuvres and feigned retreats through hill country in a manner that might be expected of a fox-hunting man. It came too late to save the Peru–Bolivia Confederation that Santa Cruz had laboriously assembled as a counter-weight to conservative Chile and the pugnacious power of Governor Rosas in Buenos Aires. However, Montenegro consolidated the present south-west border of Bolivia as well as allowing the Hibernian commander to retire from military service for the third time – he always refused to serve in times of peace – and recover his farms, which the invaders had occupied, slaughtering and selling off cattle that in those same times of peace were rustled only by the Chiriguano Indians.

At one point Santa Cruz had placed his hopes for the Confederation's future in the purchase of a new European warship for one million pesos, which he asked O'Connor to take to Britain.[32] The reply received by the president indicates that Francisco was never going to revert to Frank:

> If any friend asked me to accept this proposition I would not accept it . . . when I left my homeland I did so with the intention of never returning to it because my family suffered the persecutions of the English government, but I owe [you] the obedience due to my commander, and [you have] the right to order me to undertake this task.[33]

Perhaps it was just as well that the money was never raised. Indeed, a few years later there arrived in Tarija a letter from Feargus which would have surely confirmed his brother's fears about political repression in Britain and probably revived others about personal eccentricity in the family.

These were no longer focused on Roger because, as Feargus reported,

> Our Father died in 1834 of apoplexy, having got up in the morning in perfect health and being dressed, he stooped to put on his boot, seized the bed post and never spoke more, although he lingered some days in perfect consciousness. He also died a Catholic and was buried according to the ceremonies of that religion.

Roger's death does, however, appear to have unleashed something in Feargus, who was described by Sir Robert Peel as a man who 'appeared to take fire very easily and boil at a very low temperature'.[34] Feargus himself told his brother in Bolivia,

> Since [1837] I have had to sustain seven government prosecutions, for two of which . . . I was sentenced to 18 months confinement in York Castle, which I spent in one of the condemned cells in solitary confinement, and upon the day of my liberation I was received by delegates from all parts of England, Scotland and Wales and honoured with a triumphal procession in a splendid triumphant car covered with velvet and drawn through the City of York with six horses . . . While I was in York Castle I read 200 volumes of the best works and wrote a number myself. I have published several works, some of which

have been stereotyped and all of which sell well . . . I should tell you that on
every occasion I have been prosecuted I have defended myself, and upon my
last trial at York I spoke for 5 hours and 37 minutes, when the judge directed
an acquittal but the special jury found me guilty . . . More I need not tell you
of myself other than that after all, and having travelled more than any other
man living during the last ten years, and having been knocked down and
awfully and brutally mangled by hired mobs with stones, stricks and iron bolts,
yet I am as well in health and constitution as when you and I used to jump
over the six feet poles . . . [at] a hopping match at the Pigeon Ground at
Battersea . . . I did 306 feet in thirty consecutive hops, never putting the
second foot to the ground.[35]

Feargus gave as good as he got to almost everybody – from the
chancellor of the exchequer, whom he ridiculed at one remove,[36] to
hissing audiences of northern aristocrats, whom he abused directly and
with relish.[37] Perhaps his greatest defeat in debate was in 1844 at the
hands of Cobden over free trade. He has certainly gone down in history
as a turbulent, unreliable braggart hated by his companions in the Chartist
leadership but loved by the masses. Even Marx's description captures a
critical contrary strain: 'He is essentially conservative, and feels a highly
determined hatred not only for industrial progress but also for the
revolution . . . He unites in his person an inexhaustible number of
contradictions which find their fulfilment and harmony in a certain blunt
common sense.'[38]

Such common sense – allied with the convictions of this most physical
of men about the superiority of moral force – led Feargus to persuade the
thousands gathered on Kennington Common on 10 April 1848 not to
march on Westminster and so avoid an almost certain massacre at the
hands of troops assembled by Wellington.[39]

Here, though, there is also tragedy because Feargus, stressed by the
pressures of 1848 beyond even his promethean limits, did eventually
go mad. The sad arena for the final collapse was the House of Commons,
where he sat for Nottingham and where his prior antics had so exasperated the Speaker that he was held in custody by the sergeant-at-arms for
a full week until, after petitions from his sister Harriet, the true nature
of his ill-health was recognised.[40] Feargus died three years later, believ-
ing, not without a certain logic, that he was still being detained by the
state.

Francisco Burdett O'Connor would have recognised his brother's common sense beneath the hype, but he must also have had reason to contrast
his own life with that lived publicly and privately on the edge and so
insistently within the idiom of heroism.

O'Connor's diary gives the lie to the image of a nineteenth century
Bolivia wracked by constant anarchy and utterly unhinged from the

residual concerns of civilization. The reality was by no means shining, just more prosaic. The entry for 17 December 1849 is quite representative:

> I went to the Fort after lunch and spent a long time with the Reverend Father and the magistrate. I made a visit to the governor with some complaints about the abuses of authority caused by reserve officers posted to this frontier – he promises me satisfaction and we leave it at that. During my visit he gave me to understand that the Reverend Father had offered him six pesos and that he, for his part, would match them towards the building of a small school-house for the village. I greatly approved of his plans, and I promised six pesos of my own.

In view of what had gone on in his life before and what he learned of events in the British Isles it is perhaps unsurprising that on 6 August 1849 – Bolivia's national day and the 25th anniversary of the Battle of Junín – the general noted,

> Now I'm a man forgotten by all . . . reduced to seeking my own subsistence at an age – 58 years – when there is little strength left in the body, and even less energy, but obliged to undertake manual work by necessity. Thanks to God, who endowed me with a disposition for this. If it had been otherwise, I'd be delivered up to sadness and revisiting my past life, and who knows what would happen to me.'[41]

I have told this tale very much for its own sake, so that O'Connor might not be forgotten by all. However, it would be idle not to make at least one wider point.

These days one discerns a certain slack-jawed hubris in the world's metropoli with respect to the phenomenon of 'globalisation'. Now, of course, we cross the Atlantic every day and night, courtesy of our televisions, our telephones and our computers linked up to the internet. This transportation is not physical, but it is real. We are told that it is producing a qualitative transformation of the human condition even if the energy required and the effect produced sometimes seem to match those of a gerbil at leisure.

It is possible that – from the perspective not of technology but of the human mind and experience – we have been here, or very near here, before. Certainly, there is a narrow sense in which I need to signal an institutional precedent. The first monograph published for the Institute of Latin American Studies thirty years ago by the Athlone Press was *The 'Detached Recollections' of General D.F. O'Leary*, edited by the founding director, Professor Robin Humphreys. Daniel O'Leary was Bolívar's principal aide-de-camp, a decade younger than his friend O'Connor but also a Cork man and capable of turning a fine phrase. It was O'Leary, not García Márquez, who described Bolívar's death in 1830 as 'the last embers of an expiring volcano, the dust of the Andes still on his garments'.[42]

Professor Humphreys himself died last month, in his 92nd year. He was not only the first Director of the Institute but also, from 1948, the first holder of the established chair in Latin American history based at University College. That chair was subsequently occupied with great distinction by John Lynch and Leslie Bethell, but in the early 1990s it was frozen. This is a great shame because it was the only established chair related to Latin America in the University, and it helped to ensure that the existence of the Institute was not used as an excuse to reduce or remove the study of the region elsewhere.

Indeed, that chair was one of only a couple in the country as a whole, so I am here concerned not just with the opportunities for our field within the new, more autonomous and less coordinated University of London but also throughout the United Kingdom. The Institute plays a critical role promoting Latin American studies at national level in collaboration with other institutes and centres with which it sometimes has to compete for scarce resources. The balance is fine and the challenge is sometimes considerable but it is also entirely consonant with our place and mission within the School of Advanced Study.

My predecessor, Victor Bulmer-Thomas, was the man who so enthusiastically and energetically oversaw our entry into the School, simultaneously expanding the Institute's activities on all fronts.

I won't even attempt to match such activity, but it gives me great pleasure to announce that the Institute will, in memory of its founding director, appoint each year to a Robin Humphreys Visiting Research Fellowship a past or present British public servant with experience of the Americas. The first holder of the Fellowship is to be Philip McLean, formerly British Consul in Boston and latterly Ambassador to Cuba, or, to borrow another title from Graham Greene,'Our Man in Havana'.

Mr McLean's prior posting in Hibernian Massachusetts reminds us that O'Connor and O'Leary were a military vanguard of a major diaspora; and that diaspora was, in turn, simply one of the more recent movements of peoples – very seldom of a voluntary nature – throughout the globe.

It is a common observation that there are in America more people of Irish ancestry than on the island itself. It is less well known that there are now in US schools more pupils of an Hispanic background than there are young African-Americans. The Irish Famine began just months before the US invasion of Mexico and the annexation of that territory now being peacefully repopulated by the descendents of those defeated in 1847. It would take the better part of two more decades before slavery was abolished in the USA, and twenty more years would lapse before the system which had over several centuries transported millions of people in chains from one continent to another would be entirely eradicated in that second place.

When we ask what's in the name 'America', then, we find a plethora of responses that gives the lie to any notion that the globe came into a complete spatial and self-knowing integrity with the advent of the micro-chip or the collapse of a wall built in Berlin after Fidel Castro came to power in Havana.

I don't mean to cast aspersions. We need fashion; it keeps us on our toes, sometimes literally. I would simply register some scepticism as to any unprecedented, seamless and centrifugal process of homogenisation. In that vein I have in this chapter employed the nearly anachronistic terms 'the Americas'. Pluralism is not just normative nicety – if, in fact, it is that at all. It is also a better class of scholarship – one that seeks excellence but without elitism. General O'Connor is, to my mind, best understood as a Jeffersonian, and there are many others and much more south of the Rio Grande profitably to be studied from that perspective of similarity as well as difference.

Indeed, a little more concern with comparison as a dual process – and a little less timidity in exploring and explaining it – would rectify the unwarranted exoticism of 'otherness' and test vacuous notions of homo-genisation-through-hybridity. It would enrich the understanding of Latin America and fortify area studies as a whole.

We cannot, after all, complain at the undoubtedly miserable funding of UK research and teaching in area studies if we do not confront the belief that they constitute little more than parochialism craftily practised abroad and protected by factors of space and language from the glare of scholarship heroically based on pure discipline. We need, in short, to enhance our disciplinary expertise (usually with a couple of others besides) and energetically to demonstrate how area studies have been made more, not less, valid in the contemporary world, where phe-nomena that we have studied for decades are now in the mainstream of daily life.

Francisco Burdett O'Connor died in Tarija on 5 October 1871. At this stage of proceedings one balks at a further tale of audacity, but it is a matter of record that at eight o'clock in the evening he refused to receive the last rites at home and was assisted to the monastery, four blocks away, where they were administered. Eighty one years of age, he died at 10 pm. Francisca and Hercilia survived him. Burdett had died a dozen years before Feargus. Now, of course, Frank dies too.

The name, we know, has been kept alive. Perhaps its most celebrated owner in recent years has been Cecilia O'Connor, who was the red-haired and post-globalist representative of Bolivian pulchritude at the Miss Universe contest of 1994, staged at Manila.

The family that's in the name of O'Connor has flourished since the patriarch died in the midst of his memoirs. For this chapter I choose as its representative Octavio, from the third generation, because he carried his forebears' educational concerns into the twentieth century that we are so noisily about to leave:

> The ceremony to mark the opening of the school year was exceptionally well attended, the teachers and populace of Tarija overflowing the stalls of the '15 April Hall'. In the wait before ascending the platform the Director of Education, Dr Octavio O'Connor d'Arlach, slowly lit his pipe and took a few contented puffs as he listened to the talk about him. Then somebody came up to him to say that people were getting impatient of waiting. O'Connor snapped to, put the pipe in his back-pocket, as you would a handkerchief, and requested the committee to take their seats.
>
> Following the solemn act of inauguration, Dr O'Connor, who was standing to the right of Don Víctor Navajas Trigo, prefect of the department, began to read his annual report. Immersed in his speech, he was unaware of the mounting consternation around him. But just as he was describing with some passion the infrastructural needs of the district, he sensed both the odour of burning and the gentle elbow of the prefect in his ribs. The smell came from his trousers, which the increasingly concerned audience could not see to be on fire. The boss was unharmed, the trousers were a write-off, and the pedagogic community most gratified.[43]

We have happily evaded the combustion which terminated that inauguration. It is not the prefect but the clock that is now nudging me. The reality principle beckons, and I must thank you all for both indulgence and attention.

1999

Notes

Chapter 1

1. There is no contemporary English edition that reproduces Plutarch's 'coupling', but for a sampling see Ian Scott-Kilvert's translations for Penguin: *The Rise and Fall of Athens: Nine Greek Lives* (London, 1960), and *Makers of Rome* (London, 1965).

2. J. H. Elliott, *Richelieu and Olivares* (Cambridge, 1984); Michael R. Beschloss, *Kennedy v. Khrushchev: the Crisis Years, 1960–63* (London, 1991); Alan Bullock, *Hitler and Stalin: Parallel Lives* (London, 1991). Elliott understandably organises his text around the Mantuan crisis whereas Beschloss is concerned only with a three-year period, within which the October 1962 'Cuban missile crisis' clearly provides a focal point. Bullock adheres to a much more precise (and extended) chronological parallelism, pausing for comparison in the year 1934, with Hitler newly established in power over a one-party state and Stalin about to embark on the purges.

3. D. A. Russell, *Plutarch* (London, 1973), p. 114.

4. Jean Lacouture, *De Gaulle: the Ruler, 1945–70* (London, 1991), p. 411.

5. *The Times*, London, 28 April 1969.

6. José Antonio Llosa, *René Barrientos Ortuño: Paladín de la Bolivianidad* (La Paz, 1966).

7. Fernando Diez de Medina, *El General del Pueblo* (La Paz, 1972), p. 15.

8. J. Fest, *Hitler* (London, 1974), p. 445.

9. Such a conjunction frequently produces a relationship described as 'charismatic'. For Charles Lindholm this is a 'concept of a compulsive, inexplicable emotional tie linking a group of followers together in adulation of their leader'. *Charisma* (Oxford, 1990), p. 6.

10. Teniente René Barrientos, *Mensaje al Ejército: Gestación Histórica de la Revolución Boliviana* (La Paz, 1948, reprinted 1965).

11. *El Diario*, La Paz, 18 April 1965.

12. Raul Peña Bravo, *Hechos y Dichos del General Barrientos* (La Paz, 1982), pp. 73–4.

13. However, the close contemporary association of 'sex appeal' with charisma is not one that would be readily recognised by Max Weber and would be difficult to square with the political standing of, say, Winston Churchill. Even

the more frequently postulated linkage with sexual abstinence and religious order provides only a partial explanation. Max Weber, 'The Nature of Charismatic Domination', in W.G. Runciman (ed.), *Weber: Selections in Translation* (Cambridge, 1978), pp. 226–50.

14. Peña, *op cit.*, pp. 120–3.

15. 'Meditación para los bolivianos', in Diez de Medina, *op cit.*, p. 289.

16. *Presencia*, La Paz, 30 November 1968.

17. *El Diario*, 11 July 1962. The animal, rarely found in this region, had been killed by local *campesinos*, whose reports excited such attention that the Chief of the US Military Mission, Colonel Paul Wiemert, went to investigate and acquired the hide – apparently without exchange of cash – in his words, 'as a reward for travelling to test sensationalist reports'. Ibid., 12 July 1962.

18. Aristotle, *Nicomachean Ethics*, 4.1.

19. Between January and May 1965 Barrientos publicly changed his position at least six times on whether he would stand in the planned presidential elections. Of course, this was partly a ritual to promote expressions of support, but close colleagues report a similar indecisiveness before the 1964 coup. Interview with Colonel Julio Sanjinés Goitia, La Paz, August 1989. Peña Bravo, a distinctly unsympathetic author, does not hesitate to charge cowardice, asserting that Barrientos was nicknamed 'huallpa Melgarejo', or a pallid, insufficient version of the nineteenth century tyrant Mariano Melgarejo, who was also from Tarata. Peña, *op cit.*, p. 29.

20. *El Diaro*, 15, 18, 19 October 1961.

21. Ibid., 25 Jauary, 26, 28 February, 1–7 March 1964.

22. Ibid., 23–28 March 1965. Far less publicity was given to a not dissimilar occurrence in 1976 when, according to immovable popular conviction, General Hugo Banzer was shot in the posterior by his formidable wife Yolanda because of his liaison with a young lady from Tarija.

23. Tcnl. Oscar Vargas Valenzuela, *La Verdad sobre la Muerte del General Barrientos a la Luz de Investigaciones Policiales, Técnicas y Esotéricas* (La Paz, 1984), p. 179. Peña also attended a seance but did not himself commune with any spirit, *op. cit.*, pp. 132–6.

24. Diez de Medina, *op. cit.*, p. 15.

25. Régis Debray, *Critique of Political Reason* (London, 1983), p. 15.

26. An excellent condensed account of Debray's trial and its background is provided in *Keesing's Contemporary Archive*, vol. XVIII, 1969/70, pp. 23493 ff. The present account of Che's guerrilla and Debray's links with it draws primarily on the following sources: Daniel James (ed.), *The Complete Bolivian Diaries of Che Guevara and Other Captured Documents* (London, 1968); Luis J. González and Gustavo Sánchez Salazar, *The Great Rebel: Che Guevara in Bolivia* (New York, 1969); José Luis Alcázar, *Nacahuazu: La Guerrilla del Che en Bolivia* (Mexico, 1969); Gary Prado Salmón, *The Defeat of Che Guevara* (London, 1990); Régis Debray, *Che's Guerrilla War* (London, 1975) and *Prison Writings* (London, 1973), together with the reports of *The Times* and *The Guardian* of London and *Le Monde*, Paris.

27. Régis Debray, 'Some Literary Reflections', in *Prison Writings*, pp. 171; 186–7.

28. Louis Althusser, *Reading Capital* (London, 1972), p. 210.

29. Benedict Spinoza, *Ethica*, II, Propositions XLIII and XXXV, quoted in Perry Anderson, *Considerations on Western Marxism* (London, 1976), pp. 64–5.

30. Althusser, *op. cit.*, p. 59.

31. Reprinted in Régis Debray, *A Critique of Arms* (London, 1977), p. 267, and also partially cited in Gregory Elliott, *Althusser: the Detour of Theory* (London 1987), pp. 68–9. In the spring of 1968 Althusser repeats the same advice to Maria Antonieta Macciocchi, a militant of the Italian Communist Party: 'Politics is a protracted war. Do not be in a hurry. Try to see things in advance, and know how to wait today. Don't live in terms of subjective urgency. Know, too, how to put your defeats to use.' But in the same letter he appears to capitulate to 'empiricism' by declaring, 'Impressions are important, but above all it is the *facts* that count.' Maria Antonieta Macciocchi, *Letters from Inside the Italian Communist Party to Louis Althusser* (London, 1973), pp. 21 and 23.

32. Régis Debray, *Revolution in the Revolution?* (London, 1968), p. 21.

33. Reprinted in Régis Debray, *Strategy for Revolution* (London, 1970).

34. Ernesto Che Guevara, *Guerrilla Warfare* (New York, 1961), p. 1.

35. See, *inter alia*, Leo Huberman and Paul Sweezy (eds), *Régis Debray and the Latin American Revolution* (London, 1969); Richard Gott, *Rural Guerrillas in Latin America* (London, 1973); Geoffrey Fairbairn, *Revolutionary Guerrilla Warfare* (London, 1974).

36. Guevara, *Bolivian Diaries*, pp. 127; 132.

37. The full speech, which was taped and released to the press the following day, is reproduced in Debray, *Strategy for Revolution*, pp. 227–73.

38. Ibid., p. 242.

39. Ibid., p. 244.

40. Ibid., p. 238.

41 A long-standing view recently restated by both General Gary Prado and CIA agent Félix Rodríguez in interviews with Amalia Barrón of *Tiempo*, Madrid, reproduced in *La Razón*, La Paz, 3 November 1991.

42. Régis Debray, *Modeste contribution aux discours et cérémonies du dixième anniversaire* (Paris, 1978), p. 15.

43. Debray, *Che's Guerrilla*, p. 11. It is perhaps telling that in this text Debray continues to use an analogy employed seven years earlier in *Revolution in the Revolution?* – that of the guerrilla as a 'small motor' (and external cause) starting up the 'large motor' of the Bolivian mass movement. Ibid., p. 143. This image is borrowed from Althusser, who states that Marx and Engels's declaration in *The Communist Manifesto* that, 'class struggle is the motor of history' is a 'basic Marxist proposition'. *For Marx* (London, 1965), p. 215. Although he pushes the point too far, E. P. Thompson is surely right to insist that it is, rather, an anology that has been misinterpreted in a dangerously functionalist fashion. *The Poverty of Theory* (London, 1978), pp. 295–6. In all events, its appearance in a text written by Debray after his return to France clearly indicates a continued Althusserian influence, even as the philosopher entered decline and, eventually, tragic illness.

44. Régis Debray, *Les Masques* (Paris, 1987), which suggests that the differences between left-wing and right-wing are due to distinct 'sensibilities' but dem-

onstrates little sensitivity towards Carmen Castillo, Debray's long-time companion who had previously been the lover of the Chilean revolutionary leader Miguel Enríquez.

45. Régis Debray, *Teachers, Writers, Celebrities: the Intellectuals of Modern France* (London, 1981).
46. Debray, *Critique of Political Reason*, p. 346.
47. José Ortega y Gasset, *On Love: Aspects of a Single Theme* (London, 1967), p. 19.
48. *Que Vive la République* (Paris, 1989). It is notable that John Berger, writing about the photographs of Guevara's corpse in December 1967, meditates upon the role of Saint-Just in introducing a 'modern heroism': 'I despise the dust of which I am composed, the dust which is speaking to you; anyone can pursue and put an end to this dust. But I defy anybody to snatch from me what I have given myself, an independent life in the sky of the centuries'. *Discours et Rapports* (Paris, 1957), p. 90, quoted in John Berger, *Selected Essays* (London, 1972), p. 49. It is perhaps telling that the last recorded words of Saint-Just were, 'I am the one who wrote that', with reference to the Constitution of 1793, whereas Danton is widely reported to have addressed his executioner, 'Above all, don't forget to show my head to the people; it's worth seeing'. Norman Hampson, *Saint-Just* (London, 1991), p. 227; *Danton* (Oxford, 1978), p. 174. This latter incident is also compellingly captured in Andrzej Wajda's film *Danton*, which properly depicts this revolutionary figure as possessing more than a touch of Barrientos's populist flair, indecision and opportunist instincts.
49. Francis Fukuyama, *The End of History and the Last Man* (London, 1992), pp. xiv–xv.
50. Ibid., p. xii.
51. Ibid., p. xiii.
52. Victor Bulmer-Thomas, 'Life after Debt: the New Economic Trajectory in Latin America', Inaugural Lecture, Queen Mary and Westfield College, University of London, 5 March 1992 (published as University of London, Institute of Latin American Studies Occasional Paper No. 1, 1992).
53. Ariel Dorfman, *Death and the Maiden* (London, 1992). See also the important essay, 'Political Code and Literary Code: the Testimonial Genre in Chile Today', in Dorfman, *Some Write to the Future* (London, 1991).
54. Interview with José Woldenberg in *La Jornada*, Mexico City, 1 April 1992. Woldenberg's first novel tackles some similar themes in its attention to the Jewish experience in Mexico: *Las Ausencias Presentes* (Mexico, 1992).
55. Gabriel García Márquez, *The General in his Labyrinth* (London, 1990), p. 124.
56. Fukuyama, *The End of History*, p. xxi.
57. Eduardo Subirats, 'Venezuela: Crónica de un golpe inacabado', *La Jornada*, 5 April 1992. The brief radical manifesto of the *Movimiento Militar Bolivariano* is reprinted in *Latin American Chasqui*, London, March/April 1992.
58. Details of the fate of those held in the Estadio Chile are recounted in *Informe de la Comisión Nacional de Verdad y Reconciliación* (Santiago, 1991), vol. I, pp. 143 ff.

Chapter 2

1. Lewis Carroll, quoted by Subcomandante Marcos, Ejército Zapatista de Liberación Nacional, letter 'from the mountains of southeastern Mexico' to the press, 15 March 1994.
2. *Utopia Unarmed: The Latin American Left after the Cold War* (Knopf, New York, 1993).
3. This view is shared by Alan Angell, 'The Left in Latin America since 1930', in Leslie Bethell, *Cambridge History of Latin America*, vol. VI. part 2 (Cambridge, 1994).
4. Alain Touraine, *La Parole et le Sang* (Paris, 1986), p. 166.
5. *El País*, Madrid, 4 April 1994.
6. At the opening of public works at the village of Yurac Yurac, southern Bolivia, Col. Simón Bolívar, C.O. Fifth Engineer Battalion, declared, 'poverty is Bolivia's worst enemy, we must fight it by building a society that is just, equitable and developed'. *Presencia*, La Paz, 2 September 1993.
7. For a brilliant psychoanalytical treatment of the Argentine military's rationales for its repressive regime, see Frank Graziano, *Divine Violence: Spectacle, Psychosexuality and Radical Christianity in the Argentine Dirty War* (Boulder, 1992).
8. Charles Hale, 'Between Che Guevara and Pachamama', *Critique of Anthropology*, vol. 14, no. 1, March 1994.
9. The issue that justifiably infuriates Castañeda was the kidnap in 1991 of a Mexican citizen within the territorial limits of Mexico and his abduction by US bounty-hunters (the absolute antithesis of the Latin *justiciero*) to US territory. This act was subsequently deemed legal by the US Supreme Court, causing uproar throughout Latin America and no little consternation amongst the international legal community. According to US Attorney-General William P. Barr, 'the extraterritorial enforcement of United States laws is becoming increasingly important to protect vital national interests'. *Washington Post*, 14 August 1991, quoted on p. 301.
10. It should be emphasised that such a critique is by no means new and was upheld with great vigour from the mid-1970s by the Working People's Alliance (WPA) of Guyana, which faced in Forbes Burnham's PNC government an authoritarian regime that masqueraded under a radical veil, controlled a bloated public sector and fixed elections as energetically and shamelessly as the most reactionary dictatorship. The WPA attempted to influence the ill-fated Grenadian revolutionaries of the New Jewel Movement over the 'democratic question', and if that effort proved an abject failure, there is probably much to be learnt from the Caribbean experience – something that Castañeda, following standard protocols, does not cover.
11. Castañeda's democratic platform centres on electoral reform (to include removal of fraud, expanded registration, introduction of emigrant voting rights, proportional representation, state financing of parties, equitable access to the media); the separation of party from government and introduction of state accountability (including enhanced powers for legislatures, independent

central banks, autonomous public companies, human rights ombudsmen, reform of the judiciary and the police); the extension of democracy to social activity previously dominated by corporatist custom. Although he hints at a preference for the 'parliamentarians' who, led by Juan Linz, identify the centralist/executive bias of Latin American systems as a core problem, Castañeda does not insist on what I believe to be a largely secondary issue. Likewise, he does not devote much space to the more immediately taxing and contentious issue of amnesty and the treatment of servants of ex-dictatorships under democratic rule.

Chapter 3

1. I have discussed this pattern in *Rebellion in the Veins: Political Struggle in Bolivia, 1952–1982* (Verso, London, 1984) and *Political Transition and Economic Stabilisation: Bolivia, 1982–1989* (Research Paper No. 22, Institute of Latin American Studies, University of London, 1990).

2. See, for example, Laurence Whitehead, 'Miners as Voters: the Electoral Process in Bolivia's Mining Camps', *Journal of Latin American Studies*, vol. 13, no. 2, 1981, pp. 313–46.

3. Robert A. Dahl, *Polyarchy: Participation and Opposition* (Yale University Press, New Haven, 1971); Laurence Whitehead, 'Bolivia's Failed Democratisation, 1977–80', in G. O'Donnell, P. Schmitter and L. Whitehead (eds), *Transitions from Authoritarian Rule: Latin America* (Johns Hopkins University Press, Baltimore, 1986).

4. *La Razón*, 29 May 1997.

5. The principal lobby in this regard was Charter 88. For a detailed appraisal, see Patrick Dunleavy, Helen Margetts, Brendan O'Duffy and Stuart Weir, *Making Votes Count* (University of Essex, Democratic Audit, paper no. 11, 1997). Bolivia still lacks a comprehensive psephological study. The polls of 1979, 1980, 1985 and 1989 are surveyed from the perspective of party results in Salvador Romero Ballivián, *Geografía Electoral de Bolivia* (CEBEM/ILDIS, La Paz, 1993). A broad summary of all results may be found in Carlos Mesa Gisbert, *Presidentes de Bolivia: Entre Urnas y Fusiles*, 2nd edn, (La Paz, 1990).

6. Slightly different figures are given in Dunleavy *et al.*, *Making Votes Count*.

7. This argument is made by S. Mainwaring and T. Scully (eds), *Building Democratic Institutions: Party Systems in Latin America* (Stanford University Press, Stanford, 1995), the editors drawing largely on that volume's chapter on Bolivia by Eduardo A. Gamarra and James M. Malloy, who themselves describe the system as patrimonialist.

8. This anecdote is recounted in a most useful analysis of recent Bolivian political developments: Eduardo A. Gamarra, 'Hybrid Presidentialism and Democratization: the Case of Bolivia', in Scott Mainwaring and Matthew Soberg Shugart (eds), *Presidentialism and Democracy in Latin America* (Cambridge University Press, Cambridge, 1997).

9. For a full account of this crisis and the wider political and institutional

landscape, see María del Pilar Domingo Villegas, 'Democracy in the Making? Political Parties and Political Institutions in Bolivia, 1985–1991' (D. Phil. thesis, University of Oxford, 1993).

10. The best analysis of the political consequences of the cocaine trade is Hugo Rodas Morales, *Huanchaca: Modelo Político-Empresarial de la Cocaína en Bolivia* (Plural, La Paz, 1997).

11. On 16 August 1997 the new administration issued an injunction to its members, supporters and civil servants including the following: 1. Strict adhesion to the law; 2. Respect for the citizen; 3. Correct use of state property (no private use of public vehicles or cellular phones; no use of sirens except by the vehicles of the president and vice-president); 4. Austerity; 5. Discipline; 6. Sobriety; 7. Sense of self-criticism; 8. Sense of modesty; 9. Democratic collegiality with opponents; 10. Honesty (*La Razón*, 17 August 1997).

12. *Presencia*, 16 February 1997.

13. Fernando Mayorga, *Max Fernández. La Política del Silencio* (UMMS/ILDIS, La Paz, 1991); Fernando Mayorga, *Discurso y Política en Bolivia* (CERES/ILDIS, Pa Paz, 1993); Carlos F. Toranzo Roca and Mario Arrieta Abdalla, *Nueva Derecha y Desproletización en Bolivia* (UNITAS/ILDIS, La Paz, 1989); Hugo San Martín, *El Palenquismo* (Amigos del Libro, La Paz, 1991); Joaquín Saravia and Godofredo Sandoval, *Jach'a Uru: ¿La Esperanza de un Pueblo? Carlos Palenque, RTP y los Sectores Populares Urbanos de La Paz* (CEP/ILDIS, La Paz, 1991); Rafael Archondo, *Compadres al Micrófono: La Resurrección Metropolitana del Ayllu*, (HISBOL, La Paz, 1991); Roberto Laserna, *Productores de Democracia* (CERES, Cochabamba, 1992); J. Antonio Mayorga, *Gonismo: Discurso y Poder* (UMSS/FACES, Cochabamba, 1996); Carlos Blanco Cazas and Godofredo Sandoval, *La Alcaldía de La Paz: Entre Populistas, Modernistas y Culturalistas, 1985–1993* (ILDIS, La Paz, 1993).

14. Santa Cruz (13%); La Paz (12%); Cochabamba (7%); El Alto (7%); Oruro (3%); Sucre (2.5%); Tarija (2%).

15. A. Solís Rada, *La Fortuna del Presidente* (La Paz, 1997).

16. By early 1997 the state had contrived to identify 1,176 '*cazabeneméritos*' of between 17 and 50 years of age. At that stage the youngest veteran of the Chaco War would have been 77 (*Hoy*, 9 March 1997). Whilst a very poor state must certainly guard against inadmissible claims on its slight resources, one feels distinctly uneasy about this particularly rigorous audit, and it is to be hoped that both younger women and elderly gentlemen derived happiness and security from even the prospect of union.

17. *Ultima Hora*, 20 April 1997.

18. As the AFPs went into operation the need for regulation of the financial sector was starkly illustrated by the revelation that the country's *Fondos de Vivienda* (building associations or cooperatives) had not been obliged to maintain proper accounts before 1993 despite holding an estimated $130 million. *Presencia*, 11 September 1997.

19. *Ultima Hora*, 18 May 1997; *Presencia*, 16 June 1997.

20. Eduardo Gamarra, 'Goni's Unsung Swansong', *Hemisphere*, Miami, April 1997.

21. *Presencia*, 20 and 26 July 1997.

22. *Presencia*, 21 June, 11 September 1997.

23. *La Razón*, 31 August 1997.
24. *Presencia*, 2 and 3 September 1997.
25. Banzer's slogan of 'Pan, Techo, Trabajo' might sound rather corporatist, but it is a good deal less so than the 'Paz, Orden, Trabajo' motif he deployed 20 years earlier and which was reminiscent of the Pétain/Laval refrain, 'Travail, Famille, Patrie'. In any event the ADN slogan was much snappier than that dreamt up by the MNR's spin-doctors: '¡Soluciones de Verdad! Para una Cosecha Generosa'.
26. Jon Lee Anderson, *Che Guevara: A Revolutionary Life* (Bantam, London, 1997).
27. Régis Debray, *Revolution in the Revolution?* (Penguin, London, 1968); James Dunkerley, 'Barrientos and Debray: All Gone or More to Come?' (University of London, Institute of Latin American Studies, Occasional Paper No. 2; reprinted as Chapter 1 in this volume).
28. Quoted in Anderson, *Che Guevara*, p. 104.
29. Javier Mendoza Pizarro, *La Mesa Coja: Historia de la Proclama de la Junta Tuitiva del 16 de Julio de 1809* (PIEB, La Paz and Sucre, 1997).
30. Bolívar, Potosí, 21 October 1825, to Santander, see H. Bierck and V. Lecuna (eds), *Selected Writings of Bolívar*, II (Colonial Press, New York, 1951), p. 543.

Chapter 4

1. For an excellent synoptic treatment of this from the perspective of Latin America, see John King, *Magical Reels: a History of Cinema in Latin America* (Verso, London, 1990).
2. It is, though, rather a moot point as to whether Mexico 'stands for' the rest of Latin America. Perhaps its frequent projection as 'other' has, rather, given it the status of 'no-man's land', at least with respect to images of *political* culture. There is a real sense in which (for political as well as cultural reasons) Mexico 'is not political' in American eyes, at least not like Central America, even if it is also no longer just a place occupied by sleepy people on donkeys.
3. *Stakeout* is more than partially a road-movie, and it depends as much as did *Five Easy Pieces* (Bob Rafelson/Richard Wechsler, 1970) on the verdant chill of the landscape of Washington State. Yet Badham's film could not be more different in its treatment of the human condition: Stowe is the total opposite of the progressively disillusioned and jilted Karen Black, whose carping 'white trash' foibles are played off Jack Nicholson as they move north with a brilliance that Stowe is seemingly not required to (and maybe cannot) display.
4. However, what her part in *Parador* misses is the essential innocence of the sensuality projected by Braga in films such as *Doña Flor and Her Two Husbands* (*Dona Flor e seus dois maridos*, Bruno Barreto, 1976) and *Gabriela* (Bruno Barreto, 1983). In this sense she could not be more different from a European actress to whom she might otherwise be seen as very similar in her candid sexual activity – the knowing, and dangerous, Maruschka Detmers, given the lead by Godard in his *Prenom Carmen* (1983).
5. Paulin Kael, *State of the Art* (Dutton, New York, 1985).

6. It is, however, worth noting that the lead character in *Stand and Deliver* is based on the Los Angeles schoolteacher Jaime Escalante, who is Bolivian and manifests many of those traits of national character of his country that stand in stark contrast to those normally associated with the Caribbean region.

7. Salman Rushdie, *The Jaguar Smile: a Nicaraguan Journey* (Picador, London, 1987), pp. 15–22.

8. Pauline Kael, *Hooked* (Dutton, New York, 1989); *State of the Art*.

9. For further reading on Central America see James Dunkerley, *Power in the Isthmus: a Political History of Modern Central America* (Verso, London, 1988).

Chapter 5

1. *Visión*, Mexico, 12 November 1965, p. 15; *Keesings Contemporary Archive*, XV, 1965–6, p. 21063.

2. *Visión*, 29 October 1965, p. 13; *Keesings*, XV, 1965–6, p. 21050.

3. *New York Times*, 21 September 1965.

4. *Visión*, 20 October 1965. Lleras contrasted the *Le Monde*-led attitude to Latin America – 'that it is an oligarchically dominated zone that has somehow to be berated' – with that of the British press, led in this instance by *The Economist*, wherein the indefatigible Norman Macrae made sharp criticisms of IMF orthodoxy in a manner that could scarcely be associated with the incurious, almost talmudic approach taken towards monetary matters by today's editions of that 'newspaper'.

5. Ibid.

6. J.L. Mecham, *Church and State in Latin America* (University of North Carolina Press, Chapel Hill, 1966); Hanke, Friede and Ramón Menéndez Pidal in *Hispanic American Historical Review* (HAHR), vol. 44, no. 3, August 1964; M. Mörner (ed.), *The Expulsion of the Jesuits from Latin America* (Knopf, New York, 1965); R. Greenleaf, 'The Inquisition and the Indians of New Spain: a Study in Jurisdictional Confusion', *The Americas*, vol. 22, no. 2, 1965; Lewis Tambs, 'The Inquisition in Eighteenth Century Mexico', *The Americas*, vol. 22, no. 2, 1965; M. León Portilla (ed.), Juan de Torquemada, *Monarquía India* (UNAM, Mexico, 1964).

7. M. León Portilla, *La Visión de los Vencidos* (Mexico, 1959) (Translated as *The Broken Spears: the Aztec Account of the Conquest of Mexico* (Beacon Press, Boston, 1962).) Elizabeth Burgos Debray (ed.), *I . . . Rigoberta Menchú* (Verso, London, 1984).

8. Charles Hale, 'José María Luis Mora and the Structure of Mexican Liberalism', HAHR, 45:2, May 1965; C. Sempat Assadourian, *El Tráfico de Esclavos en Córdoba, 1588–1610*, Univ. Córdoba, 1965; 'Modos de producción, capitalismo y subdesarrollo en América Latina', in J.C. Garavaglia (ed.), *Modos de Producción en América Latina* (Ediciones de Pasado y Presente, Córdoba, 1973); José Barán and Benjamín Nahúm, *Bases Económicas de la Revolución Artiguista* (Banda Oriental, Montevideo, 1964); *Historia Rural del Uruguay Moderno*, 4 vols (Montevideo, 1967–72).

9. Miron Burgin, *The Economic Aspects of Argentine Federalism, 1820–1852* (Harvard

University Press, Cambridge Mass., 1946); J. Scobie, *Revolution on the Pampas: a Social History of Argentine Wheat, 1860–1910* (University of Texas Press, Austin, 1964); T. Halperín Donghi, 'La exportación ganadera en la campaña de Buenos Aires, 1810–1852', *Desarrollo Económico*, vol. 3, no. 12, April–Sept. 1963; *Politics, Society and Economics in Argentina in the Revolutionary Period* (Cambridge University Press, Cambridge, 1975); *Historia Contemporánea de América Latina* (Mexico, 1967) (English translation: *The Contemporary History of Latin America* (Macmillan, London, 1993). Halperín Donghi acted as guest editor of the special issue of the *Journal of Latin American Studies* (JLAS) for the 500th anniversary of Columbus' arrival in the continent.

10. See the generous (and dangerous?) admission in F.H. Cardoso and E. Faletto, *Dependency and Development in Latin America* (University of California Press, Berkeley, 1979). It is very important to note that this English edition was issued a full decade after the original Spanish text, not least in terms of its reception in the USA, the much-changed historiographical landscape, and the more developed debate on international political economy prevailing at the later date.

11. R.A. Humphreys and J. Lynch, *The Origins of the Latin American Revolutions, 1808–1826* (Knopf, New York, 1965).

12. In this and subsequent references to UK Latin Americanists I will, where possible, give their date of birth to indicate generation – something, as I suggest below, that is more important than all but the autobiographical literature recognises. In the cases of individuals mentioned in the text – such as Humphreys and Lynch – more than two publications may be cited. Otherwise, I have endeavoured – under the guise of both 'representativeness' and 'fairness' – to provide two publications that I believe best reflect each scholar's work. This is, of course, most arbitrary and can hardly be the best way to win friends, but I do hope that my selection of both people and publications will be met with at least initial indulgence. To those who cannot sustain this or encounter serious errors of fact I apologise in advance. For help over this as well as more general assistance, I am most grateful to Rory Miller, who bears no responsibility for any prejudice or errors. R.A. Humphreys (1907) (ed.), *British Consular Reports on the Trade and Politics of Latin America, 1824–1826* (Camden Third Series, London, 1940) (reprinted 1973, 1981); *The Evolution of Modern Latin America* (Oxford, 1946); *Liberation in South America, 1806–1827: the Career of James Paroissien* (Athlone Press, London, 1952); (ed. with G. Graham), *The Navy and South America, 1807–1823: Correspondence of the Commanders-in-Chief on the South American Station* (Navy Records Society, London, 1962); *Tradition and Revolt in Latin America and Other Essays* (Weidenfeld and Nicholson, London, 1964); *Latin America and the Second World War*, 2 vols (Athlone, London, 1981 and 1982). For an exhaustive bibliography, see Simon Collier, 'An Interview with R.A. Humphreys', HAHR, vol. 62, no. 2, 1982. For Humphreys's own reflections on his career and the development of Latin American studies, see R.A. Humphreys, *Latin American Studies in Great Britain. An Autobiographical Fragment* (ILAS, London, 1978).

13. John Lynch (1927), *Spanish Colonial Administration, 1782–1810: the Intendant*

System in the Viceroyalty of the Rio de la Plata (Greenwood Press, New York, 1958 and 1969); *Spain under the Habsburgs*, 2 vols (Blackwell, Oxford, 1964–9 and 1981); *The Spanish American Revolutions, 1808–1826* (Norton, New York, 1973 and 1986); *Argentine Dictator: Juan Manuel Rosas, 1829–1852* (Clarendon Press, Oxford, 1981); *Spain, 1516–1598: from Nation-State to World Empire* (Blackwell, Oxford, 1991); *The Hispanic World in Crisis and Change, 1598–1700* (Blackwell, Oxford, 1992); *Caudillos in Spanish America, 1800–1850* (Clarendon Press, Oxford, 1992).

14. J.H. Parry (1914–82), *The Audiencia of New Galicia in the Sixteenth Century* (CUP, London, 1948, 1968); *The Age of Reconnaissance* (Weidenfeld and Nicholson, London, 1966). Educated at King Edward's School, Birmingham, Clare College, Cambridge, and Harvard, Parry was appointed to a chair at UWI, Jamaica, in 1949, became Vice-Chancellor of Ibadan University in 1956, and Principal of University College, Swansea in 1960. In 1965, after the publication of his Report, he was appointed to the Gardiner Chair of Oceanic History and Affairs at Harvard.

15. David Joslin (1925–70), *A Century of Banking in Latin America* (OUP, London, 1963). John Street (1922–91), *Artigas and the Emancipation of Uruguay* (CUP, London, 1959). Joslin and Street provided the initial dynamism behind Latin American studies at Cambridge, Street serving on the Parry Committee and acting as the Cambridge Centre's first director (1966–70), Joslin dying very young shortly after succeeding to that post and being appointed joint editor of the JLAS. In neither case was early promise in Latin American studies fulfilled in terms of publications, and according to an obituary of Street by his doctoral student Brian Hamnett (assisted by Geoffrey Walker), he was sorely affected by the death of his wife in 1967 – long before his retirement in 1982. *Bulletin of Latin American Research* (BLAR), vol. 10, no. 3, 1991. Following Joslin's death, D.C.M. Platt briefly occupied the Cambridge directorship before moving to that at Oxford. Thereafter the University appears to have resisted making senior appointments in the area, notwithstanding the existence of the one-year Simón Bolívar professorship, open to visiting Latin Americans. Obituaries for David Joslin may be found in HAHR, vol. 51, no. 2, 1971; JLAS, vol. 3, no. 1, 1971. (The JLAS has published obituaries only of its editors.)

16. J.H. Elliott (1930), *Imperial Spain, 1469–1716* (Edward Arnold, London, 1963); *The Old World and the New, 1492–1650* (CUP, Cambridge, 2nd ed. 1992). D.A.G. Waddell (1927–1990), *British Honduras: a Historical and Contemporary Survey* (OUP, London, 1961); 'International Politics and Latin American Independence', in L. Bethell (ed.), *Cambridge History of Latin America* (CHLA), vol. III (CUP, Cambridge, 1985). H.S. Ferns (1913–1992) *Britain and Argentina* (OUP, Oxford, 1960). Alistair Hennessy (1926), *The Frontier in Latin American History* (Edward Arnold, London, 1978); (ed.), *Intellectuals in the Twentieth Century Caribbean*, 2 vols (Macmillan, Basingstoke, 1992). C.R. Boxer (1903), *The Golden Age of Brazil, 1695–1750* (University of California Press, Berkeley, 1962, reprinted 1995).

17. A variously titled general history course has been taught at ILAS since 1966 (by Christopher Abel, Leslie Bethell, Harold Blakemore, Robin Humphreys,

Colin Lewis, John Lynch, and Eduardo Posada as the principal teachers). In addition, the following options have been offered: Brazil Empire and Republic, 1822 to the Present Day (Leslie Bethell); The Evolution of Chile, 1833 to the Present Day (Harold Blakemore); The Archaeology of Prehispanic Mesoamerica (Warwick Bray); The Aztecs and the End of Mexican Civilisation (Warwick Bray); The Argentine Economy from the mid-Nineteenth Century to the Present Day (Colin Lewis); Aspects of the Historical Geography of Latin America (Linda Newson); Imperialism, the State and National Identity in Latin America and the Caribbean (Colin Lewis and Christopher Abel); Welfare, Poverty and Politics in Latin America since 1920 (Colin Lewis and Christopher Abel); The Latin American Colonial Experience (Linda Newson); Democracy and Violence in the History of Colombia (Eduardo Posada).

18. S. Collier, 'Interview with R.A. Humphreys', HAHR, vol. 62, no. 2, 1982, p. 186.
19. 'Weapons and Arches in the Mexican Revolutionary Landscape', in G. Joseph and D. Nugent (eds), *Everyday Forms of State Formation: Revolution in the Negotiation of Rule in Modern Mexico* (Duke University Press, Durham North Carolina, 1994), p. 25. I suspect that the following quote, from two senior US political scientists, lies firmly in the sober sector of the kind of writing that Professor Knight has in mind:

> *Statecraft* is broadly defined as the elaboration of procedural rules and public policies by agents empowered to act in the name of the state, which mandates and regulates the basic relationships among actors in the state, civil society, and market. *Governance* is used more narrowly to refer to the capacity of governments to resolve problems through the formulation and implementation of public policies.

(Catherine Conaghan and James Malloy, *Unsettling Statecraft: Democracy and Neoliberalism in the Central Andes* (University of Pittsburgh Press, Pittsburgh, 1994), p. 14.)

20. Alan Knight (1946), *The Mexican Revolution*, 2 vols (CUP, Cambridge, 1986); 'Social Revolution: a Latin American Perspective', BLAR, vol. 9, no. 2, 1990.
21. 'Latin America – History and Historiography: Interview with Alan Knight', *History Workshop Journal*, no. 34, Autumn 1992, p. 162.
22. In addition to the unusually extensive consideration of Latin America in Hobsbawm's surveys of world history in the modern era (a consideration that increases somewhat in the later volumes), he has published on the region from a variety of perspectives: 'South American Journey', *Labour Monthly*, vol. XLV, no. 7, 1963; 'Peasants and Rural Migrants in Politics', in C. Veliz (ed.), *The Politics of Conformity in Latin America* (OUP, London, 1967); 'A Case of Neo-feudalism: La Convención, Peru', JLAS, 1, 1969; 'Ideology and Social Change in Colombia', in June Nash, Juan Corradi and Hobart Spalding (eds), *Ideology and Social Change in Latin America* (Gordon and Breach, New York, 1977); *Bandits* (Weidenfeld and Nicholson, London, 1969); 'Guerrillas in Latin America', *Social Register 1970* (Merlin Press, London, 1970); 'Latin American Guerrillas: a Survey', *Latin American Review of Books 1* (in fact the only issue), London, 1973. A recent work of British history on Latin American

banditry is John Dawe, 'The Socio-economic and Political Origins of Banditry in Chile and Peru, 1870–1930', PhD, University of Liverpool, 1996.

23. The Essex programme was very much the work of Simon Collier (1938), *Ideas and Politics of Chilean Independence, 1808–1833* (CUP, Cambridge, 1967); *The Life and Times of Carlos Gardel*, (University of Pittsburgh Press, Pittsburgh, 1986). A student of John Street, Collier was appointed at the university's foundation. He moved to the University of Tennessee after more than twenty years at Essex. Alan Knight was his colleague at Essex for a number of years before himself moving to Austin and then Oxford. The Essex history programme is now headed by Brian Hamnett (1942), *Roots of Insurgency: Mexican Regions, 1750–1824* (CUP, Cambridge, 1986); *Juárez*, (Longman, London, 1994). The Warwick programme was initiated through the Department of History by Alistair Hennessy, who retired in 1993 having concentrated in recent years on building up a complementary Centre for Caribbean Studies. For the last twenty years the teaching of Latin American history at Warwick has been in the hands of Anthony McFarlane (1946), *The British in the Americas, 1480–1815* (Longman, London, 1994); *Colombia before Independence: Economy, Society and Politics under Bourbon Rule* (CUP, Cambridge, 1994); and Guy Thomson (1949), *Puebla de los Angeles: Industry and Society in a Mexican City, 1700–1850* (Westview, Boulder, 1989); 'Bulwarks of Patriotic Liberalism: the National Guard Philarmonic Corps and Patriotic Juntas in Mexico, 1847–88', JLAS, vol. 22, part 1, 1990.

24. At Essex Mathias Röhrig Assunção, a specialist in nineteenth century Brazil, and at Warwick Rebecca Earle, a specialist in nineteenth century Colombia. One talented historian for whom the UK university system could find no work was David Cahill, 'Crown, Clergy and Revolution in Bourbon Peru: the Diocese of Cuzco', PhD, University of Liverpool, 1984; 'Curas and Social Conflict: the *Doctrinas* of Cuzco, 1780–1814', JLAS, vol. 16, part 2, 1984.

25. Harold Blakemore (1930–90), *British Nitrates and Chilean Politics, 1886–1896: Balmaceda and North* (Athlone, London, 1974); *From the Pacific to La Paz: the Antofagasta (Chili) and Bolivia Railway Company* (Lester Crook, London, 1990). Blakemore was a founding editor of the JLAS, serving 18 years in that post. Independence of spirit, chronic illness and the possession of a conservative outlook at a time when Chile, the country in which he specialised, was ruled first by Allende and then by Pinochet made Harold Blakemore a more controversial figure than he wanted (or deserved) to be. This is reflected in David Fox's too diplomatic obituary: BLAR, vol. 10, no. 3, 1991, and in the response it provoked in the following issue. In fact, Blakemore actively patronised the magazine *Nueva Historia*, run by exiles from Pinochet's dictatorship. (The editorial committee for the journal's 18 issues, 1980–89, was Leonardo León, Manuel Fernández, Luis M. Ortega, Enrique Reyes, and Gabriel Salazar.) Andrew Barnard (1939) was also for many years associated with the London Institute: 'Chilean Communists, Radical Presidents and Chilean Relations with the United States', JLAS, vol. 13, part 2, 1981; 'Chile', in Leslie Bethell and Ian Roxborough (eds), *Latin America between World War Two and the Cold War, 1944–1948* (CUP, Cambridge, 1992).

26. *International Air Passenger and Flight Transport. Latin America and the Caribbean* (Montreal, 1978); Rigas Doganis, *Flying Off-course: the Economics of International Airlines* (London, 1985); A. Ellison and E. Stafford, *The Dynamics of the Civil Aviation Industry* (Saxon House, London, 1974).

27. *Historia; Historia y Cultura; Data. Historia Boliviana,* founded in 1981, expired before the end of the decade, not least because it depended on the efforts of just one man – Josep Barnadas, whose example greatly encouraged and influenced the others. The Hisbol editorial house, headed by Javier Medina, produces a wide range of texts from pocket-books to extensive monographs. It is, of course, a healthy sign that not all academic work of quality passes through the same publisher's hands, and perhaps the strongest piece of Bolivian history in recent years was published by Plural: Ana María Lema *et al.* (eds), *Bosquejo del estado en que se halla la riqueza de Bolivia con sus resultados presentados al examen de la Nación por un aldeano hijo de ella. Año de 1830* (La Paz, 1993) – a text that combines original nineteenth century documentation with a collective effort at detective work and commentary of the highest order.

28. The first issue of the JLAS contained articles by Leslie Bethell, Peter Calvert, Brian Hamnett, Eric Hobsbawm, Francis Lambert, and John Lynch. Only Robert Freeman Smith represented the USA. Such a balance at the start is unsurprising, but it does demonstrate the local capacity to sustain an international publication.

29. There are, of course, important and honourable exceptions. In the 1960s and 1970s, when the debate over 'dependency' was at its peak, *Past and Present* and *The Economic History Review* published key contributions.

30. David Joslin and John Street were the first editors of the series, which opened with Simon Collier's *Ideas and Politics of Chilean Independence* (see note 23) in 1967. They were joined by Clifford T. Smith in 1970 after 11 volumes, Malcolm Deas joining in 1971 after Joslin's death. This group oversaw the publication of some twenty titles during the following decade. Malcolm Deas then edited the series alone (with advisory committees including Werner Baer, Marvin Bernstein, Rafael Segovia, Al Stepan and Bryan Roberts) for five years and some twenty titles before handing over to Simon Collier, whose advisory board included Deas, Bernstein, Clark Reynolds and Arturo Valenzuela. Alan Knight replaced Simon Collier as editor of the series in 1995.

31. Paperback editions include: Celso Furtado, *Economic Development of Latin America: Historical Background and Contemporary Problems* (1970); James Lockhart and Enrique Otte, *Letters and People of the Spanish Indies in the Sixteenth Century* (1974); Verena Martínez Alier, *Marriage, Class and Colour in Nineteenth Century Cuba* (1974); Leslie Rout, *The African Experience in Spanish America* (1976); James Lockhart and Stuart B. Schwartz, *Early Latin America: a History of Colonial Spanish America and Brazil* (1983); Victor Bulmer-Thomas, *The Political Economy of Central America since 1920* (1987); Daniel James, *Resistance and Integration: Peronism and the Argentine Working Class, 1946–1976* (1988/93) and Victor Bulmer-Thomas, *The Economic History of Latin America since Independence* (1994). Alan Knight's two-volume *The Mexican Revolution,* issued in 1986,

was published in paperback in 1990 by the University of Nebraska Press. Oxford University Press, by contrast, has published a generally strong list of general country studies, but since these were commissioned by its New York office there are no British authors.

32. Scholars of Latin American history and politics who left (and sometimes returned to) the UK, principally for the USA, include: Simon Collier, Alan Knight, Peter Bakewell, Gerald Martin, Gordon Brotherston, Barry Carr, J.H. Elliott, Daniel James, W. Mathew, Susan Deans-Smith, Ken Duncan, David Cahill, Kenneth Maxwell, George Lovell, Norman Long, Bryan Roberts, David Rock, Ian Roxborough, A.J.R. Russell-Wood, David Slater, Peter Winn. The volumes of the CHLA issued to date are as follows: Vols I and II *Colonial Latin America* (1984); Vol. III *From Independence to c.1870* (1985); Vols IV and V *From c.1870–1930* (1986); Vol. VI *Latin America since 1930: Economy, Society and Politics* (two parts 1994); Vol. VII *Latin America since 1930: Mexico, Central America and the Caribbean* (1990); Vol. VIII *Latin America since 1930: Spanish South America* (1991); Vol. X *Latin America since 1930: Ideas, Culture and Society* (1995); Vol. XI *Bibliographical Essays*. Vol. IX *Latin America since 1930: Brazil* (part 1) and *International Relations* (part 2) is outstanding. A separate *Cambridge History of the Native Peoples of the Americas* is to be published.

33. S. Collier, review of Bethell, CHLA, Vol. VI in *Times Higher Education Supplement*, 6 October 1995.

34. The 'classic' example of cliometrics is R.W. Fogel and S.L. Engerman, *Time on the Cross: the Economics of Negro Slavery*, 2 vols (Little, Brown, Boston, 1974). (This volume is instructively reviewed by Hobsbawm in *The Guardian*, 10 October 1974). Peter Laslett, *The World We Have Lost* (Methuen, London, 1965). Perhaps the most prominent exponent of this approach is Herbert S. Klein, (with J. Kelly) *Revolution and the Rebirth of Inequality: a Theory Applied to the National Revolution in Bolivia* (University of California Press, Berkeley, 1981).

35. John J. TePaske and H.S. Klein, *Royal Treasuries of the Spanish Empire in America*, 3 vols (University of North Carolina Press, Chapel Hill, 1982).

36. Linda Newson, *The Cost of Conquest: Indian Societies in Honduras under Spanish Rule* (Westview, Boulder, 1986); *Indian Survival in Colonial Nicaragua* (University of Oklahoma Press, Norman, 1987). George Lovell (1951), *Conquest and Survival in Colonial Guatemala* (McGill-Queen's University Press, Montreal, 1992).

37. Tristan Platt (1945), *Estado boliviano y ayllu andino: tierra y tributo en el norte de Potosí* (Instituto de Estudios Peruanos, Lima, 1982); 'Liberalism and Ethnocide in the Southern Andes', *History Workshop Journal*, no.17, 1984.

38. Olivia Harris (1948), 'Labour and Produce in an Ethnic Economy: Northern Potosí, Bolivia', in D. Lehmann (ed.), *Ecology and Exchange in the Andes* (CUP, Cambridge, 1982); editor (with Brooke Larson and Enrique Tandeter), *La Participación Indígena en los Mercados Surandinos: Estrategia y Reproducción Social. Siglos XVI a XX* (CERES, La Paz, 1987). (I am told that a similarly catholic approach to method and analysis may be found in archaeology, of which the leading UK practitioner in this field is Warwick Bray (1936), *Everyday Life of*

the Aztecs (Batsford, London, 1968); (ed.), *The Meeting of Two Worlds: Europe and the Americas, 1492–1650* (OUP, Oxford, 1993).) Harris is a member of a generation of anthropologists of the Andes greatly influenced by the work of John Murra. See his collection of essays, *Formaciones económicas y políticas del mundo andino* (Instituto de Estudios Peruanos, Lima, 1975) and interview in HAHR, vol. 64, no. 4, 1984. Brian Roberts (1939) and Norman Long (1936), *Miners, Peasants and Entrepreneurs: Regional Development in the Central Highlands of Peru* (CUP, Cambridge, 1984); *Peasant Cooperatives and Capitalist Development in Central Peru* (University of Texas Press, Austin, 1978). Kenneth Duncan and Ian Rutledge with Colin Harding (eds), *Land and Labour in Latin America: Essays in the Development of Agrarian Capitalism in the Nineteenth and Twentieth Centuries* (CUP, Cambridge, 1971).

39. Peter Winn, *Weavers of Revolution: The Yarur Workers and Chile's Road to Socialism* (OUP, New York, 1986). For an appreciation of Winn's book, see Perry Anderson, 'The Common and the Particular', *International Labour and Working Class History*, no. 36, 1989.

40. D.C.M. Platt (1934–89), *Latin America and British Trade, 1806–1914* (A. and C. Black, London, 1972); (ed.) *Business Imperialism, 1840–1930: an Inquiry Based on British Experience in Latin America* (Clarendon Press, Oxford, 1977). For a sense of Platt's involvement in this debate, see his articles 'The Imperialism of Free Trade: Some Reservations', *Economic History Review*, 2nd series, vol. 21, no. 2, 1968; 'Further Objections to an "Imperialism of Free Trade", 1830–1860', *Economic History Review*, 2nd series, vol. 26, no. 1, 1973; 'Dependency in Nineteenth Century Latin America; an Historian Objects', LARR, vol. 15, no. 1, 1980, both of which go beyond a Latin American based critique of John Gallagher and Ronald Robinson, 'The Imperialism of Free Trade', *Economic Historical Review*, 2nd series, vol. 6, no. 1, 1953. For an obituary of Platt, by Rory Miller, see BLAR, vol. 9, no. 1, 1990.

41. This is particularly evident in the work of Platt's doctoral student Colin Lewis (1944): editor (with Christopher Abel) *Latin America: Economic Imperialism and the State* (Athlone, London, 1985) (paperback edn. 1988); *Public Policy and Private Initiative: Railway Building in São Paulo, 1860–1899*, ILAS, Research Paper no.26, 1991. Charles Jones (1949), 'The State and Business Practice in Argentina, 1862–1914', in Abel and Lewis, *Economic Imperialism and the State*; *International Business in the Nineteenth Century: the Rise and Fall of a Cosmopolitan Bourgeoisie* (Wheatsheaf, Brighton, 1987). Rory Miller (1949), *Britain and Latin America in the Nineteenth and Twentieth Centuries* (Longman, London, 1993); (ed.), *Region and Class: Modern Peruvian History* (ILAS, Liverpool, 1987). Henry Finch (1941), *A Political Economy of Uruguay since 1870* (Macmillan, London, 1981); editor (with Rory Miller), *Technology Transfer and Economic Development in Latin America, 1850–1930* (ILAS, Liverpool, 1986); Luis Ortega (1950), 'Crisis and Change in Chile's Economy and Society', PhD, University of London, 1979; 'The First Four Decades of Chile's Coal Industry', JLAS, vol. 14, no. 1, 1982. Robert Greenhill (with Rory Miller), 'The Peruvian Government and the Nitrate Trade, 1873–1879', JLAS, vol. 5. part 1, 1974. Roger Gravill, *The Anglo-Argentine Connection, 1900–1939* (Westview, Boulder,

1985); 'State Intervention in Argentina's Export Trade between the Wars', JLAS, vol. 2, part 2, 1970.

42. Andrew Thompson, 'Informal Empire? An Exploration in the History of Anglo-Argentine Relations, 1810–1914', JLAS, vol. 24, no. 2, 1992; A.G. Hopkins, 'Informal Empire in Argentina: an Alternative View', JLAS, vol. 26, no. 2, 1994.

43. See, for instance, the introduction to Paul Gootenberg, *Imagining Development: Economic Ideas in Peru's 'Fictitious Prosperity' of Guano, 1840–1880* (University of California Press, Berkeley, 1993).

44. Bill Albert (1942), *South America and the World Economy from Independence to 1930* (Macmillan, London, 1983); *South America and the First World War: the Impact of War on Brazil, Argentina, Peru and Chile* (CUP, Cambridge, 1988).

45. John Fisher (1943), *Commercial Relations between Spain and Spanish America in the Era of Free Trade* (ILAS, Liverpool, 1985); editor (with A. Kuethe and A. McFarlane), *Reform and Insurrection in Bourbon New Granada and Peru* (Louisiana State University Press, Baton Rouge, 1990).

46. Victor Bulmer-Thomas (1948), *The Political Economy of Central America since 1920* (CUP, Cambridge, 1987); *The Economic History of Latin America since Independence* (CUP, Cambridge, 1995).

47. One should, though, make mention of Maxine Molyneux's 'No God, No Husband. Anarchist Feminism in Nineteenth Century Argentina', *Latin American Perspectives*, vol. 13, no. 1, 1986. Dore and Stubbs work on politics as well as history, wherein their focus has been on economics: E. Dore, *The Peruvian Mining Industry: Growth, Stagnation and Crisis, 1900–1977* (Westview, Boulder, 1988); J. Stubbs, *Tobacco on the Periphery: a Case Study in Cuban Labour History, 1860–1958* (CUP, Cambridge, 1985). For US studies on gender, see R. Radford Ruether and R. Skinner Keller (eds), *Women and Religion in Latin America* (Harper and Row, San Francisco, 1983); C.R. Boxer, *Women in Iberian Expansion Overseas, 1415–1815* (OUP, New York, 1975); Silvia Arrom, *The Women of Mexico City, 1790–1857* (Stanford University Press, Stanford, 1985); Asunción Lavrin (ed.), *Latin American Women: Historical Perspectives* (Greenwood Press, Westport, 1978); Patricia Seed, *To Love, Honor and Obey in Colonial Mexico* (Stanford University Press, Stanford, 1988); Donna Guy, *Sex and Danger in Buenos Aires: Prostitution, Family and Nation in Argentina* (University of Nebraska Press, Lincoln, 1991); Jean Franco, *Plotting Women: Gender and Representation in Mexico* (Verso, London, 1989). For race, T. Skidmore, *Black into White: Race and Nationality in Brazilian Thought* (Duke University Press, Durham North Carolina, 2nd ed. 1993); M. Mörner (ed.), *Race and Class in Latin America* (Columbia University Press, New York, 1970); Richard Graham (ed.), *The Idea of Race in Latin America, 1870–1940* (University of Texas Press, Austin, 1990); Leslie Rout, *The African Experience in Spanish America* (CUP, Cambridge, 1976).

48. Valerie Fraser (1949), *The Architecture of Conquest: Building in the Viceroyalty of Peru, 1535–1635* (CUP, Cambridge, 1990); (with O. Baddeley), *Drawing the Line: Art and Cultural Identity in Contemporary Latin America* (Verso, London, 1989). Dawn Ades, *Art in Latin America: The Modern Era, 1820–1950* (Yale

University Press, New Haven, 1989). John King (1950), *Sur: A Study of the Argentine Literary Journal and its Role in the Development of a Culture, 1931–1970* (CUP, Cambridge, 1986); *Magical Reels: a History of Cinema in Latin America* (Verso, London, 1990). The present author should declare an interest – he is an editor (with John King) of the Verso series in which the Fraser/Baddeley and King volumes have been published. A recent addition to that series is a rare title on sport – Tony Mason (1938), *Passion of the People? Football in South America* (Verso, London, 1995).

49. Gerald Martin (1944), 'The Literature, Music and Art of Latin America, 1870–1930', in Bethell (ed.), CHLA, IV, 1986; *Journeys through the Labyrinth: Latin American Fiction in the Twentieth Century* (Verso, London, 1989).

50. Stephen Greenblatt, *Marvelous Possessions: the Wonder of the New World* (Clarendon Press, Oxford, 1991); Doris Sommer, *Foundational Fictions: The National Romances of Latin America* (University of California Press, Berkeley, 1991).

51. Peter Hulme, *Europe and the Native Caribbean, 1492–1797* (Routledge, London, 1986); Benedict Anderson (1936), *Imagined Communities. Reflections on the Origins and Spread of Nationalism* (Verso, London, 2nd ed. 1991).

52. Gordon Brotherston (1939), *The Emergence of the Latin American Novel* (CUP, Cambridge, 1977); *Book of the Fourth World: Reading the Native Americans through Their Literature* (CUP, Cambridge, 1992). Anthony Pagden, *The Fall of Natural Man: the American Indian and the Origins of Comparative Ethnography* (CUP, Cambridge, 1982); *Spanish Imperialism and the Political Imagination* (Yale University Press, New Haven, 1990). Malcolm Deas (1941), *Del Poder y la Gramática y Otros Ensayos sobre Historia, Política y Literatura Colombianas* (Tercer Mundo Editores, Bogotá, 1993); editor, Eloy Alfaro, *Narraciones Históricas* (Corporación Editora Nacional, Quito, 1983). (Deas has supervised over a dozen doctorates to completion over the last decade, which may be a record within humanities research on Latin America.) David Brading (1936), *The First America: the Spanish Monarchy, Creole Patriots and the Liberal State, 1492–1867* (CUP, Cambridge, 1991); (ed.), *Church and State in Bourbon Mexico: the Diocese of Michoacán, 1749–1810* (CUP, Cambridge, 1994). Amongst Brading's research students obtaining their doctorates in inauspicious times one should note Dudley Ankerson and Ian Jacobs, who contributed to D. Brading, *Caudillo and Peasant in the Mexican Revolution* (CUP, Cambridge, 1980).

53. 'Bolívar and the Caudillos', HAHR, vol. 63, 1983.

54. Michael Costeloe (1939), *Response to Revolution: Imperial Spain and the Spanish American Revolutions, 1810–1840* (CUP, Cambridge, 1986); *The Central Republic in Mexico, 1835–1846* (CUP, Cambridge, 1993).

55. Rebecca Earle (1964), 'Indian Rebellion and Bourbon Reform in New Granada: Riots in Pasto, 1780–1800', HAHR, vol. 73, no. 1, 1993; 'The Spanish Political Crisis of 1820 and the Loss of New Granada', *Colonial Latin American Historical Review*, vol. 3, no. 3, 1994. Will Fowler (1966), 'Dreams of Stability: Mexican Political Thought during the "Forgotten Years": an Analysis of the Beliefs of the Creole Intelligentsia, 1821–1853', BLAR, vol. 14, no. 3, 1995; 'Valentín Gómez Farías: Perceptions of Radicalism in Independent Mexico, 1821–1847', BLAR, vol. 15, no. 1, 1996. Matthias Röhrig Assunção

(1955), *A Guerra dos Ben-te-vis: A Balaida na memoria oral* (SIOGE, São, Luis 1988); 'Popular Culture and Regional Society in Nineteenth-century Maranhao, Brazil', BLAR, vol. 14, no. 3, 1995. Adolfo Bonilla,'Liberalism and the Enlightenment in Central America, 1759–1839', PhD, University of Manchester, 1996. A colleague of Michael Costeloe's, who belongs to the same younger generation but has directed his attention to the history of ideas in a broader sense (in keeping with his training at Cambridge), is Fernando Cervantes, *The Devil in the New World: the Impact of Diabolism in New Spain* (Yale University Press, New Haven, 1994); 'The Impact of Christianity in Spanish America', BLAR, vol. 14, no. 2, 1995. Paula Alonso, also taught at Bristol in the early 1990s; her speciality is late nineteenth century Argentina: *The Origins of the Argentine Radical Party, 1889–1898*, DPhil, University of Oxford, 1993; 'Politics and Elections in Buenos Aires, 1890–1898: the Performance of the Radical Party', JLAS, vol. 25, no. 3, 1993.

56. Eduardo Posada-Carbó (1956), *The Colombian Caribbean: a Regional History* (OUP, Oxford, 1996); editor, *Elections Before Democracy: the History of Elections in Europe and Latin America* (Macmillan, Basingstoke, 1996).

57. Christopher Abel (1946), editor (with Nissa Torrents), *José Martí: Revolutionary Democrat* (Athlone, London, 1986); *Iglesia, Partidos y Política en Colombia* (Universidad Nacional, Bogotá, 1987).

58. Murdo MacLeod, *Spanish Central America: a Socioeconomic History, 1520–1720* (University of California Press, Berkeley, 1973); editor (with Robert Wasserstrom), *Spaniards and Indians in Southeastern Mesoamerica: Essays on the History of Ethnic Relations* (University of Nebraska Press, Lincoln, 1983). David Browning, *El Salvador: Landscape and Society* (Clarendon Press, Oxford, 1971).

59. I belong myself to this second group – James Dunkerley (1953), *Power in the Isthmus: a Political History of Modern Central America* (Verso, London, 1988); *Rebellion in the Veins: Political Struggle in Bolivia, 1952–1982* (Verso, London, 1984).

60. In addition to the work of Knight, Brading, Bulmer-Thomas, Dunkerley, see Ian Roxborough (1947), 'Theories of Revolution: the Evidence from Latin America', *LSE Quarterly*, vol. 3, no. 2, 1989; Paul Garner, *La Revolución en la Provincia: Soberanía Estatal y Caudillismo en las Montañas de Oaxaca, 1910–1920* (FCE, Mexico, 1988); 'Regional Development in Oaxaca during the Porfiriato (1876–1911)' (ILAS, Liverpool, 1995).

61. Robin Blackburn, *The Overthrow of Colonial Slavery, 1776–1848* (Verso, London, 1988). Amongst the doctorates supervised by Leslie Bethell are: Luis Carlos Soares, 'Urban Slavery in Nineteenth Century Rio de Janeiro', PhD, University of London, 1988; Maria Teresa Ribeiro de Oliveira Versiani, 'The Cotton Textile Industry of Minas Gerais, Brazil: Beginnings and Early Development', PhD, University of London, 1991; Eduardo da Silva, 'Slaves, Freedmen and Free Men of Colour in the Transition from Slavery in Brazil: a Case Study in the Life, Times and Ideas of Dom Oba II d'Africa, Prince of the People, c.1845–1890', PhD, University of London, 1992. Maria de Fátima Silva Gouvea, 'Politics in Rio de Janeiro Province under the Empire (1822–89)', PhD, University of London, 1989. See also, Jaime Reis, *Abolition*

and the Economics in North East Brazil, ILAS, University of Glasgow, Occasional Paper no. 11, 1974.

62. Hugh Thomas (1931), *The Spanish Civil War* (Penguin, Harmondsworth, 3rd ed. 1977); *Cuba, or the Pursuit of Freedom* (Eyre and Spottiswode, London, 1971); *The Conquest of Mexico* (Hutchinson, London, 1993).

63. David Nicholls (1936–96), *From Dessalines to Duvalier: Race, Colour and National Independence in Haiti* (Macmillan, Basingstoke, 1979); *Haiti in Caribbean Context: Ethnicity, Economy and Revolt* (Macmillan, Basingstoke, 1985); *Deity and Domination: Images of God and the State in the Nineteenth Century* (Routledge, London, 1989).

64. John Hemming (1935), *The Conquest of the Incas* (Macmillan, London, 1970); *Amazon Frontier: the Defeat of the Brazilian Indians* (Macmillan, London, 1987).

65. Richard M. Morse (1922), *From Community to Metropolis: a Biography of São Paulo* (Florida University Press, Gainesville, 1958); *New World Soundings: Culture and Ideology in the Americas* (Johns Hopkins University Press, Baltimore, 1989). See, for instance, W.H. Prescott, *The Conquest of Mexico* (New York, 1844), and *The Conquest of Peru* (New York, 1847); H.H. Bancroft, *Native Races of the Pacific States of North America* (New York, 1875); F. Parkman, *France and England in North America* (New York, 1866–85).

66. Glen Dealy, *The Public Man: an Interpretation of Latin American and Other Catholic Countries* (University of Massachusetts Press, Amherst, 1977); *The Latin Americans: Spirit and Ethos* (Westview, Boulder, 1992); Claudio Véliz, *The Centralist Tradition in Latin America* (Princeton University Press, Princeton, 1980); *The New World of the Gothic Fox: Culture and Economy in English and Spanish America* (University of California Press, Berkeley, 1994).

67. Howard J. Wiarda (ed.), *Politics and Social Change in Latin America. Still a Distinct Tradition?* (Westview Press, Boulder, 3rd. ed. 1992), p. 5. For comparable cultural generalisations which are more 'time-constrained' but less geographically restricted, see Francis Fukuyama, *The End of History and the Last Man* (Hamish Hamilton, London, 1992); Samuel Huntington, *The Third Wave: Democratisation in the Late Twentieth Century* (University of Oklahoma Press, Norman, 1991).

68. J.H. Elliott, reply to Claudio Véliz, *New York Review of Books*, 17 November 1994. For a comprehensive consideration of British relations with Latin America, see Victor Bulmer-Thomas (ed.), *Britain and Latin America: a Changing Relationship* (CUP, Cambridge, 1989).

69. Ian Roxborough, 'Unity and Diversity in Latin American History', *JLAS*, vol. 16, no. 1, 1984.

70. Selective quotation is usually unfair but does not always bear false witness: 'the history of capital accumulation is the history of class struggles, of political movements, of the affirmation of ideologies, and of the establishment of forms of domination and reaction against them.' F.H. Cardoso and E. Faletto, *Dependency and Development in Latin America* (University of California Press, Berkeley, 1979), p. xviii (original Spanish version, 1969). 'Earlier the marxist tradition, especially Hegelian marxism, rose above analysis of the 'who governs?' type associated with Dahl, asserting that power and government are

not the same thing and even that the phenomenology of government and the substantive identity of the groups and individuals who hold office did not explain the structure of domination upholding the government. Today, however, doubts over the revolutionary dynamic of social classes and the relations between classes, parties and the state have left the marxists orphaned, deprived of a proud and omniscient knowledge.' ('Régimen Político y Cambio Social. (Algunas Reflexiones a Propósito del Caso Brasileño)', in Norbert Lechner (ed.), *Estado y Política en América Latina* (Siglo XXI, Mexico, 1981), pp. 273–4.) 'Since the left has not been capable of a self-critique which takes into account what is going on in Eastern Europe, it also continues to propose a variation of the old therapy. Hence the debate often is a very ideological one of liberalism against statism, while probably neither liberalism nor statism is the solution . . . we have to desacralize the state and to recognise that the state is an instrument . . . the process of income concentration is going on, on and on. Inflation serves very well as an instrument of income concentration . . . And, again, unfortunately, the left continues to approach the problem in an old-fashioned way, as if the control of inflation would only benefit capital.' ('The Crisis of Development in Latin America', in *Eight Essays on the Crisis of Development in Latin America* (CEDLA, Amsterdam, 1991), pp. 139; 141.) 'The market solves some problems, but not that of poverty. You have to have a state and an effective reform of the apparatus of the state.' *The Guardian*, London, 5 October 1994.

71. 'The Dark Side of Brazilian Conviviality', *London Review of Books*, September 1994.

72. This is tricky territory that I am unqualified to survey. However, it is plain that any definition of 'intellectual' in Latin America cannot usefully be limited to 'academic'. If it were the list of those members who pursued a political career it would be very brief and contemporary, including few more than Cardoso, Alejandro Foxley, Guido Di Tella and Víctor Hugo Cárdenas (although more took up university posts after holding power). A wider category could embrace Sarmiento, Mitre, Mariátegui, Sergio Ramírez, Rómulo Gallegas, Octavio Paz, Mario Vargas Llosa, Francisco Weffort (who all more or less actively sought some kind of public office) but not, in my view Fuentes, Cortázar, Galeano, García Márquez or Jorge Castañeda (who write about politics before all else), still less individuals such as José Sarney, who happen to write in their spare time to indifferent effect (even Batista wrote a book . . .). The main point is of a higher political profile given to intellectuals than in the UK or North America. See the suggestive chapter on this in Jorge Castañeda, *Utopia Unarmed: The Latin American Left after the Cold War* (Knopf, New York, 1993); Daniel Pécault, *Entre le Peuple et la Nation: Les Intellectuels et la Politique au Brésil* (Maison des Sciences de l'Homme, Paris 1989).

73. In January 1995 Riordan Roett, Director of Latin American Studies at Johns Hopkins School of Advanced International Studies, wrote a four-page newsletter for the Emerging Markets Group of the Chase Manhattan Group.

Perhaps too excited by the prospect of an audience of aggressive bankers, Prof. Roett noted that the Zapatista uprising in Chiapas had increased the price of 'Indian blood': 'Not long ago, it was valued less than two chickens, now it is the condition for the largest loan of ignomy in history.' However, the article caused a scandal because of Roett's expressed opinion that the Mexican government 'will need to eliminate the Zapatistas to demonstrate their effective control of the national territory and of security policy'. The bank immediately distanced itself from these comments. Examples of Roett's academic work include *The Politics of Foreign Aid in the Brazilian Northeast* (University of Tennessee Press, Nashville, 1972), and the edited volume *Brazil in the 1960s* (University of Tennessee Press, Nashville, 1972). Of course, members of the left too offer their views in non-academic forums, and quite often are employed in 'think-tanks' and para-academic non-governmental organisations, sometimes provoking polemic: J. Petras and M. Morley, 'The Retreat of the Intellectuals', in *Latin America in the Time of Cholera* (Routledge, London, 1992).

74. *Latin American Studies in the Universities and Polytechnics of the United Kingdom, 1988–89* (ILAS, London, 1989); *Research on Latin America in the Humanities and Social Sciences in the Universities and Polytechnics of the United Kingdom, 1988–91* (ILAS, London, 1992) and *Latin American and Caribbean Studies in the Humanities and Social Sciences in the United Kingdom* (ILAS, London, 1996). Although their work will be listed below, it is here worth identifying the principal teachers of politics (interpreted broadly) at the main centres outside London: Essex – Christian Anglade, Joe Foweraker and Ernesto Laclau; Glasgow – Peter Flynn, Phil O'Brien, David Stansfield; Liverpool – Walter Little, Benny Pollack and Lewis Taylor; Oxford – Alan Angell, Malcolm Deas, Andrew Hurrell and Laurence Whitehead. (Al Stepan was appointed Gladstone Professor of Government at the University of Oxford in 1996).

75. A variously entitled general politics course has been taught by Richard Moseley-Williams; David Rock; George Philip; and James Dunkerley. International Relations was long taught by Fred Parkinson, followed by another member of the UCL staff, Nicola Miller. Political Sociology was established by Ian Roxborough, who was succeeded, after some hiatus, by Maxine Molyneux. Indian and Peasant Politics was set up by Olivia Harris and Stephen Nugent of Goldsmiths' College. Amongst the specialist options taught in the last thirty years are: Latin American Legal Systems (Ian Kennedy); Contemporary Politics of Argentina (Richard Moseley-Williams); The Military in Latin America (George Philip); Politics of Central America (James Dunkerley and Rachel Sieder); Latin American Security Issues (Virginia Gamba-Stonehouse); Political Ideas (James Dunkerley); and Gender and Politics (Maxine Molyneux).

76. 'We prefer for purposes of analysis to reject the idea of a continuum from democracy to totalitarianism, and to stress the distinctive nature of authoritarian regimes . . . regimes which are not clearly democratic or totalitarian will be treated merely as deviations from these ideal-types.' 'An Authoritarian

Regime: Spain', in S. Rokkan (ed.), *Mass Politics* (Free Press, New York, 1970). Even 25 years later this approach is analytically plausible (provided that one allows for an exceptionally fluid exchange between 'authoritarian' and 'totalitarian', in a manner explicitly repudiated by Jeane Kirkpatrick, see below). However, apart from its evident vulnerability to manichean appropriation in the Cold War epoch, I believe that such a viewpoint was as conducive to obscuring the nature of the regimes in the small Central American and Andean countries as it was helpful in understanding those in the Southern Cone. Rachel Sieder and James Dunkerley, 'The Military in Central America: the Challenge of Transition', ILAS, Occasional Paper No. 5, 1994.

77. In December 1995 the date of the constitution prevailing in each Latin American republic was as follows: Argentina 1853 (with significant reforms in 1994); Bolivia 1967; Brazil 1988; Chile 1980; Colombia 1991; Costa Rica 1949; Cuba 1976; Dominican Republic 1966; Ecuador 1978; El Salvador 1983; Guatemala 1985; Haiti 1987; Honduras 1965 (with reforms in 1981–2); Mexico 1917 (with reforms in 1992); Nicaragua 1987; Panama 1972 (with reforms in 1983); Paraguay 1967; Peru 1993; Uruguay 1967; Venezuela 1961.

78. Since the importance of the Cuban Revolution in Europe was more symbolic (of both 'decolonisation' and 'anti–imperialism') than to do with narrow partisanship, it attracted some sympathy from a broad political spectrum although many preferred to pass silently over the details of its internal political regime. Of those that did not, here are two British examples of what I consider typical 'solidarity' and 'critical comprehension' positions with respect to the democratic question.

> The changes wrought by the internal politics of Cuba in the 1970s have been as dramatic as the foreign policies. The period, aptly characterised by Fidel Castro as a "phase of intense legality", has been particularly marked by the process of institutionalising the Revolution. A new, socialist Constitution has been formulated, debated and adopted by the Cuban people. Popularly elected assemblies of *People's Power*, at local, provincial and national level, are now operating throughout the country. As a result, decision-making and the organisation of the economy have been decentralised. The roles of the main organisations have been clearly defined and enhanced. And the Cuban Communist Party (PCC) has held its first, truly revolutionary congress.

(John Griffiths and Peter Griffiths, *Cuba: the Second Decade* (Writers and Readers, London, 1979), pp. 9–10.)

> After more than thirty years in power, Castro is still far from achieving the Utopian goals that he set in the Moncada programme and in the heady days of revolutionary triumph. But Cuba has achieved a degree of development in the economic and above all social fields that surpasses that of most countries of Latin America ... the Cuban Revolution was an authentic response to the problems of underdevelopment and neo-colonial dependency by a nationalist elite drawn mainly from the middle-class and backed by popular support ... because many of its leaders came from a class closely bound up with the state, the new regime tended to see the state as the fundamental instrument for the

transformation of society. Political and economic centralisation in one degree or another was in many cases unavoidable because of internal contradictions or external pressure.

(Sebastian Balfour, *Castro* (Longman, London, 1990), pp. 161–2.)

79. It is worth taking the risk of tiring the reader with another couple of quotations on this theme, which may now seem most anachronistic but at the time excited hot debate in Europe, which, after all, was living in the wake of the protest movements of 1968–9 that had exercised a disproportionate impact on the universities. This was scarcely less true for the UK than for the continental countries, and although the CPGB was far less influential than its counterparts, intellectual Trotskyism was not. First, Allende's concise formulation of his strategy:

> People speak of *La Via Chilena* – the Chilean road to socialism. What the Chilean people are doing has not yet been done in other countries. In our political model, starting from pluralism, democracy, and liberty, we want to use the bourgeois institutional framework to achieve the changes in the political, economic and social fields which the country is demanding and to achieve socialism. In the Chilean case the use of legal institutions is possible because they are open to the possibility of change. It was by using these bourgeois institutions, skilfully handled by the workers, that we got into government in the first place, and these same institutions have enabled us to achieve certain of the objectives which we set ourselves.

(Salvador Allende, 'The Chilean Road to Socialism', in J. Ann Zammit (ed.), *The Chilean Road to Socialism* (University of Texas Press and the Institute of Development Studies, University of Sussex, London, 1973), p. 19.)

(This volume resulted from a 10-day round table jointly organised by ODEPLAN and the IDS at Sussex University in March 1972. Amongst the participants from the UK other than Ann Zammit were Emanuel De Kadt, David Lehmann, Dudley Seers, Francis Seton, Brian Van Arkadie, Adam Watson.) Somewhat over a year before he made this statement Allende had two long conversations with the young French Marxist Régis Debray, whose confident attachment to Leninism had been little affected by three years in a Bolivian jail. Although displaying a distinct gallic tincture, Debray's general attitude is quite typical of the British 'new left' of the day:

> *Debray*: Comrade President, allow me to look ahead a little. You know that Leninism has nothing against compromise, as long as tactical compromises serve as a useful purpose in the revolutionary struggle of the proletariat, as long as they are absolutely necessary and do not jeopardize the long-term development of the class struggle. The conciliatory conditions under which the process which we are seeing today is progressing doubtless correspond to the objective and specific conditions of Chile. The problem now is whether these conditions can continue to favour the advancement of this process; in other words, how can the transition from a bourgeois system to another more democratic, more revolutionary, more proletarian system be achieved without a break? History contains many examples of a social class which, to avoid being overthrown, prefers to sacrifice a finger or two to save the hand and the arm. One may wonder whether the proletariat and their allies are going to be hemmed in by

the bourgeois institutions, and pacified with a few reforms here and there, or whether at a given moment the framework will be broken to create a proletarian democracy? Is the proletariat going to assert itself over the bourgeoisie, or will the bourgeoisie gradually remould the proletariat and reabsorb it into its world. Doubtless, I'm over-generalizing, but basically my question would be: 'Who is using who? Who is taking who for a ride?' That's putting it brutally and perhaps a little provocative . . .

Allende: I don't believe that a comrade can ask me questions whose intention is to provoke.

Debray: Well, there are those who say I'm a professional agent provocateur, Comrade President.

Allende: I shall not allow myself to be provoked.

Debray: The question is important.

Allende: And the answer is short – the proletariat.

(Régis Debray, *Conversations with Allende* (New Left Books, London, 1971), p. 122.)

80. John J. Johnson, *Political Change in Latin America: the Emergence of the Middle Sectors* (Stanford University Press, Stanford, 1958), p. 5.

81. David Apter, *The Politics of Modernization* (University of Chicago Press, Chicago, 1965), p. 452.

82. Samuel Huntington, *Political Order in Changing Societies* (Yale University Press, New Haven, 1968); *The Third Wave: Democratisation in the Late Twentieth Century* (University of Oklahoma Press, Norman, 1991); Jeane Kirkpatrick, *Dictatorships and Double Standards: Rationalism and Reagan in Politics* (Simon and Schuster, New York, 1982).

83. The first volume, published by OUP, collected papers given at Chatham House in February 1965 by Latin Americans of distinctly progressive, 'dependista' stripe: Aníbal Pinto, Torcuato Di Tella, Jacques Chonchol, Víctor Urquidi, Osvaldo Sunkel, Celso Furtado, Helio Jaguaribe, Orlando Fals Borda, Moisés González Navarro, Felipe Herrera. The second book, also issued by OUP, was more mixed in origin and political outlook, the contributors being Richard Adams, Eric Hobsbawm, José Nun, Alistair Hennessy, François Chevalier, Emanuel De Kadt, Oscar Cornblit, and Hugh Thomas.

84. Alan Angell (1939), *Politics and the Labour Movement in Chile* (OUP, Oxford, 1972); *Chile de Alessandri a Pinochet en busca de la Utopía* (Editorial Andrés Bello, Santiago, 1993).

85. Kenneth Medhurst (1938) (ed.), *Allende's Chile* (Hart-Davis, London, 1972); *The Church and Labour in Colombia* (Manchester University Press, Manchester, 1984).

86. Peter Flynn (1935), *Brazil: A Political Analysis* (E. Benn, London, 1978); 'Collor, Corruption and Crisis: Time for Reflection', JLAS, vol. 25, no. 2, 1993.

87. Celia Szusterman (1947), *Frondizi and the Politics of Developmentalism: Argentina, 1955–62* (Macmillan, Basingstoke, 1993); 'Soldiers of Perón (Review and Commentary)', JLAS, vol. 16, no. 1, 1984. María D'Alva Kinzo (1951), *Legal Opposition Politics under Authoritarian Rule in Brazil: the Case of the MDB, 1966–1979* (Macmillan, Basingstoke, 1988); (ed.), *Brazil: the Challenge of the*

1990s (ILAS, London, 1993). Carol Graham (1962), *Peru's APRA: Parties, Politics and the Elusive Quest for Democracy* (Westview, Boulder, 1992); *Safety Nets, Politics and the Poor: Transitions to Market Economics* (Brookings Institution, Washington, 1994). Anita Isaacs (1958), *Military Rule and Transition in Ecuador, 1972–92* (Macmillan, Basingstoke, 1993). Jenny Pearce, *Under the Eagle: US Intervention in Central America and the Caribbean* (Latin America Bureau, London, 1981); *Promised Land: Peasant Rebellion in Chalatenango, El Salvador* (Latin America Bureau, London, 1986).

88. Given the extraordinarily influential role of *The Civic Culture* in post-war western political analysis, it is worth noting that the case of Mexico was a last-minute replacement for Sweden (the authors make no real explanation for this very odd transfer) in a comparative survey (with USA, UK, Germany, Italy) in which 1,000 people in each country responded to a wide-ranging structured questionnaire in June/July 1959 (March 1960 in the USA) and some 125 respondents were subsequently re-interviewed. Almond and Verba's findings should not shock:

> What has been most striking about the Mexican pattern of political culture are the imbalances and inconsistencies. Mexico is the lowest of all five countries in the frequency with which impact and significance are attributed to government and in its citizens' expectations of equal and considerate treatment at the hands of the bureaucracy and the police. At the same time, the frequency with which Mexicans express pride in their political system is considerably higher than that of Germans or Italians.

(Gabriel Almond and Sidney Verba, *The Civic Culture: Political Attitudes and Democracy in Five Nations* (Princeton University Press, Princeton, 1963, 3rd. ed. Sage, London, 1980), p. 310.)

In 1980 a set of chapters reviewing the original volume was published, Ann Craig and Wayne Cornelius producing a string of respectful but quite decisive and detailed methodological criticisms of Almond and Verba:

> Their measures of political involvement are ... limited to questions about frequency and perceived freedom of discussing politics, attentiveness to and feelings about political campaigns, perceptions of citizens' responsibilities for community involvement, and an assortment of questions about partisanship. In short, they are questions which essentially tap *cognitive* involvement in politics and public affairs.

(*The Civic Culture Revisited* (Sage, London, 1980), p. 339.)

89. G. O'Donnell, P. Schmitter and L. Whitehead (eds), *Transitions from Authoritarian Rule: Prospects for Democracy*, 4 vols (Johns Hopkins University Press, Baltimore, 1986); 'On the state, democratisation and some conceptual problems: a Latin American view with glances at some post-communist societies', Helen Kellogg Institute for International Studies, University of Notre Dame, Working Paper no. 192, 1993.

90. I am here striving to describe a *style* that rises above, and aside from, these systems whilst embodying the better elements of them. It is a style perhaps best expressed by Adam Przeworski, who has no British counterpart. 'Democracy as a Contingent Outcome in Conflicts', in J. Elster and R. Slagstad (eds),

Constitutionalism and Democracy (CUP, Cambridge, 1988); *Democracy and the Market: Political and Economic Reforms in Eastern Europe and Latin America* (CUP, Cambridge, 1991). A more explicitly left-wing revisionist approach from the USA is J. Cohen and J. Rogers, *Associations and Democracy* (Verso, London, 1995). The most sure-footed British commentator on the changing global scenario and its theoretical aspects is David Held (ed.), *Prospects for Democracy* (Polity, Oxford, 1993); *Models of Democracy* (Polity, Oxford, 1987).

91. Laurence Whitehead (1944) (ed. with G. Di Palma), *The Central American Impasse* (St Martin's Press, New York, 1986); 'The Imposition of Democracy', in A. Lowenthal (ed.), *Exporting Democracy: the United States and Latin America* (Johns Hopkins University Press, Baltimore, 1991). See also notes 89 and 98.

92. Charles Gillespie (1958–91), *Negotiating Democracy: Politicians and Generals in Uruguay* (CUP, Cambridge, 1991); 'Democratic Consolidation in the Southern Cone and Brazil: Beyond Political Disarticulation?', *Third World Quarterly*, vol. 11, no. 2, 1989. For Uruguay see Francisco Panizza, *Uruguay: Batllismo y Después* (Banda Oriental, Montevideo, 1990); Aidan Rankin, 'Reflections on the Non-Revolution in Uruguay', *New Left Review*, no. 211, 1995.

93. Giovanni Sartori's *Political Parties* (CUP, Cambridge, 1976) has been out of print in the UK for several years. In late 1995 there was no copy in Britain's 'premier' social science library – that of the LSE, which had it on order – nor any in the University's Senate House library. The only copy in London – at QMW – had gone missing. Until this situation is rectified the curious can consult the chapter by Giovanni Sartori, 'The Influence of Electoral Systems: Faulty Laws or Faulty Method?', in B. Grofman and A. Lijphart (eds), *Electoral Laws and their Political Consequences* (Agathon, New York, 1986); 'Neither Presidentialism nor Parliamentarianism', in J. Linz and A. Valenzuela (eds), *The Failure of Presidential Democracy: Comparative Perspectives* (Johns Hopkins University Press, Baltimore, 1994). The second volume of this book is dedicated to Latin American case studies.

94. Pamela Lowden, *The Vicariate of Solidarity: Moral Opposition to Authoritarian Rule in Chile, 1973–90*, DPhil, University of Oxford, 1993. Alexandra Barahona De Brito, *Truth or Amnesty: Human Rights and Democratization in Latin America (Chile and Uruguay)*, DPhil, University of Oxford, 1994. Rachel Sieder (1966) (ed.), *Impunity in Latin America* (ILAS, London, 1995); (ed.), *Central America: Fragile Transition* (Macmillan, Basingstoke, 1996). Pilar Domingo, 'Democracy in the Making? Political Parties and Political Institutions in Bolivia, 1985–1991', DPhil, University of Oxford, 1993. 'Rule of Law and Judicial Systems in the Context of Democratisation and Economic Liberalisation: a Framework for Comparison and Analysis in Latin America', mimeo, CIDE, Mexico, 1994.

95. R. Andrew Nickson (1948), 'The Overthrow of the Stroessner Regime: Re-establishing the Status Quo?', BLAR, vol. 8, no. 2, 1989; *Local Government in Latin America* (Lynne Rienner, Boulder, 1995). Walter Little (1945), 'Political Corruption in Latin America', *Corruption and Reform*, vol. 7, 1992; 'Corruption and Reform in Venezuela', in W. Little and E. Posada-Carbó (eds), *Political*

Corruption in Europe and Latin America (Macmillan, Basingstoke, 1996). Ronaldo Munck (1951), *Revolutionary Trends in Latin America* (McGill University, Montreal, 1984); *Latin America: the Transition to Democracy* (Zed, London, 1989). Benny Pollack (1941) (with H. Rosenkranz), *Revolutionary Social Democracy: the Chilean Socialist Party* (Pinter, London, 1986); (with Alan Angell), 'The Chilean Elections of 1993: from Polarisation to Consensus', BLAR, vol. 14, no. 2, 1995.

96. *The Guardian*, London, 12 August 1995.
97. Fernando Rojas, 'Political Transition in Latin America', in *Eight Essays on the Crisis of Development in Latin America* (CEDLA, Amsterdam, 1991), p. 113. It is not surprising that much radical writing on this question is rather peevish in tone when so many who previously stood on the left appear to have 'swapped sides', some with positively damascene decision. Francisco Weffort, now a minister in the Cardoso administration, is quite typical: 'I do not think that it can be denied that democracy is the only path which Latin American countries can follow to modernity.' 'A América Errada', *Lua Nova*, São Paulo, 21, p. 39. According to José Nun,

> Some time ago, when the class paradigm was in vogue, it was quite common to proceed from the study of economic specificities of dependent capitalism in Latin America to social and political conclusions based on the operation of a class dynamic akin to the one that social scientists in the 'first world' were then discussing for their countries. In this way, it ended up looking as if economic dependency in fact had little concrete effect on the class structure.

('Democracy and Modernisation Thirty Years Later', *Latin American Perspectives*, vol. 20, no. 4, 1993).
98. I have borrowed the term 'democracy by default' from an important essay by Laurence Whitehead, 'The Alternatives to "Liberal Democracy": a Latin American Perspective', *Political Studies*, vol. XL, 1992 (reprinted in Held, *Prospects for Democracy*).
99. David Rock, 'The Survival and Restoration of Peronism', in D. Rock (ed.), *Argentina in the Twentieth Century* (Duckworth, London, 1975). Walter Little, 'The Popular Origins of Peronism', in ibid. Daniel James, *Resistance and Integration*.
100. Robin Blackburn, 'Prologue to the Cuban Revolution', *New Left Review*, no. 4, 1963; P. Binns and M. Gonzalez, 'Cuba, Castro and Socialism', *International Socialism*, no. 8, 1980; R. Blackburn, 'Class Forces in the Cuban Revolution', *International Socialism*, no. 9, 1980. Richard Gott, *Rural Guerrillas in Latin America* (Penguin, Harmondsworth, 1973). Twenty years later Gott would subvert literary genres rather than governments in *Land without Evil: Utopian Journeys across the South American Watershed* (Verso, London, 1993).
101. Toni Kapcia (1949), 'Martí, Marxism and Morality: the Evolution of an Ideology of Revolution', in R. Gillespie (ed.), *Cuba after Thirty Years: Rectification and the Revolution* (Cass, London, 1990); 'Thirty Years of Cuban Socialism', *Journal of Communist Studies*, vol. 6, no. 2, 1990. Jean Stubbs, *Cuba: the Test of Time* (Latin America Bureau, London, 1989). Mention should also be

made here of Peter Turton's study *José Martí. Architect of Cuba's Freedom* (Zed, London, 1986).

102. P. O'Brien (1943), I. Roxborough and J. Roddick, *Chile: the State and Revolution* (Macmillan, London, 1977); P. O'Brien and J. Roddick, *Chile: The Pinochet Decade* (Latin America Bureau, London, 1983).

103. D. Hojman (1946) (ed.), *Chile after 1973: Elements for the Analysis of Military Rule* (ILAS, Liverpool, 1985); *Chile: the Political Economy of Development and Democracy in the 1990s* (Macmillan, Basingstoke, 1992).

104. Colin Henfrey and Bernardo Sorj (eds), *Chilean Voice: Activists Describe their Experiences of the Popular Unity Period* (Harvester, Hassocks, 1977).

105. Alistair Horne, *Small Earthquake in Chile* (Macmillan, London, 1972 and 1990). Robert Moss, *Chile and the Marxist Experiment* (David and Charles, London, 1973).

106. George Black (1949), *Triumph of the People* (Zed, London, 1981). Maxine Molyneux (1948), 'The Nicaraguan revolution', BLAR, vol. 7, no. 2, 1988. Elizabeth Dore and John Weeks, *The Red and the Black: the Sandinistas and the Nicaraguan Revolution*, ILAS Research Paper no. 28, London 1992. Hazel Smith (1954), *Nicaragua* (Zed, London, 1993). Mike Gonzalez, *Nicaragua: What Went Wrong?* (Bookmarks, London, 1990).

107. Philip J. Williams (1959), *The Catholic Church and Politics in Nicaragua and Costa Rica* (Macmillan, Basingstoke, 1989); 'The Catholic Hierarchy in the Nicaraguan Revolution', JLAS, vol. 17, part 2, 1985. Mandy Macdonald and Mike Gatehouse, *In the Mountains of Morazán: Portrait of a Returned Refugee Community in El Salvador* (Latin America Bureau, London, 1995). Diana Pritchard (1960), 'The Legacy of Conflict: Refugees and Returnees in Central America', in Rachel Sieder (ed.), *Central America: Fragile Transition*.

108. Ian Roxborough, 'Theories of Revolution: the Evidence from Latin America', *LSE Quarterly*, vol. 3, no. 2, 1989.

109. Colin Harding (1945), 'Antonio Díaz and the Ideology of Sendero Luminoso', BLAR, vol. 7, no. 1, 1988. Lewis Taylor (1949), *Maoism in the Andes: Sendero Luminoso and the Contemporary Guerrilla Movement in Peru* (ILAS, Liverpool, 1983); *Bandits and Politics in Peru: Land and Peasant Violence in Hualgayoc, 1900–1930* (Centre for Latin American Studies, Cambridge, 1986). Neil Harvey (1961), *The New Agrarian Movement in Mexico*, ILAS Research Paper no. 23, London 1990; (ed.), *Mexico: Dilemmas of Transition* (I.B. Tauris, London, 1993). Richard Gillespie (1952), *Soldiers of Perón: Argentina's Montoneros* (Clarendon, Oxford, 1982).

110. Alan Angell, *Peruvian Labour and the Military Government since 1968*, ILAS Research Paper no.3, London 1980. John Humphrey (1950), *Capitalist Control and Workers' Struggle in the Brazilian Auto Industry* (Princeton University Press, Princeton, 1982); *Gender and Work in the Third World: Sexual Divisions in Brazilian Industry* (Tavistock, London, 1987). Ian Roxborough, *Unions and Politics in Mexico* (CUP, Cambridge, 1984).

111. The speakers at this conference were F.H. Cardoso (at the time Simón Bolívar Professor at Cambridge), L. Castillo, E.V.K. Fitzgerald, C. Fortín, M.

Kaplan, E. Laclau, D. Lehmann, M. Murmis, P. O'Brien, G. O'Donnell, A. Quijano, J. Wells.

112. Ernesto Laclau was initially registered at Nuffield College, Oxford to write a doctorate under the supervision of Ron Hartwell on 'The Sheep-breeding Industry in the Province of Buenos Aires, 1850–1900'. Perhaps it is both a good thing that he did not proceed along those lines and also a source of some relief to those who find his prose very difficult to know of this anterior, ovine phase in its development. Two essays focusing on Latin America – 'Feudalism and Capitalism in Latin America' and 'Towards a Theory of Populism' – formed the core of *Politics and Ideology in Marxist Theory* (Verso, London, 1977), which may be contrasted with *New Reflections on the Revolutions of our Time* (Verso, London, 1990) (particularly 'A Letter to Aletta').

113. David Lehmann, *Democracy and Development in Latin America: Economics, Politics and Religion in the Post-War Period* (Polity, Oxford, 1990); (with Leonardo Castillo), 'Chile's Three Agrarian Reforms: the Inheritors', BLAR, vol. 1, no. 2, 1982.

114. Colin Henfrey, 'Dependency, Modes of Production and the Class Analysis of Latin America', *Latin American Perspectives*, vol. 30/31, 1981; 'Rethinking Crisis and Social Change: Some Recent Studies of Latin America', *Third World Quarterly*, vol. 8, no. 2, 1986.

115. Paul Cammack (1950), 'The Political Economy of Contemporary Military Regimes in Latin America: From Bureaucratic Authoritarianism to Restructuring', in P. O'Brien and P. Cammack (eds), *Generals in Retreat: the Crisis of Military Rule in Latin America* (Manchester University Press, Manchester, 1986); 'Democracy and Development in Latin America', *Journal of International Development*, vol. 3, no. 5, 1991.

116. Cristóbal Kay (1944), *Latin American Theories of Development and Underdevelopment* (Routledge, London, 1989).

117. Christian Anglade (ed. with Carlos Fortín), *The State and Capital Accumulation in Latin America*, 2 vols (Macmillan, Basingstoke, 1985, 1990); 'Sources of Legitimacy in Latin America', *Essex Papers on Politics and Government*, no. 38, 1987.

118 Towards the end of his comprehensive paper to the 1976 Cambridge conference David Lehmann briefly breaks away from a theoretical review of political economy: 'And yet one still has doubts. The doubts have to do with that absence of any analysis of the real mechanisms which connect international capital with the national state in Latin America, above all the military.' 'The Emperor has no Clothes: Class and State in Latin America', p. 20. George Philip (1951), *The Military in South America* (Croom Helm, London, 1985); *Oil and Politics in Latin America: Nationalist Movements and State Companies* (CUP, Cambridge, 1982). Two members of the 'third generation' have produced useful work on the armed forces. Philip Somervell, 'Naval Affairs in Chilean Politics, 1910–1932', JLAS, vol. 16, no. 2, 1984; Varun Sahni (1964), 'Not Quite British: a Study of External Influences on the Argentine Navy', JLAS, vol. 25, no. 3, 1993. 'The Resurgence of Naval Political Power in Argentina,

1976–83', Research Unit for European-Latin American Relations (RUELAR), University of Bradford, 1991.

119. Fred Parkinson, *Latin America, the Cold War and the World Powers, 1945–1973* (Sage, Beverly Hills, 1974); 'Latin America and the Antarctic: an Exclusive Club', JLAS, vol. 17, no. 2, 1985. Gordon Connell-Smith, *The Inter-American System* (OUP, Oxford, 1966); *The United States and Latin America: an Historical Analysis of Inter-American Relations* (Heinemann, London, 1974). Peter Calvert (1936) (ed.), *The Central American Security System* (CUP, Cambridge, 1988); *The International Politics of Latin America* (Manchester University Press, Manchester, 1994).

120. Laurence Whitehead, 'Explaining Washington's Central American Policies', JLAS, vol. 15, no. 2, 1983.

121. Peter Beck, *Antarctica in International Politics* (Croom Helm, London, 1986); *The Falkland Islands as an International Problem* (Routledge, London, 1988). Walter Little (ed. with C. Mitchell), *In the Aftermath: Anglo-Argentine Relations since the War* (University of Maryland Press, 1989); 'The Falklands Affair: a Review of the Literature', *Political Studies*, vol. XXXII, 1984. Alistair Hennessy and John King (eds), *The Land that England Lost: Argentina and Britain, a Special Relationship* (British Academic Press, London, 1992). Laurence Freedman and Virginia Gamba-Stonehouse, *Signals of War* (Faber and Faber, London, 1990). Virginia Gamba-Stonehouse, *Strategy in the Southern Oceans: a South American View* (Pinter, London, 1989).

122. Edward Best, 'Mexican Foreign Policy and Central America since the Mexican Revolution', DPhil, University of Oxford, 1988. Joe Smith (1945), *Unequal Giants: Diplomatic Relations between the United States and Brazil, 1889–1930* (Princeton University Press, Princeton, 1991); *Illusions of Conflict: Anglo-American Diplomacy towards Latin America, 1865–1896* (Pittsburgh University Press, Pittsburgh, 1979). Mónica Serrano (1960), *Common Security in Latin America: the 1967 Treaty of Tlatelolco*, ILAS Research Paper no.30, London 1992; (ed. with Neil Harvey), *Party Politics in 'An Uncommon Democracy': Political Parties and Elections in Mexico* (ILAS, London, 1994).

123. Victor Bulmer-Thomas, Nikki Craske and Mónica Serrano (eds), *Mexico and the North American Free Trade Agreement: Who Will Benefit?* (Macmillan, Basingstoke, 1994). Blanca Muñiz, 'EEC Strategies towards Latin America: Hegemony and International Economic Relations', PhD, University of Essex, 1989. Hazel Smith, 'European Community Policy Towards Central America in the 1980s', PhD, University of London, 1993.

124. Colin Clarke (1938), *Society and Politics in the Caribbean* (Macmillan, Basingstoke, 1991); 'Europe in the Caribbean: from Colonial Hegemony to Geopolitical Marginality', in A. Bryan, J. Greene and T. Shaw (eds), *Peace, Development and Security in the Caribbean: Perspectives to the Year 2000* (Macmillan, Basingstoke, 1990). Anthony Payne (1952), *The International Crisis of the Caribbean* (Croom Helm, London, 1984); 'The Belize Triangle: Relations with Britain, Guatemala and the United States', *Journal of Inter-American Studies*, vol. 32, no. 1, 1990. Paul Sutton (ed.), *Europe and the Caribbean* (Macmillan, Basingstoke, 1991); 'The Caribbean as a focus for strategic and resource

rivalry', in P. Calvert (ed.), *The Central American Security System* (CUP, Cambridge, 1988). Jean Grugel, *Politics and Development in the Caribbean Basin: Central America and the Caribbean in the New World Order* (Macmillan, Basingstoke, 1995); Tony Thorndike, *Grenada: Politics, Economics and Society* (Lynne Reiner, Boulder, Col., 1985).

125. Nicola Miller (1960), *Soviet Relations with Latin America, 1959–1987* (CUP, Cambridge, 1987); 'The Impact of US Policy in Central America', in P. Shearman and P. Williams (eds), *The Superpowers, Central America and the Middle East* (Brassey's, London, 1988).

126. Andrew Hurrell, (ed. with Benedict Kingsbury), *The International Politics of the Environment: Actors, Interests and Institutions* (Clarendon, Oxford, 1992); 'The Politics of Amazonian Deforestration', JLAS, vol. 23, no. 1, 1991.

127. Nikki Craske, *Corporatism Revisited: Salinas and the Reform of the Popular Sector*, ILAS Research Paper no. 37, London 1994. George Philip, *The Presidency in Mexican Politics* (Macmillan, Basingstoke, 1992).

128. Jorge Larraín (1942), *Ideology and Cultural Identity: Modernity and the Third World Presence* (Polity, Cambridge, 1994); *Theories of Development: Capitalism, Colonialism and Dependency* (Polity, Cambridge, 1989). J.G. Merquior, *The Veil and the Mask: Essays on Culture and Ideology* (Routledge, London, 1979); *From Prague to Paris. A Critique of Structuralist and Post-structuralist Thought* (Verso, London, 1986). Roberto Mangabeira Unger, *False Necessity: Anti-necessitarian Social Theory in the Service of Radical Democracy* (CUP, Cambridge, 1987); *Plasticity into Power: Comparative-historical Studies on the Institutional Conditions of Economic and Military Success* (CUP, Cambridge, 1987).

129. David Slater, *Territory and State Power in Latin America: the Peruvian Case* (Macmillan, Basingstoke, 1989); (ed.), *New Social Movements and the State in Latin America* (CEDLA, Amsterdam, 1985).

130. John Gledhill, *Power and its Disguises: Anthropological Perspectives on Politics* (Pluto, London, 1994). Richard Wilson (1964), *Maya Resurgence in Guatemala: Q'eqchi Experiences* (University of Oklahoma Press, Norman, 1995).

131. Joe Foweraker, *The Struggle for Land: a Political Economy of the Pioneer Frontier in Brazil from 1930 to the Present Day* (CUP, Cambridge, 1981); *Popular Mobilisation in Mexico: the Teachers' Movement* (CUP, Cambridge, 1993); *Theorizing Social Movements* (Pluto, London, 1995).

132. Maxine Molyneux, 'Mobilisation without Emancipation? Women's Interests, the State and Revolution', *Feminist Studies*, vol. 11, no. 2, 1985; 'The Politics of Abortion in Nicaragua', *Feminist Review*, vol. 29, 1988; *State, Gender and Institutional Change in Cuba's 'Special Period': the Federación de Mujeres Cubanas*, ILAS Research Paper no. 43, London 1996. Jo Fisher (1954), *Mothers of the Disappeared* (Zed, London, 1989); *Out of the Shadows: Women, Resistance and Politics in South America* (Latin America Bureau, London, 1993). Georgina Waylen, 'Rethinking Women's Political Participation and Protest: Chile 1970–1990', *Political Studies*, vol. 60, no. 2, 1992; 'Women and Democratization: Conceptualizing Gender Relations in Transition Politics', *World Politics*, April 1994. Sarah Radcliffe, *'Así es una mujer del pueblo': low-income women's organisations under APRA, 1979–1987*, Centre for Latin American Studies,

University of Cambridge, Working Paper no. 43, 1988; (ed. with Sallie Westwood), *'Viva': Women and Popular Protest in Latin America* (Routledge, London, 1993).

133. Peter Wade (1957), *Blackness and Race Mixture: the Dynamics of Racial Identity in Colombia* (Johns Hopkins University Press, Baltimore, 1993).

134. Richard Bourne, *Getúlio Vargas of Brazil, 1883–1954: Sphinx of the Pampas* (C. Knight, London, 1974); *Political Leaders of Latin America: Ché Guevara, Alfredo Strössner, Eduardo Frei Montalva, Carlos Lacerda, Juscelino Kubitschek, Eva Perón* (Penguin, Harmondsworth, 1969). Sue Branford (1944) (with Oriel Glock), *The Last Frontier: Fighting over Land in the Amazon* (Zed, London, 1985); (with Bernardo Kucinski), *Carnival of the Oppressed* (Latin America Bureau, London, 1995). Eduardo Crawley, *Dictators Never Die: a Portrait of Nicaragua and the Somoza Dynasty* (C. Hurst, London, 1979). Phil Gunson (with Andrew Thompson and Greg Chamberlain), *The Dictionary of Contemporary Politics of South America* (Routledge, London, 1989); (with Greg Chamberlain), *The Dictionary of Contemporary Politics of Central America and the Caribbean* (Routledge, London, 1991). Colin Harding, *Colombia in Focus* (Latin America Bureau, London, 1986). For Richard Gott, see note 100. Hugh O'Shaughnessy, *Grenada: Revolution, Invasion and Aftermath* (Hamilton, London, 1984); *Latin Americans* (BBC, London, 1988). James Painter (1956), *Bolivia and Coca: a Study in Dependency* (Lynne Rienner, Boulder, 1994); *Paraguay in the 1970s: Continuity and Change in the Political Process*, ILAS Research Paper no. 9, London 1983. Simon Strong, *Shining Path: the World's Deadliest Revolutionary Force* (HarperCollins, London, 1992).

135. In addition to his own book on guerrillas and Bourne's on political leaders (see note 134), this series included *Fidel Castro Speaks*, ed. J. Petras and M. Kenner, 1970; Thomas and Margorie Melville, *Guatemala: Another Vietnam?* 1971; Régis Debray, *Revolution in the Revolution?* 1969 and *Strategy for Revolution*, 1970.

136. The University of London Library lists 48 titles issued by LAB since 1978. Since many of these have been noted above, I shall mention here only those that reflect the organisation's vocation to cover relatively ignored topics: Jenny Pearce (ed.), *The European Challenge: Europe's New Role in Latin America*, 1982; James Ferguson, *The Dominican Republic: Beyond the Lighthouse*, 1992; David Corkill and David Cubitt, *Ecuador, Fragile Democracy*, 1988; *El Salvador under General Romero: an Analysis of the First Nine Months of the Regime of President Romero*, 1979; Caipora Women's Group, *Women in Brazil*, 1993; *Guyana: Fraudulent Revolution*, 1984; Richard Lapper and James Painter, *Honduras: State for Sale*, 1985; Chico Mendes, *Fight for the Forest*, 2nd ed. 1992; John Weeks and Phil Gunson, *Panama: Made in the USA*, 1991; *Paraguay: Power Game*, 1980; *The Thatcher Years: Britain and Latin America*, 1988; Jenny Pearce, *Uruguay: Generals Rule*, 1980.

Chapter 6

1. Buchanan, Washington, to John Appleton, 1 June 1848, in J.B. Moore (ed.), *The Writings of James Buchanan*, vol. 8 (J.B. Lippincott, Philadelphia, 1911) pp. 75–6

2. Buchanan, Washington, to Secretary of State Clayton, 17 April 1849, in ibid., pp. 360–6.

3. Peter H. Smith, *Talons of the Eagle. Dynamics of US-Latin American Relations* (Oxford University Press, New York and Oxford, 1996).

4. Rodolfo Cerdas Cruz, 'Nicaragua: One Step Forward, Two Steps Back', in Guiseppe Di Palma and Lawrence Whitehead (eds), *The Central American Impasse* (St. Martin's Press, New York, 1986).

5. NAM/G77 is the 'non-aligned' movement that was created in the 1950s.

6. For Morse the years 1760–1920 in Latin America are 'colonial'. See Richard Morse, 'Independence in a Patrimonial State', in J. Tulchin (ed.), *Problems in Latin American History. The Modern Period* (New York, 1973), p. 12. For Véliz the years 1850 to 1930 constitute a 'liberal pause' in a general centralist, corporatist history. See Claudio Véliz, *The Centralist Tradition in Latin America* (Princeton University Press, Princeton, 1980).

7. Samuel Flagg Bemis, *The Latin American Policy of the United States* (Harcourt, Brace & Co., New York, 1943), p. 6.

8. W. Peden (ed.), Thomas Jefferson, *Notes on the State of Virginia* (University of North Carolina Press, Chapel Hill, 1955), pp. 267–7.

9. John Quincy Adams, *Writings of John Quincy Adams*, vol. VII (Macmillan, New York, 1913), pp. 272–3.

10. 'Spatialities of Power and Post-modern Ethics – Rethinking Geographical Encounters', *Environmental Planning*, vol. 15, 1997.

11. Carl J. Richard, *The Founders and the Classics. Greece, Rome and the American Enlightenment* (Harvard University Press, Cambridge, Mass., 1994), pp. 163–4; José Enrique Rodó, *Ariel* (University of Texas Press, Austin, 1988).

12. *North American Review*, vol. XXXI, 1821. This article is anonymous, but my strong suspicion is that the author is either Edward Everett, president of Harvard in the 1840s and secretary of state in the early 1850s, or his brother Alexander, who was appointed ambassador to Spain by Adams.

13. Quoted in Dexter Perkins, *A History of the Monroe Doctrine* (Little, Brown, Boston, 1927) pp. 84–5. For a discussion of the background, see Piero Gleijeses, 'The Limits of Sympathy: The United States and the Independence of Spanish America', *Journal of Latin American Studies*, vol. 24, part 3, 1992, pp. 481–505.

14. Quoted in Ernest May, *The Making of the Monroe Doctrine* (Harvard University Press, Cambridge, Mass., 1975).

15. Frederick Merk, *The Monroe Doctrine and American Expansionism, 1843–1849* (Knopf, New York, 1966)

16. Roosevelt to Elihu Root, Washington, 20 May 1904. W. H. Harbaugh (ed.), Theodore Roosevelt, *The Writings of Theodore Roosevelt* (Bobbs Merrill, Indianapolis, 1967) p. 73.

17. Although Thoreau opens his *Resistance to Civil Government* with the claim that, 'the people would not have consented to [the Mexican war]', he goes on to state that, 'the opponents to . . . reform in Massachusetts are not a hundred thousand politicians at the South, but a hundred thousand merchants and farmers here, who are more interested in commerce and agriculture than they are in humanity, and are not prepared to do justice to the slaves and to Mexico, *cost what it may*'. Nancy Rosenblum (ed.), *Thoreau. Political Writings* (Cambridge University Press, Cambridge, 1996) pp. 1, 5.

18. Quoted in Frederick Merk, *Manifest Destiny and Mission in American History* (Knopf, New York, 1963), p. 59. Calhoun saw any major annexation as positively dangerous: 'Can we incorporate a people so dissimilar to us in every respect – so little qualified for free and popular government – without certain destruction to our political institutions?' Quoted in Albert K. Weinberg, *Manifest Dstiny* (Quadrangle, Chicago, 1968), p. 361. At the other end of the political spectrum Emerson opined, 'The United States will conquer Mexico, but it will be as a man swallows the arsenic, which brings him down in turn. Mexico will poison us'. Emerson's primary fear here was not the incorporation of 'alien' populations but the expansion and acceleration of the US conflict over slavery. See Ralph Waldo Emerson, *The Journals and Miscellaneous Notebooks of Ralph Waldo Emerson*, vol. VII (Harvard University Press, Cambridge, Mass., 1969) p. 206.

19. Quoted in Alexander Deconde, *Ethnicity, Race and American Foreign Policy. A History* (Boston, 1992), p. 34.

20. James Russell Lowell, quoted in Deconde (1992), p. 55.

21. Thomas Tennery, *The Mexican War Diary of Thomas D. Tennery* (University of Oklahoma Press, Norman, 1970), pp. 37–8. The enlistment figures are given in C.S. Ellsworth, 'The American Churches and the Mexican War', *American Historical Review*, XLV, 1940, p. 318. According to my Rand McNally US road atlas, seven of the twelve towns in the country called Polk are in former slave states. (The president himself was from Tennessee.) This is what the most advanced scholarship might call a 'correlative imaginary', which generates and sustains, 'an ideational horizontal integration with a shared space, through a form of interpellation which correlates with social spaces'. See Sarah Radcliffe and Sallie Westwood (eds), *Remaking the Nation: Place, Identity and Politics in Latin America* (Routledge, London, 1996), p. 28.

22. *Del Gobierno en Sud América*, quoted in W.W. Pierson, 'Alberdi's View on the Monroe Doctrine', *Hispanic American Historical Review*, vol. 3, 1920, pp. 366; 371.

23. Message of 7 December 1847, reprinted in *British and Foreign State Papers, 1846–47*, XXXV, p. 170.

24. Message of 31 January 1845, reprinted in *British and Foreign State Papers, 1845–46*, XXXIV, p. 1251.

25. Russell F. Weigley, *History of the United States Army* (Indiana University Press, Bloomington, 1984), p. 597; W.A. Ganoe, *The History of the United States Army* (New York, 1964), p. 208; Report of Navy Secretary John P. Kennedy to the President, 26 August 1852, in *British and Foreign State Papers, 1851–52*, XL, pp. 114–5.

26. R.A. Johnson, *The Administration of United States Foreign Policy* (University of Texas Press, Austin, 1971), p. 50; G.H. Stuart, *The Department of State: A History of its Organization, Procedure and Personnel* (Macmillan, New York, 1949), pp. 110; 414. In 1850, the year in which the trans-Atlantic slave trade was effectively suppressed, the Slave Trade Department of the British Foreign Office comprised one superintendent and four clerks. In 1853 the total establishment of the Foreign Office based in London was 53, including chambers keepers, porters and doorkeepers. Roger Anstey, 'The Pattern of British Abolitionism in the Eighteenth and Nineteenth Centuries', in C. Bolt and S. Drescher (eds), *Anti-Slavery, Religion and Reform* (Dawson, Folkestone, 1980), p. 33.

27. Michael Mann, *The Sources of Social Power*, vol. II (Cambridge University Press, Cambridge, 1993) p. 283.

28. Quoted in Thomas Schoonover, *Dollars over Dominion. The Triumph of Liberalism in Mexican United States Relations, 1861–1867* (Louisiana State University Press, Baton Rouge and London, 1978), p. 141. It should not be forgotten that Chile, Peru and Ecuador were menaced by the Spanish fleet in the 1860s.

29. For Ephraim Squier, ex-ambassador to Nicaragua for the USA and now a railroad promotor in Honduras, 'The southern troubles are directing the attention of northern capital and enterprising men to Central America and the West Indies as a source whence to draw future tropical staples. Secession will be good for sugar and cotton production.' Quoted in Thomas Schoonover, *The United States and Central America, 1860–1911* (Duke University Press, Durham, North Carolina, 1991), p. 17.

30. Walter LaFeber, *The New Empire. An Interpretaion of American Expansionism, 1860–1898* (Cornell University Press, Ithaca, 1963), p. 1.

31. Quoted in Walter LaFeber, *The Cambridge History of American Foreign Relations. Vol. 2: The American Search for Opportunity, 1865–1913* (Cambridge University Press, Cambridge, 1993), p. 9.

32. Quoted in Walter LaFeber, *The New Empire*, pp. 25–6.

33. Quoted in Peter H. Smith, *Talons of the Eagle*, p. 45.

34. Rostow had British 'take-off' in 1783–1802; that of the USA, France and Germany in 1830–50; Sweden, Japan, Russia/USSR, Italy, Canada and Australia in 1870–1901; and Argentina, Brazil and Mexico, Turkey, Iran, India, China and South Korea from 1933 onwards. W. W. Rostow, *The Stages of Economic Growth* (Cambridge Univerity Press, Cambridge, 1960), p. xviii. For a recent radical reconsideration of LaFeber, see Charles Bergquist, *Labor and the Course of American Democracy: US History in Latin American Perspective* (Verso, London, 1996).

35. Ian Clark argues for the *primacy* of the Pacific/Asiatic theatre for the USA in 1895–1905, with the non-partition of China and the rapidly growing Russian interest there and in Japan:

   It offered a stage for the United States to convert its growing economic and technical muscle into a degree of diplomatic leverage: its stake in the Philippines in 1898, the Hay 'Open Door' note in relation to China, and the hosting of the Portsmouth peace settlement between Russia and Japan all bear witness to America's coming of international age.

Ian Clark, *The Hierarchy of States. Reform and Resistance in the International Order* (Cambridge University Press, Cambridge, 1989), p. 5.

36. Quoted in Peter H. Smith, *Talons of the Eagle. Dynamics of US–Latin American Relations* (Oxford University Press, New York and Oxford, 1996), p. 100.

37. 'The Washington Pan-American Congress', *La Nación*, 19–20 December 1889, reprinted in José Martí, *Inside the Monster. Writings on the United States and American Imperialism* (Monthly Review Press, New York, 1975), pp. 356–7.

38. Clark, *The Hierarchy of States*, pp. 96–7.

39. Quoted in J.W. Gautenbein (ed.), *The Evolution of our Latin American Policy. A Documentary Record* (New York, 1950), p. 97.

40. 'La Unidad de la América Indo-Española', *Variedades*, Lima, 6 December 1924, in José Carlos Mariátegui, *Temas de Nuestra América* (Biblioteca Amanta, Lima, 1988), pp. 16; 28.

41. Kenneth Grieb, *The Latin American Policy of Warren G. Harding* (Fort Worth, 1977).

42. Secretary of State Hughes, 18 May 1922, quoted in Robert Freeman Smith, *The United States and Revolutionary Nationalism in Mexico, 1916–1932* (University of Chicago Press, Chicago, 1972), pp. 190–1.

43. Cordell Hull, *The Memoirs of Cordell Hull*, II vols (Hodder & Stoughton, London, 1948), p. 308; David Sheinin, *Argentina and the United States at the Sixth Pan-American Conference (Havana 1928)*, (Research Paper No. 25, Institute of Latin American Studies, London, 1998).

44. Hull, *The Memoirs of Cordell Hull*, p. 308.

45. Kellogg to Bliss, 7 November 1927, quoted in Sheinin, *Argentina and the United States at the Sixth Pan-American Conference*, p. 6.

46. Writing from London in 1852, the US Whig leader Thurlow Weed commented wryly,

> There is a fable, I believe, of a fox who, having lost his own tail, persuaded his friends that tails were quite useless. England has got to the end of protection, and is now endeavouring to persuade America, a nation that possesses, like England, all the elements required for manufacturing independence, that as she can manufacture for us, we should abandon the protective policy. She does not tell us, however, that when, deluded by the popular theory of Free Trade, we shall have withdrawn the pressure of American competition, John Bull, generous as he is, will consult his own rather than our interests, in his prices.

(Thurlow Weed, *Life of Thurlow Weed*, vol. II (Houghton Mifflin, Cambridge, Mass., 1884), p. 202.)

47. Speech of 12 April 1933, quoted in Gautenbein (ed.), *The Evolution of our Latin American Policy*, pp. 160–1.

48. Walter LaFeber, *Inevitable Revolutions. The United States and Central America*, 2nd. ed. (Norton, New York and London, 1993), p. 83.

49. Latin American countries had taken one of three positions with respect to the Central Powers by 1918: declaration of war (Brazil, Cuba, Costa Rica, Guatemala, Haiti, Honduras, Nicaragua, Panama); breaking of diplomatic

relations (Bolivia, Dominican Republic, Ecuador, Peru, Uruguay); declaration of neutrality (Argentina, Chile, Colombia, Mexico, Paraguay, El Salvador, Venezuela).

50. Only some states declared war on all the Axis powers: Cuba, Haiti, Dominican Republic, Panama, Costa Rica, Honduras, Nicaragua, El Salvador, and Guatemala (all in December 1941); Mexico (May 1942); and Bolivia (April 1943). Some declared war on Germany alone: Brazil (August 1942) and Colombia (November 1943). Ecuador declared war on Japan only (February 1945) and a significant group of countries remained neutral until 1945: Chile, Venezuela, Uruguay (February), and Argentina and Paraguay (March).

51. Hull, *The Memoirs of Cordell Hull*, p. 1380.

Chapter 7

1. Julio Díaz A., *Historia del ejército boliviano, 1825–1932*, (La Paz 1971), p. 65.

2. In 1850 he wrote to his old friend Marshal Otto Philip Braun that his wife had lost 'six or seven' girls, '*todas muertas de resfrío*', and was then nursing a son of 10 months with great apprehension. O'Connor, Tarija, to Braun, 12 December 1850, in J. Barnadas (ed.), *El Mariscal Braun a través de su epistolario*, (Cochabamba 1998), p. 204.

3. Graham Wallas, *The Life of Francis Place*, (London 1898), p. 51.

4. Johan Huizinga, *Homo Ludens*, (London 1949), p. 148.

5. Marianne Elliott, *Partners in Revolution: the United Irishmen and France*, (New Haven 1982), pp. 100; 173.

6.
> My Heart's Beloved, knowing how anxious you will be, I send [this], though the trials will be over some time tonight. Matters, we think, look good for O'Connor, but I am resolved not to be sanguine. I got to speak to him this morning. His mind is composed, but his nerves badly shaken. He was greatly affected when his poor brother was brought into court yesterday, and when the other took his hand, he burst into tears. The usage of Roger O'Connor, who is one of the finest fellows I ever saw, has been merciless beyond example. We are all very anxious and very busy, for the counsel want assistance. Here is Fox, Grey, Erskine, Grattan, Moira, Norfolk etc.

(Quoted in Walter Sichel, *Sheridan*, (London 1909), II, p. 284. See also Fintan O'Toole, *A Traitor's Kiss: the Life of Richard Brinsley Sheridan*, (London 1997), pp. 325–337.)

7. Thomas Packenham, *The Year of Liberty: the History of the Great Irish Rebellion of 1798*, (London 1972), pp. 129–30. In his maiden speech of March 1797 Burdett declared to the Commons, 'Good God, that treason to Ireland and the name of O'Connor should be preposterously linked together, as he is capable of everything that is great, generous and noble for his country's good'. Quoted in M.W. Patterson, *Sir Francis Burdett and his Times (1770–1844)*, vol. II, (London 1931), p. 58.

8. Having met Arthur in January 1805, Benjamin Constant noted in his diary:

'O'Connor is a sophisticated man. When joking he has a lighter touch than foreigners usually do, and so has something of the French defect of joking about one's own opinions. He is more ambitious than he is a friend of liberty, and yet a friend of liberty nevertheless, because to be so is the refuge of ambitious men who have missed success.

(*Journaux Intimes*, (Paris 1952), p. 189.)

9. James Livesey (ed.), *The State of Ireland*, (1798) (Dublin 1998). Frank Mac-Dermott calls *Monopoly*, 'a boring mixture of economics, politics and anti-clerical rant'. 'Arthur O'Connor', *Irish Historical Studies*, vol. XV (1966–67), p. 67. In his introduction to the pamphlet Livesey quotes Lady Wycombe, writing in March 1798 to Lady Holland, in similar vein: 'when he is in company, by the aid of a good memory he talks a few pages out of Adam Smith in lieu of conversation'. *The State of Ireland*, p. 9. MacDermott makes no mention of the pamphlet and is much more interested in matters of espionage than those of ideology.

10.

The press is the palladium of Liberty. What has heretofore made England celebrated over the nations of Europe? – the press. What overturned the Catholic despotism of France? – the press, by the writings of Montesquieu, Voltaire, Rousseau, Diderot, Seyes, Raynal and Condorcet. What has electrified England and called down its curses on a Pitt? – that press he in vain attempted to silence. What illumined Belfast, the Athens of Ireland? *The Press* and the *Northern Star*. Why did America triumph over tyranny? – a journeyman printer fulminated the decree of nature against the giants of Engalnd – and the pen of a Franklin routed the armies of the King.

(Quoted in D. Dickson, D. Keogh and K. Whelan (eds), *The United Irishmen: Republicanism, Radicalism and Rebellion*, (Dublin 1993), pp. 275–6.) In 1843 Feargus wrote to Frank:

The press of this country is much more shackled than ever the French press was – the difference is just this – that of France had to undergo governmental censorship; while the aristocracy and middle classes hold the press of England in close and close and much more destructive bonds.

(Feargus, London, 28 September 1843, to Francisco Burdett O'Connor, original in possession of Eduardo Trigo O'Connor d'Arlach, to whom I am most grateful for access to this and other papers belonging to General O'Connor.)

11. In a letter to Braun some three years after his marriage O'Connor wrote that, having lost most of his men in a small-scale operation to capture some rebels, he himself was about to be lanced down and tried to kill himself but his pistol failed. He was spared and managed to escape but later suffered a collapse:

En fin, mi amigo, los trabajos que padecí ese día me reventaron el corazón. Desde entonces no me conozco a mí mismo, ni Usted me conociera: estoy lastimado interiormente y expuesto a continuos ataques de enfermedad. Regresé a Tarija, en donde pasé tres meses en cama, merecí mil atenciones de la familia, en la cual me casé por gratitud, pensando morirme y dejar lo que poseía en esa familia. Tal no fue mi suerte. Aún existo . . . Mi mujercita es apreciable, porque – pobre! – no me trajo un real, y es por eso que la elegí.

(O'Connor, Retiro-Frontera de Tarija, to Braun, 13 March 1830, in *El Mariscal Braun*, pp. 50–1.)

12. G.D.H. Cole, *Chartist Portraits*, (London 1941), p. 308.

13. Elliott, *Partners in Revolution*,p. 329.

14. Patterson, *Sir Francis Burdett*, vol. II, p. 433; D. Read and E. Glasgow, *Feargus O'Connor: Irishman and Chartist*, (London 1961), p. 13; Francisco Burdett O'Connor, *Recuerdos* (1895) (La Paz 1972), p. 5.

15. Quoted in Patterson, *Sir Francis Burdett*, p. 441.

16. The space between reality and invention is shown to be magically minimal in this letter from Roger to Lady Burdett:

> Dear Lady Burdett,
>
> Your good opinion is most gratifying to me. The greatest misfortune of my life would be the loss of it. I did not think to write now, but a note I wrote in my wild mountains (which I pray Heaven that you will look upon next Summer) in answer to one Burdett wrote to me calls for a little history. Of these mountains I can give you no idea – the messenger handed me the letter, which demanded an answer, a written one from me for fear of mistake. How was this to be done was the point; people there were to hand, but they were all on the chance trip to meet Sir Francis. What am I to do lads, say I; is it possible to get pen, ink and paper anywhere near? What, says one, is there no pen among you? No. Is there no goose here, says another? Yes. Off with the speaker from his horse, catches a goose – plucks a quill – no knife – may be the smith (there chanced to be a smith's forge not far off) has a razor. The pen was made. There was no ink. Run down one of you boys to the forge and make up some forge water pretty strong. Up came ink; there happened to be a pedlar who had a little book – out goes a leaf of a little bit of paper – a fellow takes off his hat for a table – and *thus* was I enabled to make out my note. Never let it be said that the Irish are not people of rare invention.
>
> Your faithful servant.

(Quoted in Patterson, *Sir Francis Burdett*, pp. 451–2.)

17. Terry Eagleton, *Heathcliff and the Great Hunger*, (London 1995), p. 9. In 1848 Aubrey de Vere wrote that 'charges made against Ireland, it is true, derive a certain verisimilitude from the stories in circulation amongst you; but you cannot be ignorant that for such tales the supply, according to the ordinary laws of trade, will always be proportionate to the demand.' *English Misrule and Irish Misdeeds*, (London 1970), p. 44.

18. James Dunkerley, *Americana: the Americas in the World, around 1850 (Or 'Seeing the Elephant' as the theme for an imaginary western)* (London, forthcoming 2000).

19. Neither uncle nor nephew confused the rights of man with the qualities of men. Francisco opens his untitled essay in distinctly sober voice:

> A true desire to render a service to the Republic of Bolivia and to all the new states of America obliges me to exercise strict control over my nature, violating it to the extreme of writing for the multitude, ungrateful though I know it to be, always to have been and always to be ... My conscience tells me that [in this] I provide a service of greater value than those ... in nine years of work in the fields of destruction of tyranny and victories for the rights of man ...'

20. Parts are reprinted in Edmund Temple, *Travels in Various Parts of Peru, Including a Year's Residence in Potosí*, vol. II, (London 1830), pp. 354 ff.

21. In the mid-1830s, arguing that the sale of public lands on the US model would not work in Latin America, O'Connor proposed to President Santa Cruz that all Bolivians who wore foreign clothes should be taxed twice as much as those with locally produced garments. Although there was evidently a huge problem with the practicality of such a scheme, O'Connor reports that Santa Cruz reacted in a positive manner:

> Do you know General, he said, that my little Simon's nurse is an Indian from the Puna, to whom my wife gives presents of yarn, shawls and scarves of foreign fabric. Her relatives see this when they come to the house in La Paz and are themselves wearing such garments when they visit the following Sunday. I expect to see all our Indians dressed in foreign clothes instead of the rude garments they now wear. And, General, it will then be necessary to find new sources of tributary tax because when the Indians who now pay it are clothed in foreign materials they will not have a *real* left to pay for their *fiestas* or ecclesiastical obligations.

(*Recuerdos*, p. 217.)

22. *Northern Star*, 3 November 1838.

23. John Miller (ed.), *Memoirs of General Miller in the Service of Peru*, vol. II, (London 1828), p. 170. According to Miller there was not a single qualified doctor in the Peruvian department of Puno, and when, after the war, San Martín's surgeon general, the Irishman Michael Crawley, set himself up at Lampa it was not as a medical practitioner but as an owner of mines. An English dentist by the name of Dudley did open a clinic in Arequipa, where he had a child with the great Argentine writer Juana Manuela Gorriti, at whose earlier wedding General O'Connor had been *padrino*.

24. *Recuerdos*, p. 28.

25. *Recuerdos*, pp. 62; 78–9; Diary entries for 22 November 1849; 27 March 1950.

26. *Recuerdos*, p. 56. Morgan O'Connell, the son of Daniel, 'the Liberator', also joined the Patriot forces in 1820, encouraging his father to stage a fervent defence of John Devereux, the Waterford man charged with illegally recruiting members of the Irish Legion. In April 1820 O'Connell wrote to Bolívar to register 'my respect for your high character and ... my attachment to that sacred cause which your talents, valour and virtue have gloriously sustained – I mean the cause of liberty and national independence'. By the end of the year, though, he was writing to his wife with more parental concern and candour:

> You have seen our darling Morgan's letter to Ricarda (*sic*) Connor. Would to God we knew where he is at present. Admiral Brion's letter which appeared in the *Freeman's* [*Journal*] of yesterday distinctly says there will not be any more troops recruited from Ireland. He calls them a *banditta*. In my opinion that gentleman has not behaved by the Irish troops as he should have done. I hope he will be made to suffer for his conduct.

(O'Connell, Dublin, to Bolívar, 17 April 1820; O'Connell, Tralee, to his wife Mary, 5 October 1820. *The Correspondence of Danial O'Connell*, vol. II, (Shannon 1972), pp. 277–8; 284.)

27. In January 1824, a month after he first met him, Bolívar wrote to Sucre, 'Major O'Connor should be detached from his batallion to oversee the carrying out of your instructions to the Grenadiers as I think he is the best officer to use at the advanced posts.' Bolívar, Pativilca, to Sucre, 24 January 1824, in V.Lecuña (ed.), *Selected Writings of Bolívar*, vol. II, (New York 1952), p. 247. In April the Liberator had enough confidence in O'Connor to think of using him as an emissary to negotiate with Viceroy LaSerna. Bolívar, Otuzco, to Sucre, 14 April 1824, in V.Lecuña (ed.), *Cartas del Libertador*, vol. IV, (Caracas 1929), p. 127.

28. 'Such was the scarcity of iron that most of the fire-arms had been converted into nails and horse-shoes', *Memoirs of General Miller*, vol. II, p. 124.

29.
> The Liberator instructs me to inform you that there are here 700 loads of wheat which should be taken to the hill, and that he does not know how this is to be checked because O'Connor does not belong to this world and knows nothing; and the intendent is worse than O'Connor because he is useless.

(Tomás de Heres, Huánuco, to Sucre, 12 July 1824, in *Correspondencia del Libertador*, (Caracas 1974), p. 240.)

30. *Recuerdos*, pp. 99–104. In fact, O'Connor had previously used his powers of persuasion to stop Sucre executing the Kessel-born Braun for disobedience when he was conducting himself in a rather teutonic and not ingratiating fashion. Aside from Miller and Braun, both of whom would serve the young Bolivian republic, O'Connor mentioned Wright, Ferguson, Harris, Gregg, Duxbury and Hallowes as foreign-born soldiers who fought at Ayacucho with distinction. Foreigners served on the other side too. O'Connor failed to extract a single intelligible word from Paul Eccles, a native of Switzerland whom he and Sandes had interrogated in French, Spanish, English and Celtic when Eccles was detained near Oruro carrying a flask of poison and instructions from General Olañeta for the murder of Sucre and the rebel guerrilla commander Miguel Lanza. Ibid., pp. 109–10; C. Arnade, *La dramática insurgencia de Bolivia*, (La Paz 1972), pp. 196–7.

31. *Recuerdos*, p. 97. Miller's account stresses the superior numbers, weapons and resources of the Royalists but also their political divisions and low morale. *Memoirs of General Miller*, vol. II, pp. 163 ff.

32. 'Señor O'Connor, because of his birth, his honour and his knowledge seems to me to be the most obvious choice to obtain a boat for us in Europe'. Vice-President Enrique Calvo, Tapacarí, to Santa Cruz, 10 June 1836, in R. Querejazu (ed.), *Oposición en Bolivia a la Confederación Peru–Boliviana*, (Sucre 1996), pp. 149–50.

33. *Recuerdos*, p. 248.

34. Quoted in Norman Gash, *Sir Robert Peel*, (London 1986), p. 661.

35. Feargus O'Connor, London, to 'My dear Frank', 28 September 1843. Typed copy in the possession of Eduardo Trigo O'Connor d'Arlach. Feargus shared the family love of equestrianism, but 'in 1834 all my horses were thoroughly licked at the races of Fermoy. I lost £750 upon them, sold them all, and gave up the Turf. Since then I have never bet a farthing on horseflesh'.

36.

Harry Brougham said they wanted no poor law as every young man ought to lay up a provision for old age, yet while he said this with one side of his mouth, he was screwing the other side to get his retiring pension raised from £4,000 to £5,000 a year. But if the people had their rights they would not long pay his salary. Harry would go to the treasury, he would knock at the door, but Cerberus would not open the door, he would ask, "Who is there?" And then luckless Harry would answer, "It's an ex-chancellor coming for his £1,250 a quarter's salary", but Cerberus would say, "There have been a dozen of ye here already, and there is nothing for ye". And then Harry would cry, "Oh! what will become of me? What shall I do?" And Cerberus would say, "Go into the Bastille that you have provided for the people". Then, when Lord Harry and Lady Harry went into the Bastille, the keeper would say, "This is your ward to the right, and this, my lady, is your ward to the left; we are Malthusians here, and are afraid you would breed, therefore you must be kept asunder".

(Quoted in R.G. Gammage, *History of the Chartist Movement, 1837–1854*, (London 1894), p. 26.)

37.

Yes – you – I was just coming to you, when I was describing the materials of which our spurious aristocracy is composed. You gentlemen belong to the big-bellied, little-brained, numskull aristocracy. How dare you hiss me, you con-temptible set of platter-faced, amphibious politicians? ... Now was it not indecent of you? Was it not foolish of you? Was it not ignorant of you to hiss me? If you interrupt me again, I'll bundle you out of the room.

(Quoted in Mark Hovell, *The Chartist Movement*, (London 1918), p. 94.) The threat would have been taken seriously, according to Gammage, who was writing when Feargus was still alive: 'No member of the prize ring could fight his way with more desperate energy through a crowd than could this electioneering pugilist; and it was not alone with his fists that he was useful to his friends.' Gammage, *History*, p. 14. In 1843 Feargus told Frank, 'I am six feet and one inch high, and weigh 14 stone ... I have had four duels in which I received three apologies on the ground, and was once fired at in the neighbourhood of Cork when the bullet wizzed by my nose.'

38. Review of May–October 1850, *Neue Rheinische Zeitung Revue*, in D. Fernbach (ed.), *Marx: the Revolutions of 1848*, (Harmondsworth 1973), pp. 308–9.

39. I take my lead in this unfashionable interpretation from John Belchem, '1848: Feargus O'Connor and the Collapse of the Mass Platform', in J. Epstein and D. Thompson (eds), *The Chartist Experience: Studies in Working-Class Radicalism and Culture, 1830–60*, (London 1982). In his 1843 letter to Frank – who as Francisco was a republican and warrior – Feargus wrote,

You must know that I am not a Republican nor would I seek for any change by violence, while you have learned enough of literary political trick to be aware that ... with the accredited power of authority, tyrannical governments always have it in their power at a given moment to bring about a futile resistance to the settled order of things.

40. Feargus had earlier eaten the supper left for the Speaker in his private office following a refusal by that officer to issue a ruling on whether a root vegetable

served to O'Connor and the O'Gorman Mahon (the MP for Ennis, Charles James Parick Mahon (1800–1891), whom Trollope once spotted on dubious business in Costa Rica) was a beetroot or a mangle-wurzel. On 8 June 1852 Feargus struck another MP in the chamber, was named and apologised. On the 9th Hansard reports,

> The Attorney General was proceeding to address the Committee, but was interrupted by the disorderly and offensive conduct of the honourable Member for Nottingham, who, on being remonstrated with by the honourable Member for West Riding, thrust a half-closed hand into the honourable Member's face.

(*Parliamentary Debates*, Third Series, vol. CXII, p. 367.)

41. O'Connor knew that local politics was not for him:

> In Tarija today there was a farce of an election for senator, and it befell General Celedonio Avila to be elected to that class of escort for General Belzu. The said general knows about as much about legislation as I do of the Chinese language, but this matters not at all; that is not the intended object of General Avila's nomination . . . These countries are ignorant of everything to do with sovereignty. Votes are given according to the orders of the leader and there's nothing more to be said of this matter.

(Diary, entry for 2 June 1850.) A year earlier O'Connor's close friend Colonel Eustaquio ('El Moto') Méndez, a guerrilla leader in the Independence Wars, had been tortured by rebels against Belzu and died in his house whilst being nursed by Francisca. Octavio O'Connor d'Arlach, *Calendario histórico de Tarija*, (La Paz 1975), p. 114.

42. R.A.Humphreys (ed.), *The 'Detached Recollections' of General D.F. O'Leary*, (London 1969), p. 48. The final sentence of García Márquez's account is less concise but still very powerful:

> Then he crossed his arms over his chest and began to listen to the radiant voices of slaves singing the six o'clock *Salve* in the mills, and through the window he saw the diamond of Venus in the sky that was dying forever, the eternal snows, the new vine whose yellow bellflowers he would not see bloom the following Saturday in the house closed in mourning, the final brilliance of life that would never, in all eternity, be repeated again.

(*The General in His Labyrinth*, (London 1991), p. 268.)

43. Antonio Paredes Candia, *Anécdotas Bolivianas*, (La Paz 1978), pp. 127–8.